MILTON and *This Pendant World*

GEORGE WESLEY WHITING:

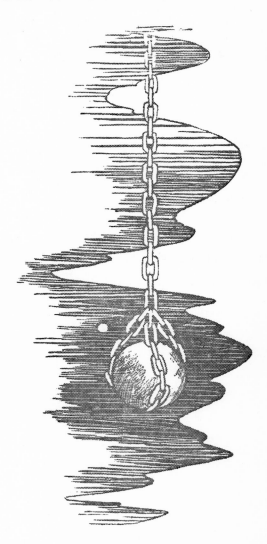

MILTON and
This Pendant World

And fast by hanging in a golden Chain
This pendant world, in bigness as a Starr
Of smallest Magnitude, close by the Moon.

1969
OCTAGON BOOKS
New York

Reprinted 1969
by special arrangement with the University of Texas Press

OCTAGON BOOKS
A Division of Farrar, Straus & Giroux, Inc.
19 Union Square West
New York, N. Y. 10003

Library of Congress Catalog Card Number: 77-97259

Printed in U.S.A. by
NOBLE OFFSET PRINTERS, INC.
NEW YORK 3, N. Y.

To Florence Barrett Whiting

Prologue

That I may see and tell

From the intensive study and analysis of individual poems the thoughtful student will acquire some understanding of the meaning and form of poetry; but it seems improbable that much real profit is to be derived from that phase of modern criticism which, without respect for tradition, is preoccupied with mere image and pattern, and which, as F. L. Lucas has observed, is overgrown with thickets of jargon and submerged in the swamps of pseudo psychology and fancy metaphysics. The prudent student will rely mainly on that historical approach which unfortunately, as we have just been reminded (*The Times Literary Supplement,* March 16, 1956), "has recently fallen out of fashion." By no means disparaging the closest scrutiny of poetic form and meaning, I urge that only a patient and thorough investigation of tradition and the historical setting will enable the student to understand fully what Milton means. For in Milton, as perhaps in no other poet, more is meant than meets the ear and the eye of the critic. A true understanding of Milton's poetry depends upon the comprehension of his thought and its relation to an extensive and complex background, literary, intellectual, and spiritual. At this distance of time and in this secular age, no one, however sedulous and resourceful, may hope to become familiar with the entire tradition which is embodied and reflected in the art and thought of this poet, who towers above the rest in thought and art, "In shape and gesture proudly eminent."

It may, however, be possible to isolate and study definite ideas and themes in various poems. In each of the following essays the method is much the same: the topic is treated historically in some detail, with full recognition of the contributions of scholars and critics but with emphasis upon interpretations based on the scrutiny of tradition and the contemporary milieu as far as these can be ascertained. The purpose is not to discover sources or to list verbal similarities but rather to trace, as precisely and as thoroughly as possible, the course of specific ideas and themes and their ultimate embodiment or transformation in Milton's poetry. I can honestly say that I have tried to be thorough and accurate; I have attempted to indicate the important stages and documents in each case; and I trust that the conclusions, though not very original, may be accepted as valid.

In these studies all the major poems except *Paradise Regained* are embraced. In the first the relation of *Comus* to Jonson's masques is re-examined and an independent critical reappraisal is attempted. In the next the central passage on the clergy in *Lycidas* is interpreted in the light of Scripture and the Protestant tradition. In the four studies that follow various aspects of the imagery, the ideas, and the structure of *Paradise Lost* are scrutinized. All the studies except the last are now published for the first time, and the last has been revised. As I have repeatedly stated, my purpose is not to discover specific literary sources of Milton's poetry but to show the relationship of the poetry to tradition or to show how Milton uses certain traditional ideas.

These studies ignore Milton's classical heritage and what has recently been called "the basic classicist meaning of Renaissance humanism." Milton's thorough assimilation of classical culture is of course indisputable. On the other hand, his profound concern with morality and religion warrants the character and the purpose of these studies, which, to be sure, do not pretend to represent all the phases of his intellectual or even his spiritual interests.

However incomplete, this work is the result of some years of study and reflection. In the later stages it was supported by the interest and appreciation of a devoted band of graduate students and especially by Miss Ann Mary Gossman, who is already an accomplished Milton scholar. To Miss Gossman I am especially grateful for "safe convoy" along the "perplex't paths" of the patristic wilderness, "The nodding horror of whose shady brows/Threats the forlorn and wandring Passinger."

It is my hope that these studies will be useful to students and that in style and thought they may not be quite unworthy of the poet whom for years I have read with unfailing interest; whose life is an inspiration and a challenge; whose poetry has led me and others in this "pendant world," in this dim spot called earth—in this universe once conceived to have been created and to be ruled by God—to believe that the Word received in faith "worketh the health of the soul," to cherish virtue and truth, to appreciate poetry for its form but more for its meaning, and sometimes to see if not to tell

> Of things invisible to mortal sight.

If I should fall into doctrinal heresy, perhaps I shall receive indulgent correction from the theologians. If I should misrepresent Milton, my sin would be less venial; for, without blasphemy be it spoken, my feeling for Milton is much like that of the psalmist before God: "Let us come before his presence with thanksgiving: and shew ourselves glad in him with Psalms." If I quote Milton freely, I do so because the quotations are in my judgment delightful, relevant, and convincing. If all this be idolatry, let the critics make the most of it.

Milton's poetry is quoted from *The Poetical Works of John Milton,* edited by H. C. Beeching; his prose, as a rule, from *The Student's Milton,* edited by F. A. Patterson.

Unfortunately, Rosemond Tuve's invaluable *Images and Themes in Five Poems by Milton* (1957) was published too late to be of service in my studies, but I should like to quote from her preface the following pregnant sentence: "Most of what the Renaissance poets learned from the Middle Ages about literary method—and this is where they learned much of what they built upon with such inventiveness and such splendor—is in him, and every sea-change that it underwent." And also this, from the chapter on *Comus,* explaining a detail of what she calls "the double reality of scenes and persons": "The Lady does not represent but presents virtue, and presents it in that one of its aspects most suitable to her literal self, for she does not cease to be Alice Egerton though she is equally the human spirit partially in the power of insidious evil." This criticism penetrates to the heart of truth and makes apparent the futility of some modern criticism of the Lady.

As related to my subject, Irene Samuel's recent study of the dialogue in heaven (*PMLA,* September, 1957) might also be mentioned. She emphasizes the importance of this dialogue, defines Milton's concept of God as the voice of Reason, Moral Law, "*the* Intelligence that comprehends the universe," and demonstrates the perfect dramatic and ethical propriety of this part of the epic. Here is the complete vindication of this dialogue; here is the conclusive refutation of all those critics who have complacently echoed Pope's quip.

Analyzing Milton's serious character and religious purpose, which in these enlightened days alienate many readers, Douglas Bush quoted Housman's lines "And malt does more than Milton can/To justify God's ways to man." This pleasantry must not pass for the truth. These lines immediately follow:

> Ale, man, ale's the stuff to drink
> For fellows whom it hurts to think:
> Look into the pewter pot
> To see the world as the world's not.

As this work is concluded and I look before and after, I recall another of Housman's poems which, it seems to me, anticipated my experience and expresses my hopes:

> I hoed and trenched and weeded,
>   And took the flowers to fair:
> I brought them home unheeded;
>   The hue was not the wear.
>
> So up and down I sow them,
>   For lads like me to find,
> When I shall lie below them,
>   A dead man out of mind.
>
> Some seeds the birds devour,
>   And some the season mars,
> But here and there will flower
>   The solitary stars.

In this context it scarcely becomes me to mention flowers and stars but rather to hope that some seed will fall, not by the wayside or in stony places, but into good ground and bring forth fruit in season. It is not for the sower to know or say what the harvest will be. Whatever its value, this study, with Milton at hand to bless, has for me not been altogether vain. It has brought its own sense of satisfaction, which, though not complacent, is not likely to be intimidated by the strictures of the learned as it is undaunted by a haunting nostalgia for that far country, the fields, the streams, the blue remembered hills, "The happy highways where I went/And cannot come again." There is, we are assured, another and a more hopeful prospect: there are hills eternal, in the memory and of the spirit, built by faith to stand, our own faith, not another's. Meanwhile, there is the conviction and the faith that Milton is the central and supreme figure in English poetry.

To Milton's poetry the public, sophisticated and unenlightened, is, we know, indifferent. And the principal reason for this lack of interest is clear. Our age, as Humphrey Kitto, in *Form and Meaning in Drama* (1956), has just recently observed, "is hardly one which is instinctively attuned to religious modes of thought." This estrangement is not by any means a recent development. "Neither today nor for centuries past have we been in immediate contact with a religious culture—with its habits of mind, its natural means of expression." Properly to understand and appreciate Milton's poetry it would, therefore, be necessary to bridge the centuries, to recall and in some measure re-create the faith and the prestige of a vanished Christian civilization, in which religion was a vital force. At the outset and as a simple test one must think of the cathedral not as an attraction for tourists but as a place of worship: the ancient fane with its gray columns soaring to the dimness of its embowed roof, the delicate traceries of the organ screen, the swelling notes of the organ, "the mellow shafts of light filtered through the stained-glass windows" with their hues of emeralds and rubies and amethysts, the hushed, reverent worshipers—all these things were familiar and precious: "And storied Windows richly dight,/Casting a dimm religious light." But of course it is manifestly impossible—and in some respects undesirable—to restore the past, to return to a precritical, dogmatic metaphysic.

Adapting the language of C. J. Sisson's introduction to his *New Readings in Shakespeare* (1956), I may say that I have tried to "creep closer" to the minds and the speech of the Reformation and that I have resisted that absorption in our modern world which has had such a pernicious effect upon recent aesthetic criticism. With the aid of others I have done what I could do to indicate specific areas and aspects of the religious tradition which is reflected in Milton's poetry. Conscious of the inadequacy if not of the imperfection of my endeavors, I can at least say that I have not spared any labor to present "My true account, lest he returning chide."

Implicit throughout this study is the assumption that life may have spiritual values and may be interpreted spiritually and that the life of the spirit presupposes the existence of the Divine as well as the human life. "Spiritual life always implies something higher than itself towards which it is ascending." Spiritual life is not opposed to mental and physical life but transforms these to a higher plane, imparts a higher quality to them, and raises them "towards the heights, towards that which is beyond life, beyond nature, beyond being." In this sense life is then a symbol of the highest value and the highest good, a symbol of true being, of the final mystery.

True appreciation of Milton's poetry demands, it is clear, some insight into this fundamental truth. It demands also a rather special temperament and a kind of religious consecration along with other qualities which are extremely rare in this age in which literature frequently has no roots and criticism no tradition. In such a degenerate time Milton's audience is inevitably limited. When we figuratively ascend to the lofty spiritual and artistic heights where Milton dwells,

> Thin, thin the pleasant human noises grow,
> And faint the city gleams;
> Rare the lone pastoral huts—marvel not thou!
> The solemn peaks but to the stars are known,
> But to the stars, and the cold lunar beams;
> Alone the sun arises, and alone
> Spring the great streams.

Milton was a superb craftsman, "by instinct first, and then by trained habit," as Helen Darbishire has recently said. But of course he was far more than a craftsman, isolated in a high and lonely tower. His poetry was inspired by and has in part satisfied the spiritual aspiration of humanity. Even in this skeptical age it still affords a superb view of the world *sub specie aeternitatis.*

For their forbearance and co-operation I thank the Department of English and the staff of the Fondren Library of The Rice Institute.

In conclusion I venture to add a more personal note. To my wife I am indebted for invaluable help and especially for her careful reading of the typescript. But, after all has been said, my greatest debt, which can never be paid, is to my mother, who revering the Word of God strove daily to be true to her Christian faith; who was "active in all that is good, industrious in all the ways in which good is to be gained"; who with patience and fortitude bore disappointment and affliction; and who many years ago resigned "this earthy load" and passed

> To where beyond these voices there is peace.

GEORGE WESLEY WHITING

Houston, Texas
January, 1958

A Note from the Author

The purpose of this study of Milton's poetry and the religious tradition is to interpret Milton in an age increasingly skeptical, in a culture dominated by the assumptions of the natural and historical sciences and by the illusions of progress and enlightenment. Its implicit thesis is that man's search for God and his struggle to overcome the material forces and prejudices that impede this search transcend in value all other human efforts. Unless "amid all the changes and chances of this mortal life, our hearts are surely fixed where true joys are to be found," life here lacks any true and final purpose or meaning. In the light of this truth I have undertaken to study some of the themes and symbols in Milton's poetry. To speak more precisely, I have attempted to trace the course of certain ideas, symbols, and themes and to show how these are embodied and are transformed in *Comus, Lycidas, Paradise Lost,* and *Samson Agonistes.*

Without tradition, which need not be static and which in any case played a vital part in the dissemination and preservation of Gospel truth, the Christian faith and church would never have reached Milton and the modern world. Tradition can be a constant witness for the Lord and His living Word, in darkness as well as in light. Christianity and tradition are really inseparable. Even when he rejects traditional ceremonies and dogmas, Milton's poetry is best understood with reference to tradition, to which it is indebted.

Drawing upon Scripture, Milton compared truth to a "streaming fountain": "if her waters flow not in a perpetual progression, they sicken into a muddy pool of conformity and tradition." He scorned and feared conformity: "I fear this yoke of outward conformity hath left a slavish print upon our necks." In Michael's preview of history in *Paradise Lost*, tradition is linked with superstition and coercion as an anti-Christian aberration, a mystery of iniquity, which corrupts the pure doctrine and story of Holy Scripture, upon which Milton, as a true Protestant, relies. The pure tradition of Scripture as interpreted by Protestants and shaped by his own intense convictions was Milton's ideal guide.

The subject is treated not as an academic problem of literary history nor as an abstract concept or occasion for sophisticated literary criticism but rather as an opportunity to show in the light of tradition the permanent spiritual and moral value of Milton's poetry. Without any loss of objectivity, this value is at all times kept firmly in mind—not in a utilitarian or dogmatic fashion but rather as a means of inviting the reader to share in a genuine understanding and appreciation of the poetry.

The kinship of poetry and religion should be emphasized. As has been said, poetry is a chief means by which religious realism is achieved. Without the aid of poetry, religious mystery can hardly be expressed. Poetry, which both enchants and informs, addresses its rhythmic and symbolic speech to regions of the mind which are inaccessible to argument.

In the present state of society the need of a genuine spiritual and religious renaissance should be apparent. Every civilization, and, not withstanding its astonishing technical achievements, even the current one—every civilization is corrupt, because each is the product of the human heart, which makes self, rather than God or what Julian Huxley calls the Sacred Reality, the center of existence. Thus every culture bears within itself the seeds of its own dissolution. Our mechanical triumphs and even our physical comforts may be the insidious foes of spiritual health.

In this tortured but complacent century, when materialism is rampant and when humanism, become gray and grim, seems to be "the last defence of the genteel tradition against chaos," we urgently need the wisest counsel, with true religion and the clear voice of conscience as our faithful guides. Some may return, spiritually if not literally, to the worship of what Evelyn Underhill calls the Universal Church: "her penitence, her supplication, her invulnerable confidence, her adoring delight in the splendour of God." In the words of Benjamin Jowett, some may repair to the example and the teaching of Christ, as to a fountain of light, "purging away the mist of eighteen centuries, which have insensibly gathered over the Christian world, yea, and over our own hearts also." It is my earnest hope that the voice and the message of Milton as here interpreted, echoing out of the distant past across the tumult of human hopes and fears, will even now to alien ears speak of things invisible to mortal sight and once more reveal how we may so pass through things temporal that we finally lose not the things eternal.

Contents

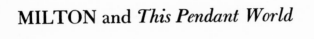

Comus, Jonson, and the Critics

Be it not don in pride, or in presumption

There is much sound criticism of Milton's masque (now invariably but incorrectly entitled *Comus*); but not infrequently conjecture or mere prejudice, "which on firm land/ Thaws not, but gathers heap," obstructs the view or fills the air with barbarous dissonance. In some cases assertion endlessly repeated seems to have been accepted as proof.

In considering, first, the literary sources or antecedents of the poem, it is imperatively necessary to emphasize the independence of Milton's mind, character, and method. In his highly individual and independent mind the material was assimilated, modified, and transmuted so that it bore in his work the stamp of his own personality and purpose. The relation of Milton's poetry to any source is, in Hanford's phrase, "distant and intangible." One has the impression that his recollection must always have been an unconscious one. This is a tested and true principle, which should be kept in mind throughout the following discussion.

Milton's masque is invariably said to be indebted to Jonson's *Pleasure Reconciled to Vertue*. The following statement is typical: "Milton read this masque, as we pointed out in our general introduction and as Miss Welsford has further shown in *The Court Masque*, pp. 314–

20."[1] It is known, however, that Jonson's masque, acted without success January 6, 1618, was first printed in the Folio of 1640, six years after Milton's masque was performed. Hence those who insist upon the indebtedness of Milton's exquisite poem to Jonson's dull and crude spectacle are forced to resort to sundry conjectures. Milton "read" Jonson's masque in the "little book," the contemporary manuscript, which is at Chatsworth, the seat of the Duke of Devonshire; or he may have read it in a privately printed quarto, which has unaccountably disappeared, leaving no trace behind; or he "must have obtained a copy from a courtier, from people like the Egertons, for instance."[2] In any case, it is insisted, Milton "read" *Pleasure Reconciled to Vertue.* It is, I admit, not impossible that through the Egertons (perhaps through Penelope, who had a part in *Chloridia,* 1630–31)[3] or through Henry Lawes, Milton had heard of Jonson's masque or at least of Comus, Jonson's repulsive dumb god of the belly. But certainly there is no proof that Milton had read Jonson's masque, which was not liked at all when it was produced and which was first published in 1640, six years after Milton's masque was produced and three years after it was published by Lawes, in 1637. The assertion that Milton read *Pleasure Reconciled to Vertue* seems to be an unwarranted assumption to buttress a theory of indebtedness which may have little or no basis in fact. Carefully and thoroughly comparing the two masques, the student who is without prejudice may find in Milton's masque little or no evidence of indebtedness to this earlier masque, which, I repeat, was a sad failure when it was produced and which, apart from its alleged influence on *Comus,* is quite negligible.

On the contrary, Milton's masque may, I think, be related to Jonson's *Hymenaei* or *Masque of Hymen,* which appeared in quarto in 1606 and again in folio in 1616, upon which Jonson and Jones lavished their best talents to celebrate a very important marriage (which was followed by a notorious scandal and divorce), and which was elaborately performed. The relationship of these masques is, I suggest, that of complete contrast: *Comus* is the converse of the *Masque of Hymen.* Jonson's masque is a pagan, worldly, discreetly amatory spectacle, with no trace or suggestion of Christian thought. Milton's masque with its theme of the "unassailable security of the virtuous mind in every circumstance of violence, and wrong,"—to borrow Hanford's apt phrasing—is devoted to the expression of a serious ethical

---

[1] Ben Jonson, *Ben Jonson,* ed. by C. H. Herford and Percy Simpson, X (Oxford, 1950), 574, Commentary.
[2] *Ibid.,* X, 575.   [3] *Ibid.,* VII, 761.

4

and religious philosophy, with specific Platonic ideas and with definite Christian overtones, and is inspired by the assurance that "if Vertue feeble were,/Heav'n it self would stoop to her." In developing his theme Milton presents, it seems, in the licentious conduct and wanton rites of Comus and his crew a deliberate parody of the stately pagan marriage ceremonies of Hymen, with similar mythological and natural images and characters, which are adapted to his purpose. There may also be a contrast between Juno, of the *Masque of Hymen,* who is adored and to whom the marriage rites are sacred, and Sabrina, of Milton's masque, who loves maidenhood and whose office is "To help insnared chastity." Moreover, in reason's control over the humors and affections or passions of men there is another important link between these masques, which are, however, so entirely different in quality, spirit, and purpose.

Before considering these points, it should be emphasized that at this time Milton's poetry was undoubtedly influenced by Jonson's. Bush—I could scarcely cite a better authority—finds in *L'Allegro* and *Il Penseroso* "the purer, more classical influence of Jonson." He describes as Jonsonian the "civilized, courtly, masque-like quality" of their mythological allusions. He says that Milton's study of Jonson is "very apparent" in the plot, tone, and even in the details of *Arcades.*[4] Sharing Bush's reluctance to "soil the pure ambrosial weeds of *Comus* with the rank vapors of annotation," I presume to suggest, first, that Comus' prologue is a kind of profane version of some parts of the *Masque of Hymen,* with the theme and the characters so changed that the relationship is not apparent to the inattentive or desultory reader.

Jonson's *Masque of Hymen,* "magnificently performed" at court for the "auspicious" celebration of the marriage of Robert, Earl of Essex, and the Lady Frances, second daughter to the "most noble" Earl of Suffolk, is presided over by Hymen and Reason, who have all the speaking parts, excluding the songs and the long epithalamion.

After the entrance of the characters, bridegroom, Hymen, bride, and attendants, the *Masque of Hymen* opens with a song warning all except those who are in sympathy with the ceremonies to depart:

> Bid all profane away;
> None here may stay
> To view our *mysteries,* . . .

---

[4] Douglas Bush, *Mythology and the Renaissance Tradition in English Poetry* (Minneapolis, 1932), p. 258.

Only those may remain who have been or in time will be the "self-same *sacrifice*." This song ends with a chorus which repeats the admonition:

> Flie then, all prophane, away,
> Flie farre off, as hath the *Day*;
> Night her cortine doth display,
> And this is Hymens *holiday*.

The time is night; all profane are banished; the rites are sacred to marriage, "In honour of that blest *Estate*,/Which all good *minds* should celebrate." Throughout, at the center of the scene, is an altar, sacred to Juno; and all the ceremonies are sacred to marriage, over which as in Rome, as a marginal note explains, Juno is "President." Later, as the darkness deepens, there is a sense of urgency, the Chorus exhorting the lingering dancers to haste, "for Hesperus his head downe bowes."

By contrast, in Milton's masque, Comus leads the profane, a "rout of Monsters" who are "in thick shelter of black shades imbowr'd." Here also, as Comus says, Hesperus is present: "The Star that bids the Shepherd fold,/Now the top of Heav'n doth hold." With gusto Comus then invokes the rites, the orgies rather, of license and lust:

> Mean while welcom Joy, and Feast,
> Midnight shout, and revelry,
> Tipsie dance, and jollity.

In both masques it is night; but the setting, the characters, and the avowed purpose are in each different. Not improbably the contrast is deliberate on the part of Milton, who, I believe, would be inclined to doubt that the union celebrated with such irreligious and idolatrous ceremonies in Jonson's masque "Was all in honour and devotion ment."

Later, in the *Masque of Hymen*, Reason, who is associated with Hymen as the master of ceremonies, invokes in this night sacred to married love the light of torches "To fright all malice from the *Night*." And Hymen calls for aid to save the virgins: "keepe your hallow'd lights/Untouch'd; and with their flame defend our *Rites*." On the contrary, Comus welcomes and loves the night, when "Strict Age, and sowre Severity" slumber, when the fairies, elves, and wood nymphs "Their merry wakes and pastimes keep"; when indeed all nature is free from moral control. Comus declares explicitly " 'Tis onely daylight that makes Sin/Which these dun shades will ne're report." Comus hopes that all their orgies will be concluded before the Morn

6

can disclose their "conceal'd Solemnity." In Jonson's masque the married couple is urged to conclude their loves "That you may both, e're day,/Rise perfect everie way." In *Hymen* the theme, frequently emphasized, is "This night is Hymen's all." For Comus and his crew, on the other hand, night is the fit time for wanton revelry and lust. For Comus in particular it is an opportunity to seduce a fair virgin.

It should be particularly noted that in Jonson's masque Reason invokes Juno and Hymen, without whom "Venus can doe nought,/Save what with shame is bought." Reason exclaims, "See, see! the bright *Idalian* starre,/That lighteth *louers* to their warre," and she repeatedly warns the dancers not to intrude upon the mysterious rites of married lovers. Comus invokes Venus for an entirely different purpose: "*Venus* now wakes, and wak'ns Love." To emphasize his purpose Comus also summons "Dark vaild Cotytto," the lewd

> Goddesse of Nocturnal sport
> . . . t'whom the secret flame
> Of mid-night Torches burns.

In *Hymen* the "personated *Bride*" wears a "gyrland of Roses," and the chaste bower of the wedded pair is strewn by Cypria (Venus) with "many a Lily, many a Rose." Comus thus instructs his followers: "Braid your Locks with rosie Twine,/Dropping odours, dropping wine." The roses of wedded lovers in *Hymen* become in *Comus* "rosie Twine" for the locks of a beastly, drunken rout of men and women, "Doing abhorred rites to *Hecate*/In their obscured haunts of inmost bowers."

In Jonson's masque when the scene is "all covered with clouds, as a night," Hymen admonishes the dancers to make an end:

> O know to end, as to beginne:
> A minutes losse, in *loue*, is sinne.
> . . . .
> The *night* hath other treasures
> Then these (though long conceal'd)
> Ere day, to be reueal'd.
> Then, know to end, as to beginne;
> A minutes losse, in *loue*, is sinne.

One is instantly reminded of Comus urging his followers to begin their rites in honor of Venus: "Night hath other sweets to prove,/*Venus* now wakes, and wak'ns Love." In both masques Venus is invoked, but, of course, for different purposes: Hymen invokes the goddess for the rites of wedded love, which are presumably, at least nominally, chaste; Comus summons her with Cotytto to preside over an orgy of tipsy dancing and lewd revelry. The contrast is, I believe, intentional: Milton contrasted the licentious rites of Comus with the ostensibly sacred rites of marriage in a masque that is entirely under the auspices of pagan deities, a masque that is barren of every sacred Christian idea and sanction. So much for contrasting character and purpose.

Some apparent verbal reminiscences may be noted. In *Hymen* a song inviting the men and women maskers to dance ends with these lines:

> Instruct your nimble feete,
> In motions, swift, and meete,
> The happy ground to beate,

and, apparently appropriating this idea and even part of the phrasing, Comus urges his crew "Com, knit hands, and beat the ground,/In a light fantastick round." In Jonson's epithalamion two lines expressing the wish that the child born of this union will have "Much of the *fathers* face,/ More of the *mothers* grace" seem to be recalled in the Attendant Spirit's description of Comus: "Much like his Father, but his Mother more."

The magnificent spectacle of the *Masque of Hymen,* with its plenitude of what Jonson calls "strangenesse of the *habites,* delicacie of *daunces,* magnificence of the *scenes,* or diuine rapture of *musique,*" was perhaps in Milton's mind when he has Comus say:

> Beauty is natures brag, and must be shown
> In courts, at feasts, and high solemnities
> Where most may wonder at the workmanship;

though these lines refer as well to court ceremonies and entertainments in general. Ignoring the proper title of Milton's masque, which has been discarded ever since Dalton's spurious and wretched version saw the light, one might even argue that Milton, to achieve his purpose, had substituted *Comus* for *Hymen* in Jonson's couplet: "On Hymen, Hymen call,/This night is Hymen's all." The titles then would be: the *Masque of Hymen* and the *Masque of Comus.* We know, however, that Comus in Milton's masque is merely the foil, the antagonist, the tempter, and that the proper title should probably be the *Masque of Chastity* or the *Masque of Vertue.* Comus should not be mentioned in the title of Milton's solemn and beautiful masque, with its exquisite tribute to virtue, which by its inherent power and the grace of heaven is victorious over temptation and is uncontaminated by "the rank vapours of this Sin-worn mould."

Milton's masque may thus in part be interpreted as a protest against such worldly spectacles as Jonson's *Masque of Hymen,* the ostentatious and profane diversions of "tapstry Halls/And Courts of Princes," where true courtesy, not to mention moral conduct and true religion, is more rarely found than "in lowly sheds with smoaky rafters." The theme of Milton's masque, the setting, the characters, the purpose, all in contrast with the *Masque of Hymen,* along with the invocation of Venus and the occasional reminiscences of style—all this seems to indicate that part of Milton's masque was written as the converse of *Hymen,* as perhaps a rejoinder to Jonson's elaborately pagan spectacle, which was as devoid of true religion as the nuptials so celebrated were barren of true love.

It is nevertheless almost an article of our literary creed that Milton's masque is much indebted to *Pleasure Reconciled to Virtue.* Welsford, who avers that Milton "owes a great deal" to this masque, indicates the details of the alleged indebtedness:[5] *Comus* resembles Jonson's masque in teaching the supremacy of virtue; the Attendant Spirit was suggested by Hercules; both masques end with praise of virtue; and in both masques children are presented to their parents by means of dances "which celebrate the happy results of youthful training in virtue." A thorough, comparative study of the masques yields little substantial evidence to support these dogmatic statements. In Jonson's masque, it is true, pleasure and virtue appear and they are reconciled; but what their nature is and what they do we never know. Certainly Jonson's gross dumb god of the belly is utterly unlike Milton's eloquent and plausible enchanter. Hercules, though praised as the servant of good and the friend of virtue, is quite unlike the Attendant Spirit, who descends from heaven to protect the innocent children. What is meant by the children's being presented to their parents is not at all clear; for the twelve princes, bred in the mountain, apparently have no parents. One comes from the "bright race of *Hesperus*" and so is not mortal. They have something to do with justice and wisdom, beauty and love; they are presented by Vertue; they return to the mountain. True it is that Hercules rebukes the "Belly-god," "voluptuous *Comus,* god of cheere," and his gross attendants, who

[5] Enid Welsford, *The Court Masque* . . . (Cambridge, 1927), pp. 314 ff.

wallow in the "stye of vice." This is all. There is here not much that resembles anything in Milton's masque. Perhaps there is a suggestion in the following lines of the concluding song praising Vertue:

> She, she it is, in darknes shines.
> 'tis she that still hir-self refines,
> by hir owne light, to eurie eye,
> more seene, more knowne, when Vice stands by.
> And though a stranger here on earth,
> in heauen she hath hir right of birth.
> There, there is Vertues seat.

In the vaguest way these lines do suggest the Lady in Milton's masque. But in general the similarities between these masques are hardly clear and definite enough to warrant the positive statements of indebtedness usually made.

On the other hand, the evidence linking Milton's masque with the *Masque of Hymen* seems to be rather definite. The relationship is one characteristic of Milton, who does not copy but freely adapts and transmutes material to suit his own purpose, to show the triumph of virtue over vice.[6] Another link between *Comus* and the *Masque of Hymen* should be mentioned. In *Hymen* the "bright Virgin," who indeed might suggest the Lady, is to be wedded, and the ceremonies precede the "mutuall" joys of the couple, the "delights" of the marriage bed. Early in the masque Reason with Hymen intervenes to restrain and subdue the Humours and Affections or Passions (who are akin to the crew of Comus), who with swords threaten to disrupt the ceremonies. After Hymen has warned that the "foure untemp'red *Humours* are broke out," Reason sternly speaks:

> Forbeare your rude attempt; what ignorance
> Could yeeld you so prophane, as to aduance
> One thought in act, against these *mysteries?*

The Humours and Passions are admonished to have reverence for these mysterious rites of marriage. In fact in the *Masque of Hymen* Reason, represented as a venerable person with white hair and blue garments "semined with starres," is the mistress of ceremonies, doing most of the speaking and directing the action of the masque.

Now it is well known that *Comus* expounds "the Platonic doctrine that reason must govern the irrational elements of the soul." In Jon-

---

[6] It is conceivable but improbable that this method applied to *Pleasure Reconciled to Vertue* would produce *Comus*.

son's masque Reason is a cold impersonal abstraction, quite lacking in any human quality whatever. In Milton's masque, on the other hand, reason is delightfully embodied in the Elder Brother, sage beyond his years; in the Lady, charming confuter if not vanquisher of the juggler Comus; and to some extent in the Attendant Spirit, the good angel dispatched from heaven for the defense and protection of threatened innocence. In Jonson's masque Reason is simply reason, moving or rather standing on the intellectual plane and not possessing any human character or emotions at all. In Milton's masque reason is dramatically embodied in the characters, who, succored by divine grace, firmly supported by their own inherent virtue, and finally aided by a bit of charming magic, subdue sensual folly and intemperance, although these are reinforced by charms and spells and baited "with reasons not unplausible." Contrasting the supple and beautiful poetry that expresses the wisdom of the Elder Brother, the Lady, and the Attendant Spirit with the dreary and mechanical verse of Reason in the *Masque of Hymen,* one must heartily agree with the Younger Brother:

> How charming is divine Philosophy!
> Not harsh, and crabbed as dull fools suppose,
> But musical as is *Apollo's* lute,
> And a perpetual feast of nectar'd sweets,
> Where no crude surfet reigns.

—a tribute that the verse of Jonson's cold Reason could never inspire.[7]

It is possible, then, that Comus and his wanton revelers, with his lust, his sophistry, and his attempted seduction of the Lady, is Milton's answer to Jonson's *Masque of Hymen,* which, with Reason presiding, ostensibly honored marriage with pagan ceremonies, which at that court may have been far from the decorous or respectable. The contrast is striking if not intentional. In Jonson we have Hymen, Reason, and the wedded pair, who anticipate the nominally chaste delights and tender blisses of the marriage bed. In Milton we have Comus presiding at first over a scene of revelry and lust, perhaps a profane version of the masque of marriage, and then proceeding in his nefarious attempt to seduce the Lady, the incarnation of innocence and saintly chastity. In the end, of course, the Lady and her Brothers, partly aided by the Attendant Spirit, triumph over "sensual Folly, and Intem-

[7] Incidentally, in Campion's *Masque of the Marriage of the Lord Hayes* (1607), with Night, Hesperus, Flora, Zephyrus, and Diana's tree, there may be a faint foreshadowing of Milton's masque. The tone of Campion's masque with its sincere praise of chastity is obviously in harmony with that of *Comus.*

perance" and are reunited with their father. Jonson ostensibly celebrates marriage; Milton praises virtue and chastity and their victory
over sensual folly and intemperance.

At court, as we know, for example from the report of Sir John Har-
rington, folly and intemperance sometimes scandalously held sway:[8]

One day, a great feast was held, and, after dinner, the representation of
Solomon his Temple and the coming of the Queen of Sheba was made, or
(I might better say) was meant to have been made, before their Majesties,
by device of the Earl of Salisbury and others. But alas! as all earthly things
do fail to poor mortals in enjoyment, so did prove our presentment hereof.
The Lady who did play the Queen's part, did carry most precious gifts to
both their Majesties; but, forgetting the steps arising to the canopy, overset
her caskets into his Danish Majestie's lap, and fell at his feet, tho I rather
think it was in his face. Much was the hurry and confusion; cloths and
napkins were at hand, to make all clean. His Majesty then got up and would
dance with the Queen of Sheba; but he fell down and humbled himself
before her, and was carried to an inner chamber, and laid on a bed of state;
which was not a little defiled with the presents of the Queen which had
been bestowed on his garments; such as wine, cream, jelly, beverage, cakes,
spices, and other good matters. The entertainment and show went forward,
and most of the presenters went backward, or fell down; wine did so occupy
their upper chamber. Now did appear, in rich dress, Hope, Faith, and
Charity: Hope did assay to speak, but wine rendered her endeavours so
feeble that she withdrew, and hoped the King would excuse her brevity:
Faith was then all alone, for I am certain she was not joyned with good
works, and left the court in a staggering condition: Charity came to the
King's feet; and seemed to cover the multitude of sins her sisters had committed; in some sort she made obeysance and brought gifts, but said she
would return home again as there was no gift which heaven had not already
given his Majesty. She then returned to Hope and Faith, who were both
sick and spewing in the lower hall. Next came Victory, in bright Armour,
and presented a rich sword to the King, who did not accept it, but put it
by with his hand; and, by a strange medley of versification, did endeavour
to make suit to the King. But Victory did not tryumph long; for, after much
lamentable utterance, she was led away like a silly captive, and laid to
sleep in the outer steps of the anti-chamber. Now did Peace make entry,
and strive to get foremoste to the King; but I grieve to tell how great wrath
she did discover unto those of her attendants; and, much contrary to her
semblance, most rudely made war with her olive branch, and laid on the
pates of those who did oppose her coming.

This was in the reign of James I, but in the following reign such

[8] Charles Williams, *James I* (London, 1951), pp. 203–204.

scenes may not have been uncommon. Though dwelling in the ominous wood, Comus and his crew are intimately related to these court revelers whose "upper chambers" were occupied with wine. Puritans, who objected to the turning of the church sacrament into a theatrical stage play, would surely be offended by such disgraceful conduct. There were, to be sure, several strains in the character of Puritans, and Milton, who may have been an exception, could, at least in imagination, contemplate with enjoyment such kinds of entertainment:

> There let *Hymen* oft appear
> In Saffron robe, with Taper clear,
> And pomp, and feast, and revelry,
> With mask, and antique Pageantry, . . .

In general, Puritans could be counted upon to condemn profane masques and pagan entertainments at court or elsewhere, for these were at least sometimes the occasion of intemperance and immorality and they certainly did not promote the cause of morality or what was considered true religion.

A particular form of vice at court, carefully studied by Sensabaugh,[9] may be mentioned here. Sensabaugh contends that Milton's masque is an attack upon the cult of Platonic love then prevalent in courtly circles, in literature, and in the theater. He presents much evidence regarding the nature of this erotic cult, which was sponsored by the Queen. The cult prescribed that men should worship the physical beauty of women. Courtiers spent much time in affected compliment, extolling the beauty and the chastity of women and adoring them as saints. But this cult of Platonic love, expressed in a kind of rhetorical jargon, was in fact a disguise for the pursuit of carnal love. The cult threw down, Sensabaugh says, "a serious challenge to traditional ethics in matters of marriage and love." Puritans and of course many other decent Englishmen deemed marriage a sacred and honorable estate which signified the mystical marriage between Christ and the church. In sermons and pamphlets Puritans attacked the reasoning and the morals of this coterie, which was also denounced as a scheme to promote popery. Sensabaugh argues that Milton, partly to justify his choice of celibacy, espoused the doctrine of virginity and that, with reference to this Platonic cult, he embodied in the speech of Comus "much current casuistry about beauty and love."

[9] George F. Sensabaugh, "The Milieu of *Comus*," *Studies in Philology*, XLI (April, 1944), 238–49.

Milton's masque may incidentally or by way of Comus' argument be an attack on this Platonic cult, but the masque as a whole cannot be restricted to that subject. It does not attack or condemn any specific vice except lust, unchastity, or in the poet's words "leud and lavish act of sin." The true theme of the masque is virtue or specifically chastity: " 'Tis chastity, my brother, chastity." Inspired by this theme and his Christian Platonism, "the uncontrouled worth/Of this pure cause" kindles the poet's spirits to a pure flame of sacred poetry, which reaches one of its peaks in the following affirmation of his faith by the Elder Brother:[10]

> against the threats
> Of malice or of sorcery, or that power
> Which erring men call Chance, this I hold firm,
> Vertue may be assail'd, but never hurt,
> Surpriz'd by unjust force, but not enthrall'd,
> Yea even that which mischief meant most harm,
> Shall in the happy trial prove most glory.
> But evil on it self shall back recoyl,
> And mix no more with goodness, when at last
> Gather'd like scum, and setl'd to it self
> It shall be in eternal restless change
> Self-fed, and self-consum'd.

Warm appreciation of this key passage, this eloquent affirmation of faith in the invincibility of virtue and the ultimate defeat of evil might reasonably be expected (though sometimes one's own faith may waver), and such approval might naturally set the tone for criticism of the masque. But the matter is not as simple as this. It is true that we have much enlightened and informative interpretation of the masque, but there is unfortunately some carping criticism and more than a little outright dogmatism. As the Lady says, the tumult is "rife, and perfet" in the listening ear, and the eye may sometimes encounter only "single darknes."

The diversity of critical opinion may be briefly indicated. Some critics declare roundly that the poem is neither a true masque nor a real drama; some aver that it is composed of incongruous elements and is sadly lacking in artistic unity; some discover in it a mixture of heterogeneous styles. One much respected critic is convinced that it is a true allegory, a Christian allegory of course, the action consti-

[10] The title *Comus* is a forgery of the depraved taste of the eighteenth century, which seemed to prefer Dalton's spurious version to Milton's exquisitely pure and chaste poem.

tuting a pilgrimage, the wild wood being the world, Ludlow town an image of heaven, the sprinkling of the water "an infusion of divine grace"; another is equally confident that the allegory is unimportant and irrelevant. One critic condemns the poem because it does not blend harmoniously the many discordant elements derived from a variety of "pre-texts" or sources (here, of course, Milton is cast in the old discredited role of mere compiler, an unimaginative pedestrian transcriber, with no originality whatever and with almost no talent). One, who should know better, finds a discordant mixture of "Greek, Jonsonian, and Augustan classicism." And so it goes. One declares that the masque is "full of monologues and lengthy tirades" and that the didactic intention is so apparent that it "deadens the required emotion and prevents anxiety." For one critic Milton's masque is a deplorable departure from true Renaissance humanism. This is illustrated by comparing the Attendant Spirit with Ariel. In the short space of twenty years Ariel, the "winged spright, trembling with eagerness to serve mankind," becomes in Thyrsis an "angel with a moral mission." (Obviously Thyrsis has no purpose of serving mankind!) At the end the "Miltonian angel ascends to heaven amid moralising, mythological visions," his last words a plea for chastity; Ariel takes flight "like a butterfly." It is all most regrettable. It has even been declared that the theme of *Comus* is "not unspottedly Christian" because some pagans believed in virtue and because the time of the action is confused between pre-Christian Albion and the Christian present. "This way the noise was, if mine ear be true."

Deafened by this din, lost in the mazes of this wilderness, the student may in desperation turn to the clear-eyed if somewhat undiscriminating critic who obviously knows his own way and mind:[11]

Comus as a masque presenting a clear story, a simple allegory, and a graceful compliment embroidered with a fluid imagery seems to me worth ten fretworks of strained conceit and forced interpretation. Perhaps when the critics have learned a little temperance in the application of their Byzantine ingenuities, we shall be able to enjoy without apology the simple beauties of obvious commonplace set in musical language.

Firmly rejecting the notion that the ideas of *Comus* are "obvious commonplace" and that the criticism of the masque is all a tissue of "strained conceit and forced interpretation," the student should welcome the critic's clarion call: back to the poem. The poem itself, un-

[11]Robert M. Adams, "Reading *Comus*," *Ikon: John Milton and the Modern Critics* (Ithaca, 1955), p. 34. Hereafter cited as *Ikon*.

encumbered by irrelevant issues and critical disquisitions, should always be the main object of study and enjoyment as well as the sole criterion for the evaluation of all criticism. This is the only way of sanity and truth. What is the student to think when he reads the following statements, the first by the dean of Milton scholars in our country, the next by the dean of Milton scholars in England?[12]

There is no real dramatic conflict. The Lady, her knightly brothers, the flushed reveler, his allegorical monsters, . . . Thyrsis stand frozen in a tableau.
. . . not a little of *Comus* is deliberately and successfully dramatic. In *Comus* he had mastered the elements of drama.

He can be genuinely dramatic in *Comus.*

What indeed! Only by reading the poem may the informed and sensitive student discover the truth.

Milton's masque has obviously occasioned or has been the innocent victim of a variety of disconcerting opinions. This is no place to survey all of this criticism, to enter what Warton calls this "chaos of controversy," this "Wilde Abyss,/The Womb of nature and perhaps her Grave." But something may yet be done to indicate the principal points of controversy and perhaps to help the student to see his way more clearly. Leaving a "calm and pleasing solitarinesse, fed with chearfull and confident thoughts," one would, in Milton's phrase, embark in this "troubled sea of noises and hoarse disputes" only, if possible, to behold in the end "the bright countenance of truth." Forward then, "And som good angel bear a shield before us."

First there is the matter of romanticism. Thomas Warton was among the first to emphasize the importance of this subject in Milton's early poems. He wrote:[13]

When Milton wrote these poems, many traditionary superstitions, not yet worn out in the popular belief, adhered to the poetry of the times. Romances and fabulous narratives were still in fashion, and not yet driven away by puritans and usurpers. To ideas of this sort, and they corresponded with the complexion of his genius, allusions often appear even in Milton's elder poetry: but it was natural that they should be found at least as largely in his early pieces, which were professedly written in a lighter strain, at a period when they more universally prevailed, and were more likely to

---

[12] John Milton, *The Poems of John Milton,* ed. by James Holly Hanford (2d ed.; New York, 1953), p. 103. E. M. W. Tillyard, *Milton* (New York, 1930), pp. 66, 74. E. M. W. Tillyard, *The Metaphysicals and Milton* (London, 1956), p. 61.
[13] *Poems upon Several Occasions, English, Italian, and Latin . . . with Notes Critical and Explanatory, . . .* by Thomas Warton (London, 1785), Preface, p. xx.

be caught by a young poet. Much imagery in these poems is founded on this source of fiction.

Warton goes on to say that Newton, an excellent scholar, was unacquainted with the "treasures of the Gothick library," this "idle track of reading" never luring him away from his "more solid and rational studies." In these early poems, however, Milton is an old English poet; and therefore Warton in his notes supplies abundant illustration of this fact. There is space for only a few examples. On the line "No savage fierce, bandite, or mountaneer" Warton remarks, "A Mountaneer seems to have conveyed the idea of somewhat very savage and ferocious." And he cites examples from *The Tempest* and *Cymbeline* and refers to "instances in B. and Fletcher." On the line "No goblin, or swart Faëry of the mine," Warton has the following note: "In the Gothick system of pneumatology, mines were supposed to be inhabited by various sorts of spirits." There are references to and material cited from several "authorities" on this subject. The celebrated passage beginning "Of calling shapes, and beck'ning shadows dire," carries this note: "I remember these superstitions, which are here finely applied, in the ancient Voyages of Marco Polo the Venetian." Warton quotes the relevant passage in Latin. The lines "when the gray-hooded Even,/Like a sad votarist in palmer's weed," is accompanied by a note pointing out a romantic-superstitious connotation: "Milton, notwithstanding his abhorrence of every thing that related to superstition, often dresses his imaginary beings in the habits of popery. But poetry is of all religions: and popery is a very poetical one." The first part of the line "Helping all urchin blasts, and ill-luck signs" is explained: from "its solitariness, the ugliness of its appearance, and from a popular opinion that it sucked or poisoned the udders of cows" the urchin or hedgehog was adopted into the demonologic system. Then follow relevant illustrations from *The Tempest*.[14]

Bush, though, perhaps thinking primarily of the myth of Circe, declares that most of the romance is "strained out" in the Miltonic version. The details are romantic, but the poem is not "romantic in spirit." Milton is restrained by his classical instincts, by the weighty discourse on virtue, and by the formal requirements of the masque. He could not, like Spenser, "wander delightfully through a world of enchant-

---

[14] Consult Warton's notes: L. C. Martin, "Thomas Warton and the Early Poems of Milton," *Proceedings of the British Academy 1934* (London, 1934); E. E. Stoll, *Poets and Playwrights* (Minneapolis, 1930), pp. 190, 194, *passim*, and his "Milton a Romantic," *From Shakespeare to Joyce* (Garden City, 1944), pp. 388–412.

ment."[15] We are grateful for Milton's classical restraint, for his sense of form, which is almost unique among English poets. But if what goes on in that ominous wood is not romantic, what is it? There is peril, for there great Comus dwells, "And in thick shelter of black shades imbowr'd,/Excells his Mother at her mighty Art." There on the tawny sands dance the fairies, elves, and wood nymphs. There is enchanting song which floats upon the wings "Of silence, through the empty-vaulted night." There or hard by in the "hilly crofts" the shepherd meditates his "rural minstrelsie." And thither comes fair Sabrina to the aid of ensnared chastity. Here surely is the sense, the reality of danger, mysterious and imminent; here there is strangeness and enchantment. All this exists not for its own sake or to provide thrills and delicious sensations of horror, as in your genuine Gothic romance. It is a setting, a proving ground for virtue, for chastity. The drear wood, "The nodding horror of whose shady brows/Threats the forlorn and wandring Passinger," is in truth an accursed place, whence the children guarded and guided by the Spirit flee "to holier ground." Perhaps there is too much real evil and too much weighty discourse to suit Bush's idea of romance. If so, one can say only that this material is not to be judged by a preconceived standard, even that of such an intelligent critic as Bush undoubtedly is. Perhaps we should abandon the word *romance,* which has such a variety of meanings. But Warton found romantic material and imagery in this poem. So undoubtedly does the intelligent and sensitive reader, who almost instinctively realizes that such material is proper here and that it adds infinitely to the meaning and strange beauty and charm of the masque.

Criticism is even more divided over Milton's alleged failure to reconcile disparate elements and to make his masque conform to the masque pattern. Bush has very justly said that *Comus* is "an excellent specimen of Milton's combining of pagan and Christian materials in harmonious purity."[16] Another critic, to be cited later, most emphatically, not to say violently, rejects this opinion. It should be said that the unique effect and power of Milton's masque is attained by contrast. On the one hand, it degrades the passions, through which the soul "grows clotted by contagion/Imbodies, and imbrutes, till she quite loose/The divine property of her first being." On the other hand, the masque exalts the spiritual and intellectual virtues, both

[15] Douglas Bush, *Mythology and the Renaissance Tradition in English Poetry,* pp. 260 ff.
[16] *Ibid.,* p. 263.

18

philosophical and Christian, to a state almost bordering on the divine. The Christian Platonism of the antithesis between sin and virtue, between the frail and feverish life in this dim spot called earth and the serene existence amongst "the enthron'd gods on Sainted seats" is steadily maintained. It is really an understatement to say that Milton "has a vision of heavenly beauty beyond the range of Jonson."[17] Jonson really has no vision of heavenly beauty. It should be obvious that Milton's firm faith in virtue and his detestation of vice underlie the extreme contrasts which make *Comus* effective. It is perverse to argue that the "contrast between the pure world of angelic spirits and the world of Comus" blurred Milton's essential idea. Heaven and the angelic world are necessarily elements in the thought of a Christian poet. How could he be expected to exclude them?

In the masque, however, the actual contrast is not so much between the celestial powers and the world of Comus as it is between virtue and vice in this world, between the Lady, whose inherent virtue and purity are so dear to heaven, and Comus, who is specifically lust. Alone the Lady is intellectually and morally more than a match for Comus although her body is manacled "while Heav'n sees good." She is really invincible. Nevertheless it is most reassuring—and not at all surprising in a Christian poem—to know that the Heavenly Spirit is near to help: to warn the Brothers, to arm them with the magical herb, to guide them to the palace of the wicked enchanter, to summon the virtuous Sabrina, and finally to conduct the children safely to their father's residence. The Spirit has a real function, and the masque would be ineffably poor and thin without him.

Through contrast Milton achieves his superb effects, artistic and moral. The Lady's purity, the "pure flame of religious and moral passion," glows steadily and brightly against the black shadows of this ominous wood, where all are in peril except those who

> by due steps aspire
> To lay their just hands on that Golden Key
> That ope's the Palace of Eternity.

This antithesis is essential. And the Attendant Spirit is essential too, for he represents the liveried angels that attend and guard the virtuous. If virtue feeble were—but virtue is not feeble—heaven itself would stoop to her. Heaven does stoop: God watches over His own.

[17] Douglas Bush, *English Literature in the Earlier Seventeenth Century 1600–1660* (Oxford, 1952), p. 364.

19

As already noted, some critics are greatly troubled by what they regard as an inept contrast, an incongruity arising from Milton's lack of judgment or taste: the contrast between the theme of *Comus* and the true spirit or character of the masque as a type. Welsford, for example, declares that Milton was unable to see that the masque, "whose presiding deity was Hymen," was most unsuitable for the unfolding of the sage and serious doctrine of virginity. Moreover, *Comus* is inconsistent with Milton's other poetry: the idea of "self-righteous asceticism" which he expounds in *Comus* is "incompatible with the ideal of the golden world of beauty which pervades so much of his poetry."[18] Recently, another critic, attacking with more violence if less discrimination, condemns *Comus* as a "mélange of various tendencies and styles that never merge into anything intensely organic." *Comus* is a hodgepodge, never achieving a satisfactory translation of the pre-texts and their motifs. To put the appalling truth into a few words, *Comus* is "an error in artistic judgment."[19] The grievous faults of the masque are enumerated and described. The conflicts are "both extrinsic and intrinsic"; *Comus* is a patchwork of styles; it lacks the formality and ritual of the masque; it is totally lacking in humorousness; it is totally lacking in suspense and character development; it converts what was considered history into a saint's legend; the Lady is a "curious mixture, half-rational and half-instinctive"; the virtues celebrated are Christian "only by adoption"; and so on ad infinitum. After all this, one is indeed surprised to come across the admission that the critic has "perhaps . . . missed the real point of the masque." Perhaps he has.

These strictures are irksome but not unanswerable. Was it really necessary for Milton to conform to the marriage conventions of the masque? Were the conventions of the masque binding and sacred? Is it not true that Milton has written the only memorable masque, long cherished by the discriminating for its serious theme and its enchanting poetry while other masques are forgotten or known only by the literary specialist? The critic speaks vaguely of the "ideal of the golden world of beauty" which pervades so much of Milton's poetry but is wanting in *Comus*. What can this mean? The idea of temperance, purity, and virtue in this poem is not unrelated to the moral, religious, and spiritual values of his major poems, the core, the central

18 Enid Welsford, *The Court Masque . . .* , pp. 320 ff.
19 Don C. Allen, *The Harmonious Vision: Studies in Milton's Poetry* (Baltimore, 1954), pp. 32 ff.

20

idea of which is not ideal beauty in a golden age but righteousness and truth and obedience to divine law. In fact, as Hanford has shown,[20] Milton's masque is a first and an important step in his treatment of temptation, the central subject or theme of his major poems. The Lady triumphs over folly and intemperance whereas Eve weakly succumbs. Unwilling to embark upon a systematic refutation of Allen's criticism,[21] which though challenging is generally unsympathetic and sometimes dogmatic, I may simply say that Allen shows no understanding of the serious thought and no appreciation of the poetry. Characteristic of this lack of insight is his remark that the masque is properly entitled *Comus,* for Comus dominates it and the theme of chastity is not "firmly brought home." It is hard to believe that Allen has actually read the poem. He says that the characters in general speak like pagans but "momently become Christian." Does he include among the characters the Lady and the Attendant Spirit? Is the fact that the conversation of the Lady and her Brothers is "studded with classical mythology" any sound reason for saying that they speak like pagans? Must the speech of Christians be restricted solely to Scripture and be clothed altogether in Biblical language? If it were, I can imagine that Allen would be prompt to find in this pious speech matter for satire. He is indeed a most difficult man to please. I am glad to hear him admit that he may have missed the real point of the masque. Fortunately others, much less learned and sophisticated, have no trouble at all in seeing the point clearly.[22] For Allen the poem is obviously a complete failure. For Adams, who takes the trouble to refute him, it meets successfully the essential requirements of the masque: to voice a compliment, to present a moral allegory, and to provide occasion for a spectacle. It can, Adams thinks, be read "consistently and satisfyingly" on the level of the masque, and it should not be "overread." Recondite allusions and metaphorical overtones should not be sought out. The masque was not written for explication. Adams is clearly right in focusing attention on the central episode, the temptation, and in emphasizing the various elements of the Lady's strength and the "convincing demonstration" of her moral self-sufficiency, in-

[20] J. H. Hanford, "The Temptation Motive in Milton," *Studies in Philology,* XV (January, 1918), 176–94.
[21] For a searching discussion the student should consult the work of Adams already mentioned: *Ikon,* pp. 30–33.
[22] In her discussion of *Comus* in *Themes and Images in Five Poems by Milton* (Cambridge [Mass.], 1957) Rosemond Tuve firmly refutes some of Mr. Allen's criticism of the masque.

directly aided by heaven. Although he may unwisely depreciate the role of grace and the spiritual sense of haemony (which Coleridge understood), Adams is right in insisting that virtue is not wholly dependent on grace—the poem in fact says so—; and it is certainly true that Miltonic temperance is not a passive and contemplative virtue. As Adams says, Milton's whole life shows that virtue was for him "an active, wayfaring, warfaring quality." Although perhaps lacking in subtlety and spiritual insight, his criticism is marked by refreshing common sense, by an emphasis on fundamental matters, and by a clear perspective on "the poem's literal architecture." Adams is particularly successful in dissecting the absurdities of Brooks and Hardy. The appreciation of spiritual values is not, however, his strong point. He lacks Milton's sense of things invisible to mortal sight. And he and Allen have, it is clear, one common quality: they are both essentially rationalistic.

For Woodhouse *Comus* has a more profound meaning: it is a consistent religious allegory moving on two levels of existence and experience, that of nature and that of grace, which to some extent interpenetrate.[23] The action is a sort of pilgrimage, and everything about the poem is symbolic: the Wood is the world, made up of good and evil, to be discriminated by reason, and thus a place of danger and trial; the palace of Comus is a crystallization of evil, one of the crises of temptation which abounds in the world; Ludlow town with the castle is the goal of the pilgrimage and the reward of virtue. The Attendant Spirit is a symbol, not of grace in its full extent, but of divine protection. Comus and his crew are symbols of the "perversion of natural goods to evil ends." The Lady symbolizes virtue and chastity which rise through "the order of grace" to virginity. Sabrina, by sprinkling pure water, that is by baptism, is the agent of "an infusion of divine grace." In this way the problem is solved on the religious level, where alone "the dynamic of true virtue" is found. The Lady is freed by the operation of grace "to make her way through the Wild Wood . . . to the Heavenly City, whose earthly image is Ludlow."

Certainly it would be strange if Milton's poem had no overtones of the religious concept of grace, which, however, is not mentioned. As a religious poet and heir of the medieval tradition, Milton may well be thought to have included more implicit allegorical and symbolic significance than the central allegory might lead the reader to suspect. But it may be objected that Woodhouse's interpretation is unwar-

[23] A. S. P. Woodhouse, "*Comus* Once More," *University of Toronto Quarterly,* XIX (April, 1950), 218–23.

ranted, that the pattern which he describes seems to be forced or superimposed upon the poem, the action of which takes place on one level, with natural magic added and with something divine far more deeply interfused, something whose dwelling is the mind and the spirit of man. From heaven or near it the Spirit, the one divine being, descends bringing divine protection and care; and when his mission is completed he returns to his celestial home above the smoke and stir of the earth. Sabrina, the river goddess, was a virgin pure on earth before she was made immortal but not divine. The other characters are and remain of this world though under divine protection. There are two levels in nature: virtuous nature in the children, who are incorruptible and victorious; depraved nature in Comus and his crew, who are enslaved and damned. The Lady and her Brothers are inherently virtuous and wise, and they merit and receive divine aid, which is unsolicited but welcome. The Lady, who alone is tempted or subject to temptation, is in character and argument invincible. In these there is no movement from a lower to a higher level, from nature to grace; but divine power (or grace, if Woodhouse insists) is present to warn the Brothers, to guide them to the wizard's palace, and to release from fetters, ensnared but spiritually and intellectually invincible, chastity. True virtue is inherent. There is no evidence in the poem that Milton meant to differentiate between chastity and virginity; the words are used synonymously. Virginity or chastity is dear to heaven but triumphs on the secular level by its own power. There is no movement from nature to grace but rather from grace to virtuous nature. Thus the Elder Brother (of whom Brooks and Hardy make such a figure of fun) is proved right in his thesis that "Vertue may be assail'd, but never hurt." There is no fall here, no need for grace to renew man's "lapsed powers, though forfeit and enthrall'd/By sin to foul exorbitant desires;" and certainly, to alter the line slightly, the Lady does not owe to God "All her deliv'rance, and to none but him." In *Comus* Milton does not emphasize so much man's need of grace as his virtue, his ability (through the ministration of grace or divine aid) to achieve and preserve moral goodness. The masque celebrates such virtue as mortals protected by heaven may achieve in this world, and it closes with the plea "Mortals that would follow me/Love vertue, she alone is free."

His task completed, the Spirit announces his intention of going back home, to the ocean and the sky, to the gardens fair of Hesperus, where in eternal summer dwell Adonis and Aphrodite, and where celestial Cupid

Holds his dear *Psyche* sweet intranc't
After her wandering labours long,
Till free consent the gods among
Make her his eternal Bride,
And from her fair unspotted side
Two blissful twins are to be born,
Youth and Joy; so *Jove* hath sworn.

It seems very simple. But Tillyard finds here an "oblique" meaning. According to him the epilogue suggests a solution of the "problem" posed in the masque.[24] The problem is that in the masque Comus advocates incontinence, the Lady abstinence. This problem, one would think, is solved by the Lady's triumph and the rout of Comus. This is not Tillyard's idea. According to him, the Spirit in the epilogue advocates the right way, the middle way, for the Lady. The right way is marriage. It can hardly be thought, however, that in the epilogue Milton would propose another course; and it is improbable that the Cupid-Psyche union is intended to suggest human marriage; for this is an ethereal union. It is not at all likely that a few lines in the epilogue could be meant to repudiate the sage and serious doctrine of chastity, the theme of the masque. There is no evidence at all that Milton came to believe that the Lady was wrong. It is improbable that the epilogue was written to "correct" the doctrine of the masque; for this doctrine needed no correction.[25] In the epilogue we in imagination ascend to the blessed realm of immortal spirits, but from that realm, which in effect is heaven, mere mortals are excluded. We or rather the true servants of virtue may enter that region of bliss only after "this mortal change," that is, after death. There is, as Adams says, "no . . . reason to suppose the young people are going to heaven" —going immediately, he must mean; for of course they must hope to go there ultimately. In any case marriage is out of the question. For in heaven, we are told, there is neither marrying nor giving in marriage; and in the masque there is not the faintest suggestion of marriage. I am afraid that we shall just have to put up with Milton's own masque, the Masque of Chastity!

The truth is that the poem itself should be the center of interest

[24] E. M. W. Tillyard, "The Action of *Comus*," *Studies in Milton* (New York, 1951), pp. 90 ff.

[25] Referring to Jonson's *Pleasure Reconciled to Vertue*, which he takes to be Milton's source, Tillyard suggests for Milton's masque the absurd title *Virtue Reconciled to Pleasure*. According to his theory the proper title should be *Virtue Reconciled to Marriage*. Milton should really have written a masque of marriage instead of a masque of chastity!

24

and of study and the test of all criticism. Doubtless the understanding of Milton's poetry owes something to the patient labors of scholars and the remarks of sundry critics, whose services I have no intention of depreciating. I do protest against the scholarship and the criticism which condemn Milton's masque for its failure to conform to the conventions, to embody the motifs of the pre-texts, or to satisfy the mere whim or fantasy of the critic. Misinterpretation of the meaning and the spirit of Milton's masque is apparently one of the most common and grievous faults. The student especially may be distracted if not exasperated by the utterances of those critics who are opinionated or captious or incompetent. Students now are obliged to consult criticism; and, as Randall Jarrell has maintained, criticism which "began by anonymously and humbly existing for the work of art" has now become "almost what the work of art exists for. . . ." The poem or story is "in some sense 'data' or 'raw material' which the critic cooks up into understanding,"—his own understanding, one must add. Now the critics "are so much better armed than they used to be in the old days: they've got tanks and flame-throwers now, and it's harder to see past them to the work of art."[26] Realizing that some criticism may be misleading and positively harmful, I plead for a return to the poetry. Realizing that I may be damned as impertinent, I dare to speak for Milton's fit audience against those false critics, those jugglers—fortunately there are not many—who think to charm the judgment as the sense, "Obtruding false rules pranckt in reasons garb."

The fit audience knows how to evaluate Milton's thought and art. As for Milton's masque, this audience understands its purpose and perceives the essential unity of feeling and style; it believes that somehow by the poet's genius and moral fervor the various elements of the poem are, in the words of a wise scholar, "fused into a pure and clear flame of religious and moral passion." It sympathizes with the children in their trials and danger and rejoices in their triumph. It is charmed by the Lady's purity and her indignant refutation of Comus' "deer Wit, and gay Rhetorick." Unimpressed by the conventions of the masque and by the alleged pre-texts, unperturbed by the petulant strictures of dogmatic critics, the fit audience persists in its admiration of Milton's thought and art and of the poem which in immortal verse enshrines his youthful ideal of virginity, his firm belief in the security of the virtuous mind, his passionate faith in virtue:

[26] Jarrell, "The Age of Criticism," *Poetry and the Age* (New York, 1955), pp. 84–85.

Vertue may be assail'd, but never hurt,
Surpriz'd by unjust force, but not enthrall'd,
Yea even that which mischief meant most harm,
Shall in the happy trial prove most glory.
But evil on it self shall back recoyl,
And mix no more with goodness, when at last
Gather'd like scum, and setl'd to it self
It shall be in eternal restless change
Self-fed, and self-consum'd.

This faith in the inviolable nature of virtue is the central doctrine and the soul of the masque. As we know, "Faith is the substance of things hoped for, the evidence of things not seen." For Milton, as for others, this faith was a substantial reality.[27] There can be no doubt that this faith in virtue and this assurance of its triumph was for perhaps two centuries the basis for the admiration of the masque, which even Johnson praised for its "vigour of sentiment, employed in the praise and defence of virtue." This faith accounts in part for the eulogies of the poem, of which in 1835 Brydges wrote enthusiastically: the sentiments are "tender, or lofty, refined, philosophical, virtuous, and wise." He considered the "chaste and graceful eloquence of the Lady enchanting" and the language "flowing, harmonious, elegant, almost ethereal"—so that, to use Cowper's words, in reading these dialogues we "dance for joy." Brydges adds that not only every verse but literally every word is "pure and exquisite poetry." At the middle of the nineteenth century Cyrus R. Edmonds declared that *Comus* had by the choicest minds of every succeeding generation been found conspicuous among the best productions of genius for its refined and exquisite purity and its "intense spirituality." In fact, as Keightley said a few years later, no one had the hardihood to deny that *Comus* is "an exquisitely beautiful poem." In the twentieth century Wright, praising the poem as Platonic in an original and genuine sense, identified virtue as "the rule of reason and knowledge" and explained that chastity illustrates this "larger theme of virtue as knowledge and of vice as ignorance."

Recently, with the change in the intellectual climate, with the triumph of rationalism, the distrust of idealism, the rejection of Puri-

[27] In the William Belden Noble Lectures delivered at Harvard University in 1947 and entitled *On the Meaning of Christ* (1947), John Knox remarks that the Revised Standard Version changes "substance" to "assurance" and "evidence" to "conviction." He thinks that this change is proper, "because faith, as well as hope, is primarily subjective," whereas "Love is the actual substance of things hoped for, the actual evidence of things not seen." (p. 109)

26

tanism and asceticism, there has been, mainly in the United States, a change in the tone of criticism. In Bush, who is generally a thoughtful critic of Milton, there is some evidence of this change. In *Comus* Bush finds Plato "a little altered by the selective instinct of a cultivated puritan of the Renaissance." Expounding the Platonic doctrine that reason must govern the irrational elements of the soul and echoing the Platonic fear of moral "contagion" in this material world, Milton, according to Bush, is in his fear of the flesh and in his "ascetic fervor" an Englishman, a Christian, and something of "an inexperienced doctrinaire." But as a matter of fact Bush finds that this asceticism or Puritanism is reflected in Milton's permanent view of life as "an unceasing moral conflict," and of sensuality as "if not the chief of sins, at least a source and symbol of most others." Sensuality is, I may add, evidence of the victory of passion over reason. Asserting that this view is only partly Platonic and scarcely Greek, Bush concludes that Milton's "rigorous dualism" is "Pauline, patristic, puritan." It is probably true that this view of Milton has influenced Allen's criticism of *Comus*. His disapproval of the idea of virtue or of chastity as a principle of moral conduct and righteousness is, I think, the real but unacknowledged basis of his strictures on *Comus* as a work of art. This is why he condemns it. He really prefers Comus to the Lady.

Woodhouse is, as I have said, the consistent champion of the religious meaning of Milton's masque. He insists that the purport of the poem is not purely negative, that it does not in fact advocate a doctrine of renunciation. He has recently restated his views: the pattern, the structure of the poem emphasizes the necessary progression "from nature to grace," and in the final vision of existence "the goods of the natural order are not rejected but comprehended and assigned to their place in a hierarchy which rises from earth to heaven."[28] Perhaps many will be unable to see this pattern, this progression from nature to grace. It is an orthodox Christian doctrine, but it is not obvious in the poem, where the Lady's virtue is very much her own, though heaven is or may be its source, as heaven, after "this mortal change," is assuredly its destination.

However this may be, the discriminating student will try to comprehend the Platonic Christian doctrine of virtue, the mystery of chastity; for, as Charles Williams has explained, "It is no use trying to deal with *Comus* and omitting chastity." Chastity is "the means, in *Comus*, by which all evils are defeated, the flesh is transmuted, and a

[28] A. S. P. Woodhouse, *Milton the Poet* (Toronto, 1955), pp. 10–11.

very high and particular Joy ensured." The student will delight in the rich, fluent, supple, and melodious verse. He will be reassured by the knowledge that today Milton's masque "enjoys classical status, and may be expected to survive the questioning even of the present subversive age." From the diligent and thorough study of Milton's thought and art he will acquire a genuine sense of values and will realize that the capacity for sensitive and profound evaluation of experience has not altogether perished from the earth.

II

Lycidas, the Corrupt Clergy, and the Reformation

He shook his Miter'd locks, and stern bespake

Lycidas is obviously more than an elegy on the death of Edward King. It is, of course, an elegy, a memorial of friendship; but the real theme of the elegy appears to be the fate of the humanist or the poet in an alien world.[1] The poem is admittedly complex, "impersonal and personal, elegiac and exultant, derivative and original, topical and universal." Once the theme is recognized, it should be clear that the poem is thoroughly unified, with occasional variations of mood but without digressions. French has recently argued that the unity of idea consists in the contrast between the naturalistic and the Christian. Three passages, on fame, the church, and eternal life, all lead to the "Christian assurance of immortality." Consoled and reassured, the poet is finally persuaded that defeat and death are not the end of life, that true worth and faith shall conquer and ultimately be rewarded by fame and immortality.[2]

In this unified poem the passage on the church, St. Peter's denunci-

[1] David Daiches, *A Study of Literature for Readers and Critics* (Ithaca, 1948), pp. 170 ff.

[2] J. Milton French, "The Digressions in Milton's *Lycidas*," *Studies in Philology,* L (July, 1953), 485–90. Don C. Allen, who practically ignores King, oracularly declares that the true form coincides with the "triple myth." (See Allen, *The Harmonious Vision: Studies in Milton's Poetry* [Baltimore, 1954], p. 61.)

ation of the false shepherds of the Anglican Church, is an essential part of the larger theme. The despicable pastors who profane the service of God and neglect His sheep are scornfully contrasted with the dedicated priest, God's faithful shepherd. We should consider the entire passage as a unit, without isolating the last two lines, "But that two-handed engine at the door,/Stands ready to smite once, and smite no more." Usually ignoring the context, critics have approached the couplet as a kind of riddle to be solved by finding pairs, pairs of almost any conceivable thing, secular, religious, political, literary, relevant, and irrelevant. To find a way out of this wild abyss of conflicting interpretations, we must analyze the passage and try to discover its Protestant background. First, however, let us recapitulate very briefly. The "two-handed engine" refers, we are told, to the axe of the headsman by which the hated Laud was to suffer;[3] to the axe of the Gospel (Matt. 3:10 and Luke 3:9); to the sword of St. Michael, the sword of God's justice; to the sword of St. John's vision (Rev. 1:16; 2:12–16); to St. Peter's sword (Matt. 26:51; John 18:10); to the sword of the romances of chivalry; to the scythe of death; to the combined forces of France and Spain, which threatened to destroy English liberty; to the shepherd's crook; to the iron flail of Talus, in *The Faerie Queene;* to the massy keys themselves, literally regarded as weapons to smite with: the key to salvation and the key of damnation —but *not* the Word of God;[4] to the Court of High Commission; to the secular and the spiritual powers of England; to the Houses of Parliament, from which Puritans expected reform of the Church. The last interpretation was apparently first proposed by Masson, who imagined that Milton realized the meaning only *after* the fulfillment of the prophecy. This interpretation was elaborated by Donald C. Dorian, who believes that the engine stands for liberty, a weapon wielded by Parliament against the corrupt clergy.

This interpretation has been conclusively refuted by Donald A. Stauffer, who says that Milton could not count on the reformation by the *two* Houses of Parliament; for the House of Lords, with the bishops, stood in the main for the established Church and state. The

---

[3] Thomas Warton first proposed this explanation. He rejected Warburton's "two-handed sword of romance," but supposed that there may be an allusion to the Saviour's metaphorical axe (Matt. 3:10; Luke 3:9). *Poems upon Several Occasions, English, Italian, and Latin . . . with Notes Critical and Explanatory,* . . . by Thomas Warton (London, 1785), p. 22.

[4] J. Milton French, "Milton's Two-Handed Engine," *Modern Language Notes,* LXVIII (April, 1953), 229–31.

bishops sat in the House of Lords.[5] Having rejected Parliament, Stauffer strangely concludes that the engine is Scotland and England, which in the civil war joined forces to deal the Church a fatal blow. This interpretation ignores the essential point that in *Lycidas* Milton obviously foresaw the reformation, not the destruction, of the Anglican Church, the sacred founder and tradition of which is represented by St. Peter, whom Ruskin called a kind of benign bishop. At any rate, it is now impossible to think of the two-handed engine as the *two* Houses of Parliament, for the House of Lords had at no time any interest or share in the reform of the Church.

Probably the most fantastic suggestion is that the engine is the Church of Rome (the Wolf), which will "reform" the English sheep. This interpretation is based partly on some lines in Sylvester's *Funeral Elegy* and *Divine Weeks* about the "two-handed Sinnes of *Profit* and of *Pleasure*" (an ingenious if irrelevant pair of entities) and partly on some parallels with Burton's *Anatomy of Melancholy*. In treating the Roman Catholic Church as the enemy triumphant rather than a punitive instrument, this interpretation spoils the sense and the climax, ignoring "But" and Milton's firm faith in the triumph of justice.[6]

Insisting that the symbol must be scriptural, Leon Howard has recently identified the two-handed engine as the two-edged sword issuing from the Lord's mouth (Rev. 1:16), a sword sometimes depicted as a great two-handed broadsword of heroic combat. Then citing a number of other Biblical passages (Eph. 6:17; Heb. 4:12; II Thess. 2:8), he confidently identifies this sword as the Word of God.[7] Howard is undecided as to how this sword is to bring about the reformation: whether at the second coming of Christ or through the power of Parliament; but he thinks it improbable that Milton envisioned the Long Parliament as the power to smite the corrupt Church, for Milton disapproved of the "violence" of Parliament. Howard then concludes that there is "no justification at all" for a more particular definition of the symbol than that it indicated a Protestant reformation by means of God's Word: "the threat is the threat of Protestant reforma-

[5] Stauffer, "Milton's Two-Handed Engine," *Modern Language Review*, XXXI (January, 1936), 57–60.

[6] George N. Shuster, *The English Ode from Milton to Keats* (New York, 1940), pp. 73–74; W. J. Grace, "Notes on Robert Burton and John Milton," *Studies in Philology*, LII (October, 1955), 583 ff.

[7] Howard, "That Two-handed Engine Once More," *Huntington Library Quarterly*, XV (February, 1952), 174 ff.

tion . . . as continued in the Puritan movement." It is probable that Howard's interpretation is correct as far as it goes. But he does not go far enough. As we shall see, the two-handed engine is the Word of God. But we must understand the background of Reformation thinking on this matter, and we must also understand the most important point or problem. Even the casual reader of *Lycidas* understands that Milton predicts the reformation of the Church and the dire punishment of the corrupt clergy. The essential point is the means of punishment and reformation, and for this Howard offers no solution at all.

On the other hand, some think that the symbol is deliberately obscure and that no explanation is possible or desirable. Trent thought that this dread instrument should be left "shrouded in the obscurity with which the poet intentionally surrounded it"; Moody thought that the obscurity only added to its dreadful terror; Wright is sure that the engine is nothing more than the sword or vengeance of God; Daiches is confident that all that is necessary is to note that retribution is certain through a device "which suggests purposive activity on the part of society."[8]

To say that the engine is a vague symbol of retribution is to leave it meaningless and the reader frustrated. Besides, one may ask, why should the two-handed engine be any more vague than the other symbols: Camus, the Pilot of the Galilean lake, the keys, and the "grim Woolf"? There is no reason unless we assume that Milton obscured the meaning out of caution, an assumption that is made invalid by the entire passage on the Church and by the headnote of the 1645 edition, as Robins has recently explained.[9] Certainly Milton is not a poet who lacked courage or who deliberately cultivated obscurity for its own sake. For Milton as a man and as an artist and for the reader of the seventeenth century, versed in Scripture and the Protestant tradition, the symbol, I am firmly convinced, was not obscure. The obscurity is surely in the minds of those who isolate these lines from the context and who have insufficiently explored the tradition and the contemporary meanings of the words. The solution may be found in the literature of the Reformation, in the writings of such men as Tyndale, John

---

[8] W. P. Trent (ed.), *John Milton's "L'Allegro," "Il Penseroso," Comus, and "Lycidas"* (New York, 1895), p. 171; William V. Moody (ed.), *The Complete Poetical Works of John Milton* (Boston, 1924), p. 394; B. A. Wright (ed.), *Shorter Poems of John Milton* (London, 1950), p. 179; Daiches, *A Study of Literature for Readers and Critics*, p. 188.

[9] Harry F. Robins, "Milton's 'Two-Handed Engine at the Door' and St. Matthew's Gospel," *Review of English Studies*, N.S., V (January, 1954), 27.

Frith, Robert Barnes, Hugh Latimer, William Perkins, and others. It has been said that we cannot "understand Milton at any point in his career without understanding his relation to Puritanism."[10] We should first carefully examine the works of those who preached the Reformation and expounded Protestant doctrine, a doctrine which was founded upon the Word of God. In their time these Protestant reformers were famous; they were called the true servants of God, and some of them were martyrs. They were praised as the apostles of England in this our later age, as the enemies of the Pope and all his works, as the founders of rational Biblical interpretation, of learning and truth. They were known as godly preachers and faithful pastors, as devoted and worthy ministers of Christ. In the writings of these men, who were the founders of the reformation of the Church, we may find the background of Milton's passage on the Church and the key to its interpretation.

To obtain historical perspective we should first survey the condition of the English Church in the early seventeenth century. With the menace of foreign invasion to restore Roman Catholicism removed and the threat of Puritanism for a time checked, the Anglican Church was at the turn of the century perhaps stronger than ever; but the Church was divided. There was a sullen truce, not a true and lasting peace. Some of the clergy were active, learned, and devout; but most of the pastors were ignorant and indolent. The worldliness and the arrogance of the Episcopal hierarchy were a standing offense to ardent Puritans. Moreover the Church was not rich, more than half of the 9,000 benefices having annual incomes of ten pounds or less. The majority of the clergy had not university degrees. Fewer than 4,000 were licensed to preach. The rest were literally dumb mouths.[11] Many parishes had very infrequent services or none at all. And some of the churches were put to profane uses. In some there was bear-baiting, in others cock-fighting. In 1641 it was certified that a vicarage between Bedford and Northampton had been pulled down, the glebe lost, the tithes detained, and the church dismantled, the chancel being turned into a kennel for greyhounds. Great men sent ministers on base errands and regarded them as their menial servants. In 1612 Thomas Adams, vicar of Willington, said in a sermon at St. Paul's in Bedford: "Every gentleman thinks the priest mean, but the priest's means hath made many a gentleman."[12] In the diocese of Lincoln

[10] William Haller, *The Rise of Puritanism* . . . (New York, 1938), p. vii.
[11] Godfrey Davies, *The Early Stuarts 1603–1660* (Oxford, 1937), p. 67.
[12] John Brown, *John Bunyan* . . . (London, 1928), p. 8.

33

there were strange doings: there were alehouses in the churchyard, and hounds and dogs were kept there; vestments were stolen; the clergy and the laity were much given to drunkenness. At Brigstock the clergyman kept his audience by the simple device of locking the door. Ministers who would not conform were silenced. People were accustomed to leaving their own churches and going to hear preachers elsewhere. Laud's strict enforcement of Episcopal discipline alienated the Puritans and increased the dread of popery. Laud's idea of religion (he became Primate in 1633) was discipline and order: to him a church "was not so much the Temple of a living Spirit, as the palace of an invisible King." He attempted to harry out of the land "the free, strong, self-dependent and self-controlling life of a practical and simple religion."[13] Laud's regular weapons were "systematic and universal inquiry, deprivation, exile, imprisonment." He tried to "stop up every hole through which Puritan feeling could find vent in the press, the pulpit, the influence of the clergyman, the legal services of the Church, or the illegal worship of conventicles." For a time almost singlehandedly he was able to accomplish his "work of universal repression" because of the prestige he enjoyed and the "fear he inspired as the King's confidant." Through the High Commission Court and the Metropolitan Visitation, Laud "set to work to silence the religious voices of England," flouting the great doctrines of toleration, which England had to learn through "fifty years of war and faction and terror."

A Puritan was not at this time a separatist or an ascetic. The marks of a Puritan were a belief in justification by faith, an insistence upon preaching as the indispensable means of grace, and an attitude of reluctant toleration or implacable hostility toward bishops. Generally Puritans accepted the Word of God as the sole authority in religion, as "a uniform manual of doctrine and an absolute law of truth." Some Puritans, like Milton and the Independents, held that the Bible is a complete revelation but that there was still room for progressive comprehension, progressive interpretation.[14] Puritans "usually remained in the Establishment and desired reform from within" according to the Word of God.

In *Lycidas* the passage on the church suggests the essence of the Protestant and the Puritan reformation. The foundation of this refor-

---

[13] George M. Trevelyan, *England under the Stuarts* (London, 1949), p. 138.
[14] A. S. P. Woodhouse, *Puritanism and Liberty* . . . (London, 1938), p. 45; C. S. Lewis, *English Literature in the Sixteenth Century* . . . (Oxford, 1954), pp. 17 ff.

mation is the Protestant doctrine of the Keys and the Word. In Protestant and Puritan thought the Word of God is both a *key* and a *sword:* the Word of God is the only means of salvation and the only instrument of damnation. In Milton's lines as in the Protestant doctrine the two symbols, the keys and the two-handed engine, are merely different aspects of the same entity, the Word of God. Thus understood, in harmony with Protestant thought, there is no mystery or obscurity: the religious symbolism emerges in impressive simplicity, grandeur, and truth.

We must begin with the keys. Of the mourners for Lycidas the last —but not the least certainly—was St. Peter.

> Last came, and last did go,
> The Pilot of the *Galilean* lake,
> Two massy Keyes he bore of metals twain,
> (The Golden opes, the Iron shuts amain).

Literally interpreted the passage is misleading. The Pilot is the symbol of the true church—he is, of course, not the pope; it is possible that he may represent the Church of England, with which Milton had not then broken and whose reformation he anticipated. The Protestant doctrine was that the keys were committed, not of course to the pope, but to Christ, to the apostles, and indeed to all true ministers. The basic text is Matthew 16:18–19, which in Tyndale's version of 1525 is as follows:[15]

And I saye unto the that thou arte Peter. And upon thys roocke I wyll bylde my congregacion: and the gates of hell shall not preveyle ageynst it. And I wyll yeve unto the the keyes of the kyngdom of heven and what soever thou byndest uppon erth yt shall be bounde in heven, and whatsoever thou lowsest on erthe yt shalbe lowsed in heven.

The marginal commentary reads in part as follows:

Peter in the greke sygnieth a stoone in englysshe. This confession is the rocke . . . whosoever then this wyse confesseth of Christe the same is called Peter . . . Then ys every christen man & woman peter.

In his *Workes* Tyndale explains that Christ is revealed by the Word of God. The Law condemns; the Gospel saves. The Law binds; the Gospel sets free. "When a preacher preacheth the Lawe he byndeth all consciences and when he preacheth the Gospell he lowseth them

[15] William Tyndale, *The Beginning of the New Testament Translated by William Tyndale, 1525* . . . with an introduction by Alfred W. Pollard (Oxford, 1926).

agayne." This binding and loosing depends on the confession of faith in Christ through the *preaching* of the Word, the Law, and the Gospel, which are the keys to the kingdom of heaven. In this way all power is transferred from the pope to the Word of God and its faithful ministers. In "A Pathway into the holy Scripture" Tyndale declares that "the law is the keye that byndeth and damneth all men, and the Evangelion is the keye that looseth them agayne."[16] In "The Practice of Popish Prelates" he insists that Christ gave to all the apostles like authority to preach the Word of God. "Whereby thou seest that to bynde and to loose is but to preache. . . ."[17] The Gospel of Christ which Peter taught is "the same doctrine of Peters keyes." In "The Obedience of a Christian Man" Tyndale declares that the authority of Peter's successors is only to preach. The keys are not secular but spiritual. They are not those of St. Peter but of Scripture and its preaching. He says: "Understand therefore that to bynde and to loose, is to preache the Lawe and the Gospell. . . ."

Other Protestant reformers agree with Tyndale's interpretation of the keys. In "What the keyes of the Church bee, and to whom they were geeven," Barnes rejects the Roman Catholic interpretation of the keys as "the doctrine of the deuill." By this doctrine no man can be saved without the authority of the priest, who opens and shuts heaven. On the contrary, the true key "is nothyng els but the holy worde of God, whereby we receave fayth into our hartes." The Word of God "must needes bee the very true keye, as you may see evidently throughout all Scripture." Man is only the minister. "Therefore the blessed Word of God is the very keye," which is given not only to Peter but to all the apostles and unto the whole church. The keys belong to all Christians. But because all men cannot use the keys, the church commits the ministration of the keys, "that is the preachyng of the Worde of God," to certain men who are most able and learned in the Word. Ministers are not lords over the church but merely "keybearers of the keyes."

John Frith, who says that the meaning of the keys has often been explained "and in maner in every treatise that hath bene put forth in the english tongue," declares that there is only one key to heaven, the key of knowledge, which is the Word of God. It is also called the key of David, "whych shutteth, and no man openeth; openeth, and no man shutteth." This is indeed the key, the Word of God, which binds

---

[16] *The Whole Workes of W. Tyndale* . . . (London, 1572–3), p. 382.
[17] *Ibid.*, p. 358.

and looses through preaching.[18] He who preacheth not the Word of God can neither bind nor loose, though he call himself the pope.

In Henry Bullinger's *A Hundred Sermons upon the Apocalips* (1561), the sixth sermon, on the text: "Feare not, I am the first and the laste, and am alyve, and was deade. And beholde I am alyve for ever more and have the keyes of hel, and of deathe, . . ." explains the doctrine of the keys:[19]

Here must we speake by the waie of the keye. The ordinary glose saieth wel: he that hath the keyes of any house, sayeth he, letteth in whome he will, and kepeth backe whom he will from entring in. Therefore Christ possesseth the keyes of death & hel, for that whom he will, he delivereth from perpetual condemnation of death: And whom he wil, he suffereth to remaine iustely in the same danger of damnation.

Bullinger goes on to explain that Christ, who has the power in the kingdom of God, did not give the apostles full power of life and death, of salvation and damnation; He also gave the keys to "his Ministers and servitors, by the preaching of the Gospell." The pope, who usurps this power, is Antichrist.

In another sermon Bullinger explains the function of preaching. Ministers "open by the preaching of the gospel the bottomlesse pitte, and hell it selfe to the ungodly, when they shew them their damnation in hell, for their ungodlines. They shutte up helle from the godly, whilest by the preachyng of the gospell they open heaven, and bring the faythfull to the ioyes celestiall." Then follows this most significant statement:

By the preachyng of Gods worde the Deuill is taken and bounde. Whereof it commeth to passe, that the common painters have painted the Deuill bounden with chaynes to certen notable preachers.

This is the heart of the matter: the Word of God is the key that opens and shuts the kingdom of heaven, and the Word of God must be preached.

For good measure several other witnesses may be cited. In John Bale's *The Image of both Churches* (1550), an exposition of Revelation and a savage attack on the pope and all his works, victory over Antichrist is reserved to Christ and His living Word. "Only shall the breath of his mouth distroy them, grinde them to dust, and throw

18 *Ibid.*, pp. 58–59.
19 Bullinger, *A Hundred Sermons upon the Apocalips,* . . . pp. 43–44.

them into hell fyre."[20] The Word of God is the key of David "which openeth the kingdome of God to them that faithfully beleeueth, and that speareth it up also from them which dwelleth in unfaithfulnes." In Rudolph Walther's *Antichrist* . . . (1556) the keys are explained as "the vertue and power of the gospell and worde of God, which proclaims pardon to the faithful but threatens everlasting damnation to unrepentant sinners."[21] The pope is an usurper. Christ, not Peter, is the rock. The office of teaching signifies not empire but teaching, reproving, exhorting, which are all comprehended "in the ministeries of the Worde." One may also consult Augustine Malorate's *A Catholike and Ecclesiasticall Exposition of the holy Gospell after S. Mathewe, gathered out of all the singuler and approved Deuines which the Lorde hath giuen to His Churche.* . . . (1570)[22] Some of the divines are Martin Bucer, Calvin, Bullinger, Augustine, Jerome, Eusebius, and Gregory. The general sense of this *Exposition* as regards the subject considered is that the ministers of the Gospel are "the porters of the kingdome of heauen, because they carry the keyes of the same. . . ." The gate of life is opened only by the Word of God. The key is given "into the hande of the ministers therof." The apostles were sent into all the world "but onely to preach." The power of the keys is in the remission and the retaining of sins through the preaching of the Word. Preaching is indispensable:[23]

For the power of binding & lousing can no more be taken from the office of teaching and Apostleship, than can the lyghte or heate be taken from the sonne.

This is the substance of the doctrine:

To be short, a wonderfull consolation and comforte is it, to the myndes of the Godlye, that the message of saluation, brought unto them by a mortall man, is confirmed and ratified before God. In the meane tyme lette the wycked and ungodlye scoffe and deryde at theyr pleasure, the doctryne whiche is preached by the commaundement of God: at the length they shall feele, how truely and seriously God threateneth them by the mouth of men.

The pope's throne is in Rome, but there is no sign of the church there. Peter was merely the porter or doorkeeper of the kingdom of heaven. The keys of the kingdom are committed to the pastors; no man can be a true successor of the apostles unless he is a preacher of

---

[20] P. 136.   [21] Fol. 175.
[22] Originally written in Latin, this was translated by Thomas Tymme.
[23] Fol. 364.

38

the Word of God. It is the duty "of all those that be teachers in the Churche, to preache plentifully to the people & to feede them with the bread of lyfe in time, and out of time."

Alas the lamentable state and condition of our time . . . in the whiche there is so great want of such prouiders & dispensators of the secrete misteries of Gods woorde, that the people are ready to starue for wante of their dayly and ordinary foode.

For a clear statement of the familiar doctrine we turn finally to William Perkins' *A Godly and Learned Exposition or Commentarie upon the Three First Chapters of the Reuelation.* The text is Revelation 3:7: "And unto the Angell of the Church which is of Philadelphia, write: These things saith hee, which is holy and true: which hath the key of Dauid, which openeth and no man shutteth, and shutteth and no man openeth." This refers to Isaiah 22:22. It means that God has given Christ absolute authority in the church, to prescribe doctrine, to expound Scripture, to save and to destroy. This power is exercised through His ministers. The following statement sums up the doctrine:[24]

This ministery of the word is a key, because it opens and shuts heauen: this it doth two wayes. First, by teaching and explaining the substance of religion, the doctrine of salvation, whereby men must come to heauen; and in that regard, is called *the key of knowledge, Luke* 11. 52. Secondly by applying the promises of the Gospell, and the threatning of the Law: For . . . then the kingdome of heauen is opened: and . . . then is the kingdome of heauen shut.

Christ granted this power of the keys to all the disciples and "to every Minister of the Gospell." But since Christ also keeps the keys, we must come to Him to enter into His kingdom. In simple words Perkins states the cardinal doctrine:

The Church is the true doore which is Christ himselfe, and the key thereof is his Word, and the ministery of the Word, which doth locke and unlocke the same.

When the faithful minister preaches God's word, he is in the room of Christ and speaks that to the church which Christ himself would speak.

The Word of God is the key to the kingdom of heaven. It is the only means of salvation, the only agent of damnation. Truly and faithfully preached the Word saves and condemns. Preaching is es-

[24] *The Workes of . . . William Perkins* (London, 1631), II, 340.

sential and indispensable. In the Word of God the faithful minister has the key which unlocks and locks the door to the kingdom of heaven. As the vicar of Christ the minister has this key in trust. Without exception the cloud of Protestant witnesses testifies that *the Word of God is the key and that the Word must be preached.* In the words of Hugh Latimer, "Gods word is a seed to be sowen in Gods field, . . . and the preacher is the sower." Therefore preaching is necessary: "For take awaye preaching, and take awaye saluation." In the ladder to heaven there are three steps: "The first is preaching, then hearing, then beleeuing, and last of all Saluation." Latimer says, "*Scala coeli* is a preaching matter." Without preaching, the Word is ineffectual. "There must be preachers if wee looke to be saued." In the Geneva Bible the text "And I wil giue unto thee the keyes of the kingdom of heauen, and whatsoeuer thou shalt bind upon earth, shall bee bound in heauen: and whatsoeuer thou shalt loose on earth shal be loosed in heauen" (Matt. 16:19) has this most important marginal commentary: "The preachers of the Gospel open the gates of heauen with the Word of God, which is the right key: so that where this word is not purely taught, there is neither key nor authoritie." This key is, of course, spiritual. It is quite preposterous to think of it as a massive physical weapon, one of great weight to smite down the guilty.

If they are deprived of the true and faithful preaching of the Word of God, the people can have no consolation, no instruction, no hope of salvation. They are literally forsaken. St. Peter's denunciation of the greedy and selfish clergy who "for their bellies sake,/Creep and intrude, and climb into the fold" echoes a profound Protestant grievance. Tyndale bitterly attacked the pope, who "Feedeth not at all: but poysoneth thir pasture with the venemous leven of hys traditions. . . ." The false prophets come in sheep's clothing, attended by the "dogges and Wolues of their Disciples with their seruants of Mammon." These false ministers rob God; and they rob men of the bread of life, of faith and trust in Christ; they feed their sheep with "the shales and coddes of the hope of their merits." These false and unfaithful preachers will not study the Scriptures or suffer others to study them. Latimer found very few faithful ministers: "Too few, too few, the more is the pity, and never so few as now." Latimer exclaimed, "Oh what a vauntage hath the Devill! what entry hath the wolfe when the shepheard tendeth not his flocke, and leades them not to good pasture?" Bale called Papists "malignant ministers of Sathan, . . . lecherous locustes leaping out of the smoke of the pit bottomlesse," deceiving the ignorant multitude with their carnal doctrines.

40

Thomas Tymme warned, "Let us therefore beware of these ravenous Woolves, which being covered with sheep skinnes, doe come to no ende, but to trouble, rent and devoure." Preaching on the text "And there were in the same Region Shepheardes abiding in the field and watching their flocke by night . . ." Latimer wished that the curates, parsons, and bishops would learn from the poor shepherds this lesson, "to abide by theyr flockes, and by theyr sheepe, . . . to feede theyr sheepe with the foode of Gods worde." These few examples from a large number may suffice to illustrate the Protestant tradition. In the light of this tradition Milton's denunciation of the selfish, mercenary, corrupt clergy takes on additional meaning. For these wretched pastors, failing to preach the Word truly and faithfully, literally robbed their poor congregations of their sole hope of salvation, the *key* to the kingdom of heaven. Latimer said, "For take awaye preaching, and take awaye salvation." The enormity of the offense of the corrupt clergy against God and man could not be exaggerated. It was an offense against the soul, which thus might be forever lost. The heinous offense of the clergy demanded the severest punishment.

Now the symbol is changed. The Word of God is no longer a key to heaven but a sword to punish and destroy the guilty. It is the instrument by which the unfaithful and corrupt ministers shall be punished. The Word is a sword of vengeance and retribution, wielded by the ministers, not by the secular power. It is a spiritual sword. As Tyndale says, "God avengeth hys doctrine himself." Punishment is of God, who is mighty to defend His own Word and Church. Barnes declares that God is omnipotent, that though all the powers on earth withstand Him, He will bring His enemies to the dust by His Word. The wicked who presume against God omnipotent are worm's meat and fuel for the fire of hell. Walther declares that the wicked shall be destroyed by the eternal and mighty Word of God. This is Protestant doctrine.

The basic scriptural authority is in Revelation. In chapter one, verses 13 and 16 we read in part: "And in the middes of the seuen Candlesticks one like unto the sonne of man . . . & out of his mouth went a sharpe two edged sword. . . . "The marginal commentary in the Geneva Bible on "the sonne of man" reads: "Which was Christ, the head of the Church." And on "a sharpe two edged sword": "This sword signified his word and the vertue thereof, as is declared, *Heb.* 4.11, 12. *Dan.* 10.8, 9." The text of Hebrews 4:12: "For the worde of God is liuely, and mighty in operation, and sharper then any two edged sword, and entreth through, euen unto the dividing asunder of the soule and the spirit...." On this, there is the marginal commentary: "For it mortally woundeth the rebellious, and in the elect it killeth the old man that they should live unto God." Another text is Revelation 19:11, 15: "And I saw heaven open, and beholde, a white horse, and he that sate upon him, was called Faithfull and true, . . . And out of his mouth went out a sharpe sword, that with it hee should smite the heathen: for hee shall rule them with a rod of iron. . . ." The commentary explains that the rider is Christ, who is the ruler of all the world, and that "the wicked shall tremble before his face." On verse 13, "And he was clothed with a garment dipt in blood, and his name is called The Word of God," the commentary runs: "Whereby is signified his victorie and the destruction of his enemies. Signifying that Jesus Christ, which is the word, is made flesh, and is our Lord, our God, and the judge of the quicke and dead." The commentary declares that the sharp sword of the Word "driveth the wicked into eternall fire."

The symbol of the key occurs in the next chapter, Revelation 20:1. An angel comes down from heaven, "having the key of the bottomlesse pit. . . ." This angel, the commentary explains, represents the order of the apostles or it may signify Christ; and the key, of course, means "the Gospell whereby hell is shut up to the faithfull, and Satan is chained that he cannot hurt them, yea, and the ministers hereby open it to the infidels, but through their impietie & stubbornnesse." Here the Gospel is a key to shut and to open hell: "(The Golden opes, the Iron shuts amain)." The symbols are very intimately associated and are in fact the same in essence. The Word of God is both a *key* and a *sword:* a key (perhaps iron) to shut and to open hell, a key (perhaps golden) to open and to shut heaven; a sword to punish the wicked. The key and the sword are merely the two forms or aspects of the Word of God, which is the sole means of salvation and the sole instrument of damnation.

In his fifth sermon, on the text "And I turned me, that I might see the voice that spake to me, . . . I sawe . . . one like unto the sonne of man . . . and out of his mouth went a sharpe two edged sworde," Bullinger states very clearly the doctrine of the Word of God:[25]

For a sharpe two edged sworde commeth out of the Lordes mouth. This swearde is the Worde of God, as it is ryght well declared in the sixt of the Ephes. and fourth of the Hebrewes. And this word or swearde hangeth not upon the walle nor sticketh fast in the sheathe, nor hangeth by the side,

[25] *A Hundred Sermons upon the Apocalips,* . . . p. 38. Italics added.

but *commeth out of the mouth.* He sayeth not it came forth, or it shall come forth: But it commeth forth, as the thing that is in continuall operation, or *perpetuall preaching* . . . throughout the worlde. And it is two edged, sharpe and pearsing, as well *in the heart of the Godly unto saluation,* as *in the heartes of the wycked to payne and condemnation.* And yet at this day *commeth out that sworde of Christ by the mouthes of Ministers.*

In Protestant doctrine nothing is more certain than that God saves and condemns by His Word, His spiritual sword, and not by any secular weapon. Latimer declares that the faithless clergy shall be damned; they shall suffer "everlasting payne of hellishe fire world without ende." The unfaithful clergy are threatened not merely by one or two passages in Scripture: "For the *whole scripture,* that is to say, *both the old and the new testament* is full of threatenings of such negligent and slouthful pastors, . . . extreame punishment shall follow. . . ."[26] Those who should feed "my sheepe" but who greedily feed themselves, from day to day "wallowing in delights and idlenesse," shall be punished with "this sworde, the true Word of God." Bale says that God will destroy the papacy and its false church "with the sweorde of my mouthe." Walther insists that Antichrist can be destroyed with "non other weapon, but the sweorde of the spirite, that is the worde of God."[27] Although James I's principle of rule was "No bishop, no king," it is worth noticing that in his "Paraphrase upon Reuelation" the two edged sword is the "Word" of God; the angel is the Word of God; the faithful and true man on the white horse is Christ.[28] James says with regard to the sword: "And from his mouth came a two-edged sword, *to wit,* the Sword of the word, which comes onely from him. . . ." It is the sword of Christ, "the Mightie King of the World, and head of his Church." James also declares that "the holy Spirit by the preaching of the Gospel doeth subdue, and bring the world under his subjection, and taketh vengeance of his enemies." In spite of persecution by the civil sword "the Euangel shall spread and flourish" through the power of God. But James does not emphasize preaching of the Word, as the Protestant reformers and the Puritans always do.

William Perkins sharply distinguishes the temporal from the spiritual power. He declares that the church is governed only by the

[26] Hugh Latimer, *Fruitfull Sermons: Preached by* . . . *Master Hugh Latimer* (London, 1584), fol. 318 f.

[27] *Antichrist,* fol. 204.

[28] *The Workes of the Most High and Mightie Prince, Iames* . . . (London, 1616), pp. 8 *passim.*

sword of the Spirit. In his *Commentarie upon the Three First Chapters of the Revelations* the familiar doctrine is clearly stated:[29]

And out of his mouth went a sharpe two edged sword. This sword that came out of his mouth, is nothing else but the doctrine of the Law and the Gospell, uttered and propounded in the writings and ministerie of the Prophets and Apostles: *Hebr.* 4.12. *The Word of God is lively, mightie in operation, and sharper than any two edged sword.* . . . This two edged sword, the Word of God, . . . woundeth the wicked at the very heart with a deadly wound, and thereby brings them to eternall death: *Isay.* 11.4. *Christ shall slay the wicked with the breath of his lips:* that is, with his Word, which is this two edged sword.

It is Protestant doctrine that the Word of God, which is the key to the kingdom of heaven and to hell, is also the sword by which Christ through His faithful ministers governs His church.

Proof of the truth of this statement is to be found in a much later commentary on Scripture. In his exposition of Revelation 1:16, "and out of his mouth went a sharp two-edged sword," Gill writes:[30]

which designs the word of God . . . This comes out of the mouth of Christ, it is the word of God, and not of man; and is a sharp sword, contains sharp reproofs for sin, severe threatenings against it, and gives cutting convictions of it, and is a two-edged one; and by its two edges may be meant law and Gospel; the law lays open the sins of men, fills with grief and anguish for them, yea, not only wounds, but kills; and the Gospel cuts down the best in man, his wisdom, holiness, righteousness, and carnal privileges, in which he trusts; and the worst in man, teaching him to deny ungodliness and wordly lusts: or the word of God may be so called, because it is a means both of saving and of destroying; it is the savour of life unto life to some, and the savour of death unto death to others; . . . it is for the defence of the saints, against Satan, false teachers, and every other enemy.

The former part of verse 16, "And he had in his right hand seven stars," is explained:

The ministers of the Gospel are compared to stars, because of their efficient cause, God, who has made them, and fixed them in their proper place, and for his glory; and because of the matter of them, being the same with the heavens, so ministers are of the same nature with the churches; and because of their form, light, which they receive from the sun, so preachers of the Gospel receive their light from Christ; . . . and chiefly for their usefulness, to give light to others, to direct to Christ, and point out the way of salvation, and to rule over the churches. . . .

[29] *The Workes of . . . William Perkins*, p. 251.
[30] John Gill, *An Exposition of the New Testament* (London, 1809), III, 691.

The ministers are Christ's instruments "to do his work." Here we have again the usual association: the Word of God, the sharp two-edged sword, and the preachers of the Gospel.

Revelation 19:15, "And out of his mouth goeth a sharp sword," is explained:[31]

The word of God, or the judiciary sentence of Christ according to it, and which he will fully execute, to the utter destruction of all his enemies; see the note on ch. i. 16. *that with it he should smite the nations;* the Gentiles, the Papists, the antichristian states, those that have adhered to Babylon, and have drunk of the wine of her fornication.

The interpretation of Revelation 1:18, "and have the keys of hell and death," is similar. This is the power of Christ, who takes away persons by death when He pleases and also delivers them from death. He will raise all the dead in the last day. His power over hell is His power over the grave or "the place of the damned and the devils." His power[32]

will be seen in opening the graves at the time of the resurrection, when death and hell, or the grave, will deliver up the dead in them, at his command; and in retaining or sending out the separate souls in *hades;* and in opening the doors of hell, and casting in the wicked, and destroying them, soul and body, there; and in shutting them up, that they cannot come out from thence who are once in; and in binding Satan, and casting him into the bottomless pit, and shutting him up there, the key of which he has in his hand; and in preserving his church and people from his power and malice, so that the gates of hell cannot prevail against them.

"This," Gill says, "is an expression of the sovereignty, power, and authority of Christ . . ." and this power is exercised in the church through the Word of God and "the pastors and ministers of the churches in all the periods of time until Christ's second coming." The ministers of the Gospel are compared to stars and to angels, which "signifies *messengers,*"

as ministers are sent forth by Christ with the message of the Gospel to publish to the sons of men; and as angels are Christ's ministering spirits, so are the preachers of the Gospel the ministers of Christ, that wait upon him and serve him in the ministry of the word, and in the administration of ordinances; and there is some agreement between them in holiness, knowledge, zeal, diligence, and watchfulness, in their work; as also they may be so called for the honour and esteem in which they are, both with

[31] *Ibid.,* III, 842.
[32] *Ibid.,* III, 692.

45

Christ and his churches; and who like the angels rejoice at the conversion of sinners, and the enlargement of the interest of Christ.

It would be difficult to find a passage that is more emphatic regarding the supreme importance and value of the ministers of the Gospel. But all their authority and power are derived from Christ, the Word of God, which is "sharper than any two-edged sword." Christ also has the keys of the bottomless pit.[33]

And the key of this becomes no hand so well as his who has the keys of hell and death, . . . who has all power in heaven and in earth, and has the power of hell, of opening and shutting it at his pleasure.

All of the Reformers emphasized the importance of preaching, but they did not all believe that the Word of God alone was sufficient for salvation. Their difference of opinion in this respect was, it is said, as great as their differences over the Eucharistic doctrine. There were two extreme groups, and between these there was Calvin's position, related to both. The question was "whether the Word (i.e. the Bible and preaching) was, with the Sacraments, the means of grace." The Zwinglians, the enthusiasts, declared that the Spirit, with all His grace, "was given immediately to the soul, that is, given independently of the Word and the Sacraments, which thus mediated grace to men." To Luther, however, "the Word of God preached meant no less than the Word of God written," for God "speaks the Word of preaching" and when a preacher proclaims the Gospel "which is found in the Scriptures, his word will be the Word of God. "For Zwingli and his disciples the Word was simply a witness to Jesus Christ, "a sign, pointing us to Jesus Christ." The Spirit was given not through the Word but immediately to the soul. Calvin had affinities with both these groups: he asserted the divine character of the Word; he declared that God illuminates our minds by the light of the Holy Spirit. He taught "both the real presence of the Holy Spirit in the Word, and also the inner witness of the Holy Spirit in the heart of the believer." "Preaching is . . . a means whereby Christ establishes His rule in the heart of His people." It is Christ's scepter and His sword.[34]

In *Lycidas* we should think not of any particular school of Reformers but only of the preaching of the Word of God by ministers who are faithful and devoted servants of God and the Church. Rather

[33] *Ibid.*, III, 844.
[34] T. H. L. Parker, *The Oracles of God. An Introduction to the Preaching of John Calvin* (London, 1947), pp. 45–49; Ronald S. Wallace, *Calvin's Doctrine of the Word and the Sacrament* (Edinburgh, 1953), pp. 83–95.

46

we should think of the false pastors who know only "how to scramble at the shearers feast,/And shove away the worthy bidden guest," and who have learned nothing "That to the faithful Herdsmans art belongs!" The essential point is that to Milton and to other Reformers preaching was indispensable; it was the essential function of the church.[35]

In England, France, and Scotland, as well as Germany and Switzerland, the preaching of the Word was recognized as being the primary task of the ministry. The Mass was dethroned from its usurped reign in the Church, and the sermon was installed in its place. The pulpit, instead of the altar, became the central point in the Lutheran, Calvinist, and Anglican Churches. Preaching was bound to the Scriptures, both in form and in substance. The purpose of preaching, the Reformers hold, was to lay bare and interpret the Word of God. Hence they set up the Scriptures as the criterion by which all their preaching must be judged.

Most pertinent here is a sermon by Joseph Hall. When Hall was Dean of Worcester he preached, on February 20, 1624, to the clergy of England, in convocation in St. Paul's a sermon in Latin, which was translated and published with the title *Noah's Dove, Bringing an Olive of Peace to the Tossed Arke of Christs Church*.[36] In this sermon the Dean points out the duties of the clergy, from bishops down, and indicts the unworthy clergy in language that presents striking similarities in thought to Milton's lines, which appeared only a few years later. The ideal of a busy and painful ministry is first stated. One governs, another teaches, a third doth both teach and govern. He that governs must sometimes strike with the rod, sometimes with the sword. Sometimes he must kindly allure, another time he must sharply punish; "hee must uphold the falling, retaine the wavering, reduce the wandering. . . ." The office of a bishop is a worthy work, but whosoever "playes in this holy Chaire, shall once waile in Hell."

From Saint Bernard the Dean then cites a passage in Latin, which he translates:

The dignity only is cared for, not the duty; Men of all Ages, and ranks in the Clergy, learned and unlearned, run to spirituall Cures, as if they might live for ever, *Sine curis,* when once they have gotten Cures of soules. . . .

This he takes as a prophecy, which has come true. He says:

[35] Parker, *The Oracles of God. An Introduction to the Preaching of John Calvin,* p. 21.
[36] *The Works of Joseph Hall. Bishop of Exceter* (London, 1634), pp. 503–21.

Would to God this were not the very disease of our times. There be some delicate peeces that thrust themselves into fat benefices, onely that they may make much of one; and give themselves over to their pleasure, and ease; Even of those Mouthes which are sacred to God, there want not some, which out of a wanton custome savour of nothing but Indian soot; and take more pleasure to put forth a cloud of smoake, than the thundrings and lightnings of the Law: some negligent pastorlings there are, which have more heed to their owne hides, than to the soules of their people. I speake plaine truth, in a plaine fashion.

These call God their Father; "God indeed, but *Deum ventrem;* that beastly deity, the belly; I tremble to adde the rest, but I must; whose glory is their shame, whose end is damnation." There come to mind the sorry shepherds who "for their bellies sake,/Creep and intrude, and climb into the fold," by whose thin and insipid songs the hungry sheep are not fed but "Rot inwardly, and foul contagion spread."

As seen by the Dean and the poet the dangers confronting the church are almost the same. There are two cruel enemies, Hall says: impiety and superstition:

Now worke; A large doore and effectual is opened unto you, and many adversaries; ye see how audacious Will-worship hath of late set upon us; how proudly the Tridentine faith hath advanced her crest, and hath dared to flie fiercely in the very face of the Gospell: The Romish forces put themselves openly into array, and have dared to sound not an alarum onely, but . . . a victory: They presume to erect here amongst us an Hierarchy emulous to yours, and in the time of your life, and health, and vigor, appoint what heires shall succeed in your Seas: What wise spectator can thinke this indignity to be endured? Is this to be smoothered in silence? Is this to be any longer winked at? Rouse up your selves, O ye holy Fathers, if there be any ardor of Piety in your breasts, and destroy this Tyberine Monster, (Popery, I meane) with the breath of your mouthes: and what ever grace and authority yee have with our Gratious King, with the Peeres, and commons of this Realme, improve it all with your best prayers and counsells, to the utter extermination of Idolatry, to the happy victory and advancement of the sincere Truth of God.

The lines in *Lycidas,* "Besides what the grim Woolf with privy paw/ Daily devours apace, and nothing sed," refer to the same "Tyberine Monster." Urging them to use their influence with the King, Lords, and Commons, Hall obviously relies mainly upon the clergy themselves and upon their preaching, "the breath of your mouthes," to exterminate popery. There can be no doubt at all that the sharp two-edged sword of the Word of God is to be their principal weapon. This agrees with the fundamental principle of the Reformers; but, as we see in Hall's sermon and in *Lycidas,* it was not the actual practice of the Anglican Church at that time.

Protestants as a rule opposed the intrusion of secular power into the church. The church should govern itself and reform its abuses without the interference of temporal power. The Reformers, both Scots and English, "believed that the Scriptures contained a perfect rule of life for all to follow in family, church, and state," and they inclined "more and more to the idea that the church is an independent domain of the spirit to which rulers as well as other men, elect and reprobate, are subject and which the magistrate is bound to respect and support."[37] In the church Christ was sovereign; and Christ's people, "sharing equally in his grace, had authority to choose whom they would to teach, care for, and govern the church in his name." The primary task of the ministry was the preaching of the Word, and preaching "was bound to the Scriptures, both in form and substance."

The two-handed engine which stands ready to smite the corrupt clergy and the marauding Romanists is obviously the Word of God, a sword to punish the guilty and the only weapon sanctioned by the church. This interpretation is fully supported by Scripture. It is demanded by the context of the passage, which excludes secular power. It is in harmony with basic Protestant doctrine. No other interpretation is acceptable or possible. The keys and the two-handed engine or the sword are the same: the Word of God, the sole authority in the church. Moreover, the Word must be truly and faithfully preached. The Word of God alone is insufficient; the Word must be preached. By preaching the kingdom of heaven is opened and shut; by preaching men are saved and damned. The church is to be governed and reformed only by the preaching of the Word of God.

In Milton's later works this interpretation is confirmed. In *The Christian Doctrine* he says that the keys were committed to all the apostles and to faithful ministers.[38] Christ is the one foundation of the church; there can be no other foundation. Pastors and teachers are the gift of the same God who gave the apostles and prophets; they

---

[37] William Haller, *Liberty and Reformation in the Puritan Revolution* (New York, 1955), pp. 4 ff. On the influence of secular power, see the Rev. F. J. Taylor, "Scripture and Tradition in the Anglican Reformation," *Scripture and Tradition* (London, 1955), pp. 55 ff.

[38] "Of the Visible Church," I, xxix.

do not derive from any human institution whatsoever. The common office of all the apostles was to feed the sheep of Christ. In spiritual matters the magistrate has no authority. The church must not be subject to the civil power. For the government and reformation of the church, Milton, like other Reformers, looked only to the Word of God. Milton believed that the Scriptures by reason of their simplicity and their divine illumination contain all things necessary to salvation and that they are adapted to the instruction of the most unlearned if they are not darkened by intricate metaphysical comments and the empty distinctions of "scholastic barbarism." Ministers are persons "appointed by divine commission to perform various offices in the church of Christ." But in *The Christian Doctrine* Milton apparently went farther than he was prepared to go in *Lycidas*. In the *Doctrine* he opposes the claim of "our modern clergy" to "the exclusive right of preaching the gospel." He now believes that the Holy Spirit, which is incorruptible, is the final judge, that "this grace" of teaching is sometimes imparted to the laity, that the ground of faith is in the hearts of believers, who are properly "the house and church of the living God." In *A Treatise of Civil Power in Ecclesiastical Causes* Milton argues that it is not lawful to compel submission in matters of religion. He declares that the commonwealth and religion can flourish only when the civil and the religious authorities are separate and distinct. The magistrate should protect the church, but "the settlement of religion belongs only to each particular church by persuasive means within itself." Christian liberty is "the birthright and outward testimony of our adoption." Christ rejects outward force, which degrades the kingdom of God "from a divine and spiritual kingdom, to a kingdom of this world."

To say that the two-handed engine in *Lycidas* refers to Parliament or to any secular power is to ignore Milton's and the Reformers' conviction that the state should not meddle in church affairs. The political or any secular interpretation of the lines violates Protestant doctrine that the Word of God as preached by His faithful ministers should govern the church, reform its abuses, and punish the guilty. This doctrine Milton firmly held. And he would surely have approved Perkins' prophecy:[39]

The state of our Church continuing as it is, nothing can be expected but judgment from the Lord. . . . Christ will fight against them with the sword

[39] *The Workes of . . . William Perkins,* pp. 302 ff.

50

of his mouth, the ministeries of his Word, . . . he will still fight against them, and with the same sword destroy them for ever . . . the Ministers of the Gospell, which bee truly called, are the very mouth of Christ, . . . the kingdom of Christ is spiritual, and not of this world; for if it were worldly, then a civill sword wielded by the hand of man should belong unto him. But he hath no such sword, he governes his Church and people by the sword of his mouth, his holy Word. . . .

To this should be added a Scriptural prophecy (Ezek. 34: 1–10) which was doubtless in Milton's mind:

1. And the worde of the Lorde came unto me, saying,
2. Sonne of man, prophecie against the shepherdes of Israel, prophecie and say unto them, Thus saith the Lord God unto the shepherdes, wo be unto the shepherdes of Israel, that feede themselues: should not the shepherdes feede the flockes?
3. Ye eate the fat, and ye clothe you with the wooll: ye kill them that are fed, but ye feede not the sheepe. . . .
5. And they were scattered without a shepherde: and when they were dispersed, they were deuoured of all the beasts of the fielde. . . .
7. Therefore ye shepherdes, heare the worde of the Lorde.
8. As I liue, saith the Lorde God, surely because my flocke was spoyled, and my sheepe were deuoured of all the beasts of the fielde, hauing no shepherd, neither did my shepherdes seeke my sheepe, but the shepherdes fed themselues, and fed not my sheepe,
9. Therefore, heare ye the worde of the Lorde, O ye shepherdes.
10. Thus saith the Lorde God, Beholde, I come against the shepherdes, and wil require my sheepe at their hands & cause them to cease from feeding the sheepe: neither shall the shepherdes feede themselues any more: for I wil deliuer my sheepe from their *mouthes,* and they shall no more deuoure them.

The bearing of this passage on the passage in *Lycidas* is obvious. The greedy shepherds, who feed themselves but not their sheep, shall be punished by the Lord, by the Word of God, the sword or the engine which "Stands ready to smite once, and smite no more."

Incidentally, the naïve statement that no interpretation accounts for the phrase "smite once"[40] may be answered by I Samuel 26:8: "Then said Abishai to David . . . I pray thee, let me smite him once with a speare to the earth, and I will not smite him again." This text has in the Geneva Bible the following note: "Meaning, he would make

[40] Northrop Frye (ed.), *Paradise Lost and Selected Poetry and Prose* (New York, 1951), p. 581.

him sure at one stroke." In the Bible the word *smite,* whether with sword or God as the agent, usually means "bring disaster to," as it does in Milton's verse.[41]

Thus the allegedly enigmatic lines in *Lycidas* are explained by reference to the entire passage on the church and by the doctrines of the Reformation, which are based upon the interpretation of Scripture. The Reformers, including Milton, set the highest value on the Word of God and the preaching of the Word, which, in Milton's words, is the "rule and canon of faith" and the "sole judge of controversies." The church is "not a rule to itself, but receives its rule from the word of God," which is also the Word of Christ. According to Robins, Christ is the engine: the "Son as God's instrument of judgement."[42] But it is obvious that Christ cannot be the immediate agent of retribution. Christ works through His Word and its faithful ministers to reform the church in time, not at His second coming at the Day of Judgment.

In the passage on the church the symbols are not obscure. They are simple and clear. And they are sanctioned by the doctrine of the Reformation. They are perfectly integrated with the theme. Milton denounces the corrupt clergy. He laments the untimely death of his friend, who would have been a faithful shepherd, a sincere minister of God's Word. But although Lycidas is dead, the future is not hopeless. Saved by the "dear might of Him that walked the waves," Lycidas is now the Genius of the shore and will be good "To all that wander in that perilous flood." He will be a living proof of God's providence. But the Word of God is not only the *key* to heaven; it is also the *sword* of retribution. It is potent to save and to punish, to preserve and to condemn. In the kingdom of the church, God through His Word and His ministers will surely watch over His own. By the sword of His Word wielded by His faithful ministers God will reform the abuses in His church: He will destroy the marauding Roman wolves and the greedy and godless shepherds, the "Blind mouthes!" who feed themselves but let His poor sheep starve.

If anything more should be required to show that the passage on the church in *Lycidas* is securely based upon Protestant doctrine, we may recall the eloquent words of Thomas Becon. Note first the em-

[41] Edward S. Le Comte, "That Two-Handed Engine and Savonarola," *Studies in Philology,* XLVII (October, 1950), 593; Robins, "Milton's 'Two-Handed Engine at the Door' and St. Matthew's Gospel," *Review of English Studies,* N.S., V (January, 1954), 30.

[42] Robins, "Milton's 'Two-Handed Engine at the Door' and St. Matthew's Gospel," *Review of English Studies,* N.S., V (January, 1954), 31.

phasis upon the pre-eminent, the supreme authority of the Word of God:[43]

God's word is the word of the eternal Father, and his only-begotten Son Jesus Christ, our Lord and Saviour; which word the congregation of God only admitteth and receiveth to be sound and true doctrine, and will be ruled by it alone; admitting and approving no kind of doctrine but that shall consent and agree with this word of God at all points.

The word of God hath sundry names in scripture; "the sword of the Spirit," "a two-edged sword," "a fiery sword," . . . a "consuming fire."[44]

"To shew the word of God," Becon says, "is to preach sincerely the Gospel." His contrast between faithful preachers and "Wolvish shepherds" offers a wordy but striking parallel with the essential ideas in Milton's famous lines:[45]

Heretofore we had such shepherds as were tender fosters of thy flock. They cherished and made much of the sheep. For such as were weak they tenderly cherished, the sick they healed, the broken they bound together, the outcasts and such as ran astray they lovingly brought home again, the lost they diligently sought, and restored them to the sheep-fold. None of thy sheep did they willingly suffer to perish. Even as a nurse among her children, so lived they among thy people. Not with the sour leaven of the Pharisees, but with the heavenly manna of thy blessed word, did they feed thy flock. Neither did they give thy sheep drink of the stinking and dirty puddles of men's traditions, but of the fountain of that "living water, which springeth unto everlasting life." But now the shepherdes, yea, rather the *wolves*, which are brast into thy sheep-fold, and with violence have unjustly *thrust out* the *faithful and fatherly pastors out of their cures,* are lordly, cruel, bloodthirsty, malicious, and spiteful against thy sheep.

They are such "wolves" as "spare not the flock," but scatter and destroy the flock. They are "thieves, robbers," murderers, and soul-slayers. "They feed themselves with the fattest, and clothe themselves with the finest wool; but thy flock they nourish not." The food wherewith they pasture thy sheep is the drowsy dreams and idle imaginations of antichrist. Instead of the *preaching of thy lively word,* they feed thy flock with Latin mumblings, with dumb images, with heathenish ceremonies, with vain sights, and such other apish toys. Instead of the ministrations of the holy and blessed communion, they feed thy sheep with vile, stinking, abominable,

[43] Becon, "The Diversity between God's Word and Man's Invention," *Prayers and Other Pieces,* . . . ed. by the Rev. John Ayre for the Parker Society (Cambridge, 1844), p. 496.
[44] *Ibid.,* "The Demands of Holy Scripture," *Prayers and Other Pieces,* . . . p. 603.
[45] *Ibid.,* "An Humble Supplication unto God," *Prayers and Other Pieces,* . . . pp. 236–37. Italics supplied.

devilish, blasphemous, and idolatrous masses. And unto these *unwholesome and pestilent and poisonful pastures* they drive the sheep, will they, nill they; and if any of thy flock refuse to come and to taste of those *pestilent poisons and poisons full of pestilence*, him they accite to appear before the *great wolf, . . .* whose mouth is full of cursed speaking and bitterness, . . . whose lips are full of deadly poison, whose throat is an open sepulchre, whose breath foameth and bloweth out threatenings and slaughter against the disciples of the Lord. . . . This *wolf*, O Lord, is so arrogant, haughty, and proud, seeing the government of the whole realm is committed unto him, that he hath cast away all fear of thee. . . .

And as this *cruel and bloody wolf* dealeth with the poor lambs, even so do the residue of that lecherous litter. He with all other of that *wolvish* kind hunger and thirst nothing so greatly, as the *devouring of the bodies and the sucking of the blood of thy poor and innocent lambs.*

Becon exclaims, "Thus seest thou, O most merciful Father, how miserably the face of the Christian commonweal of England is beyond all measure defaced. Thus seest thou how thy godly doctrine and most holy ordinances are utterly abolished, and men's traditions set up in place of them. . . . Thus seest thou how the faithful bishops and faithful pastors are unjustly put out of their cures, . . . and in the stead of them . . . *blind* Pharisees, subtile hypocrites, unlearned asses, Romish foxes, *ravening wolves*, lordly tyrants, and such-like *pestilences*, are appointed to rule over thy flock . . . while they are compelled, will they, nill they, to taste their *pestilential and poisonful pastures*, to eat their pharisaical leaven, and to drink their dirty and miry puddles."

"Ah," Becon implores,

Lord, how long wilt thou be angry? shall thy jealousy burn like fire for ever? Pour out thine indignation upon the heathen which know thee not, and upon the kingdoms that call not upon thy name. . . . Help us, O God our Saviour, for the glory of thy name. O deliver us, and forgive us our sins, for thy name's sake . . . "O turn thee again, thou God of hosts: look down from heaven, behold and visit thy vineyard."

And, that thy blessed word may have the more free passage, take away from us those idolatrous massmongers, those idle Latin mumblers, . . . those *wolves*, those thieves, . . . which do nothing else than *poison* thy flock, whom thy most dear Son purchased with his most precious dear heart-blood, and *make havoc* of thy silly simple sheep . . . and in the stead of them place thou godly bishops, *learned preachers, christian ministers, faithful teachers, true spiritual fathers, loving pastors*, even such as will willingly seek up the lost sheep, whom the *wolvish papists* in the time of their tyranny have most wretchedly scattered abroad. . . .

54

In a style that reminds one of Milton's denunciation, Becon then calls down divine vengeance upon the enemies of the church:[46]

But these, O Lord, which are thy sworn enemies, . . . haste thee to root them up from the face of the earth. . . . "Destroy thou them, O God: let them perish through their own imaginations. . . . " Rain thou snares, fire, brimstone, storm, and tempest upon them: let this be their portion to drink. "Let them be confounded and put to shame, that seek after the lives of the faithful. . . . " Let them be as dust before the wind, "and the angel of the Lord scattering them . . . yea, let sudden destruction come upon them unawares. . . . " Let the swords that they draw out go through their own hearts. . . . Destroy them for ever, and pluck them out of their dwelling, and root them out of the land of the living. But let all those that love thee and thy blessed word be joyful, merry, and glad. Let them continue, prosper, flourish, and triumph in thee their Lord God for ever.

These excerpts from Becon provide an almost indispensable commentary on the passage in *Lycidas.* Without noting the detailed resemblances, one may emphasize the point that Becon's "Wolvish shepherds" who with violence "thrust out the faithful and fatherly pastors out of their cures" are the spiritual brothers of Milton's brazen intruders who know nothing "That to the faithful Herdsmans art belongs!" and have no other care "Than how to scramble at the shearers feast,/And shove away the worthy bidden guest." The "wolves," that "great wolf," and the "cruel and bloody wolf" in Becon's "Supplication" clearly show that "the grim Woolf" in *Lycidas* is the symbol of the pope and the Romanists, enemies of the English Church. The phrases "poison thy flock" and "pestilent poisons and poisons full of pestilence," "deadly poison" and "unwholesome and pestilent and poisonful pastures" must, of course, remind one of the lines "But swoln with wind, and the rank mist they draw,/Rot inwardly, and foul contagion spread." Similarly Becon's insistent emphasis on the divine authority and omnipotent power of the Word of God will suggest the true interpretation of the two-handed engine, at the door, which "Stands ready to smite once, and smite no more."

The last illustration is most important. In 1583, about a half century before *Lycidas*, the issue of to preach or not to preach brought the Church and the State into open conflict: Archbishop Grindal opposed to Queen Elizabeth. Briefly, the story, as told by John Strype, is that Archbishop Grindal, himself one of the most eminent preachers, to redress "the Ignorance and Sloth of the Clergy" and to further "Priests

46 *Ibid.,* p. 249.

and Curates" in knowledge, earnestly supported the Exercises called "Prophesyings," in which groups of preachers expounded to the people selected texts of Scripture. These Exercises tended, he was convinced, to improve the clergy and to edify the people. But they were opposed by the Queen, who thought that they stimulated dislike of the Established Church and fomented turbulence and even sedition. The Queen ordered the suppression of the Exercises. In his letter to the Queen "Concerning Suppressing the Prophesies, and Restraining the Number of Preachers" the Archbishop, who was not a Puritan but fervently believed in the preaching of the Word of God, firmly but humbly admonished the Queen. Declaring that he knew of her "Piety Godward" and her "Gentleness toward Men," he went on:[47]

I cannot marvail enough, how this strange Opinion should once enter into your Mind, that it should be good for the Church to have few Preachers.

Alas! Madam, Is the Scripture more plain in any one thing, than that the Gospel of Christ should be plentifully preached; and that Plenty of Labourers should be sent into the Lord's Harvest: Which being great and large, standeth in Need not of a few, but many Workmen?

Christ, when he sendeth forth his Apostles, saith unto them, *Ite, praedicate Evangelium omni Creaturae;* i.e. *Go ye, Preach the Gospel to every Creature.* But all God's Creatures cannot be enstructed in the Gospel unless all possible Means be used, to have Multitude of Preachers and Teachers, to preach unto them.

After citing other evidence from Scripture, including St. Paul's command, "Preach the Word, be instant in Season, out of Season, reprove, rebuke, exhort," the Archbishop says:

Public and continual Preaching of God's Word, is the ordinary Mean and Instrument of the Salvation of Mankind. St. *Paul* calleth it the *Ministry of Reconciliation* of Man unto God. By Preaching of God's Word, the Glory of God is enlarged, Faith is nourished, and Charity is encreased. By it the Ignorant is instructed, the Negligent exhorted and incited, the Stubborn rebuked, the weak Conscience comforted, and to all those that sin of malicious Wickedness, the Wrath of God is threatened.

The good Archbishop goes on to declare that by preaching "due Obedience to Princes and Magistrates" is "planted in the Hearts of Subjects." And he insists that for his part he is very careful to allow "such Preachers only, as be hable and sufficient to be Preachers, both

[47] John Strype, *The History of the Life and Acts of the Most Reverend Father in God, Edmund Grindal,* . . . (London, 1710), Book II, Appendix, pp. 76–77.

for their Knowledge in the Scriptures, and also for Testimony of their good Life and Conversation."

For Puritans and for some sincere Protestants the condition of the English Church in the latter half of the sixteenth century was not encouraging. With others Becon was persecuted, Archbishop Grindal was suspended, and the Queen's decree suppressing prophesyings was enforced. But Becon did not despair. He said, "We shall see the glorious gospel of our Saviour Christ spring again. . . . We shall see God truly honoured. . . . We shall see antichrist, the son of perdition, slain with *the breath of the Lord's mouth. . . .*" The Archbishop, who resisted both "Papistry and Puritanism," admonished the Queen to "go forward in the zelous setting forth of God's true Religion, always yielding due Obedience and Reverence to the Word of God, the only rule of Faith and Religion." In the true Protestant tradition Milton with confidence predicts that the preaching of the Word of God will bring about the swift reformation of the Church and the dire punishment of the corrupt clergy.

In *Lycidas* the thought and the symbols in the passage on the Church conform, it is obvious, to a definite Protestant pattern. The righteous indignation against wrongs and the confidence in the triumph of right parallel the grief and the final consolation which make the pattern of the elegy, the general movement of which is from deep sorrow and despair to triumphant faith and hope, a movement which reflects Milton's own thoughts and feelings about his past, present, and future, and "about the great Taskmaster's will." In Bush's words:[48]

Thus beneath the smooth surface of a conventional elegy, ebbing and flowing with the motives of the pastoral pattern, the waves of regret, anger, despair, and resolution roll upon one another. The spiritual struggle goes on before our eyes, rising steadily in intensity, momentarily assuaged and aggravated by the irregularly sweet and thunderous music, until the last movement asserts the victory of faith in a triumphant glimpse of the sure glory of heaven.

In this incomparable poetic symphony with its subtly varied pattern of rhyme and thought, in this monody with its unobtrusive reflection of the conventions of the pastoral elegy, the poet's sorrow and despair are tempered and chastened by faith. Eclipsed at first by his acute realization of loss and partly masked by the classical pastoral imagery, this theme emerges plainly in the closing lines of those in-

[48] Douglas Bush, *English Literature in the Earlier Seventeenth Century 1600–1660* (Oxford, 1952), p. 367.

tensely personal passages which were once classified as digressions but which are now recognized as integral parts of the subject: sorrow for the untimely death of a friend and fellow-poet and anxious reflections on the poet's fate in an alien world. In the concluding consolation, on the immortality of Lycidas, the elegy soars to a secure and serene assurance that with Lycidas, in "the blest kingdoms meek of joy and love," all is well and that all who wander in the "perilous flood" of this world shall be blessed by his benign influence. Thus is the poet sustained by faith. Faith brings confidence that poetic merit shall ultimately receive its due reward. Faith brings conviction that the corrupt pastors shall surely be smitten by the omnipotent Word of God. Faith mitigates the poet's sorrow, removes his doubt, and at the end brings consolation with renewed courage and hope. "At last he rose, and twitch'd his Mantle blew:/To morrow to fresh Woods, and Pastures new."

III

The Mysterious Stairs

That scal'd by steps of Gold to Heav'n Gate

Some critics are apparently insensitive to the spiritual truth of Milton's poetry. They are obviously not enchanted by his vision "Of things invisible to mortal sight." Undoubtedly some of these critics are skillful, ingenious, learned, and sophisticated; but it is clear that preoccupied as they are with aesthetic considerations they tend to ignore the vital subject: that to Milton the life of the spirit was the most important, the veritable reality. Material objects were to Christians "transient and distracting." To a Christian the "barren physical thing or fact was as the 'letter which killeth'; it had no salvation in it. That lay in the spiritual significance which the fact shadowed forth. Herein was the veritable essence, the real fact. Reality lies not in the veil, but in what the eye of the spirit sees beneath the veil."[1] The reality of spiritual truth, based on faith, a reality so difficult to comprehend in our age but so essential in the reading of Milton's poetry, is simply and clearly stated in the following sentence (p. 5) from William Perkins' *Cloud of Faithfull Witnesses, Leading to the Heavenly Canaan* (1608). Faith is

an evidence: that is, whereas life everlasting and all other things hoped

---

[1] Henry Osborn Taylor, *The Classical Heritage of the Middle Ages* (3d ed.; New York, 1911), p. 105.

59

for are invisible, and were never seen of any beleever since the world began: this saving faith hath this power and property, to take that thing in it selfe invisible, and never yet seene, and so lively to represent it to the heart of the beleever, and to the eye of the mind, as that after a sort he presently seeth and enjoyeth that invisible thing, and rejoyceth in that sight, and enjoying of it: and so the judgment is not onely convinced, that such a thing shall come to passe, though it be yet to come: but the minde (as farre as Gods word hath revealed, and as it is able) conceives of that thing, as being really present to the view of it.

What this saving faith meant, especially to the poor, the humble, the simple, the sick, Perkins explains (p. 21):

Art thou *poore?* thy faith doth make thee *rich* in God.

Art thou *simple,* and of meane reach? thy faith is true *wisedome* before God.

Art thou any way *deformed?* faith makes thee *beautifull* unto God.

Art thou weake, feeble, or *sicke?* thy faith doth make thee *strong* in God.

Art thou *base* in the world, and of no account? thy faith makes thee *honourable* in the sight of God and his holy Angels. Thus thou art poore, and foolish, and deformed, and sicke, and base in the world; but marke how God hath recompensed thee: he hath given thee faith, whereby thou art rich, and beautifull, & wise, and strong, & honorable in heaven with God: say therefore with *Dauid,* the *lot is fallen unto thee in a faire ground, and thou hast a goodly heritage*: Namely, thy faith, which thou wouldest not change for all the glory of the world. Faith is the true riches, the sound strength, the lasting beauty, the true wisedome, the true honour of a Christian man.

This passage, which reminds one of Jerome's letter to Heliodorus, surely contains a storehouse of comforts for all believers.

In Milton's words, "*Faith, or the Knowledge of God;*—and *Love, or the Worship of God*" together comprehend Christian doctrine, which is the highest truth. "We walk by faith, and not by sight. And what is the hope & happinesse of a Christian man, but to receiue at last the saluation of our soules, which is the end of our faith, and period of this walke." Milton had "that key, whereby Gods heauenly treasures" were opened. It is the simple truth that the essence of his poetry, its spiritual and moral value, can be appreciated only by the reader who has (or who can imaginatively fashion) "a sound key: that is, a true and sound faith, which may strongly turn about the lockes of Gods treasury." The realization of this truth, which some critics blithely ignore, transcends all aesthetic considerations, of style, imagery, pattern, and so forth, which are interesting but comparatively peripheral. The fact, the figure in itself is barren; "the letter killeth, but the spirit giveth life."

Now the works of the flesh are manifest. . . .

But the fruit of the Spirit is love, joy, peace, longsuffering, gentleness, goodness, faith, Meekness, temperance: against such there is no law. . . . If we live in the Spirit, let us also walk in the Spirit.   (Gal. 5: 19–25)

Henceforth, "led of the Spirit" and with this text as our guide, we may humbly venture to "unfould" the secrets of a world now become somewhat unfamiliar, a world beyond the reach of human sense.

Even those who admire the unique scope and magnificence of the imagery of *Paradise Lost* may sometimes not appreciate or understand fully its spiritual significance. This is, I believe, true of the image of the stairs, which has been accepted as a magnificent external property, a grand approach to the empyreal heaven, but one almost exclusively conventional and quite unrelated to other parts of the epic. In fact the figure of the stairs is not definitely correlated with or associated with its traditional spiritual values. It is left suspended in space in lonely and mysterious grandeur. The reader familiar with Christian doctrine would, however, readily perceive its profound meaning; for it illustrates a fundamental Christian principle, which Lovejoy has stated: "The one God was the goal of the 'way up,' of that ascending process by which the finite soul, turning from all created things, took its way back to the immutable Perfection in which alone it could find rest."[2] Except the cross, Christianity perhaps offers no more compelling and inspiring figure than that about to be scrutinized—a figure derived from the Old Testament and interpreted to include the New, sanctioned and expounded by the Fathers of the church and by famous preachers, exemplified in belief and conduct by the saints and a host of devout and sincere Christians unknown to fame. Milton said that this world is a wilderness, a wide wilderness, between a lost state of innocence and a golden age to be restored. It is a temporal span between two eternities. In Petrarch the blessed life is on the highest peak, to which by a narrow way we must proceed, "from vertue to vertue." St. Thomas Aquinas, the angelic doctor, held that the "sole reason" for being in the universe was the realization by man of "that supreme good which consists in assimilation to

[2] Arthur O. Lovejoy, *The Great Chain of Being* . . .(Cambridge [Mass.], 1936), p. 83.

God." Progress toward truth is the structural principle of human life. The pattern of *Paradise Lost* has been described as one of movement from the depths of darkness and ignorance to the fountain of light. By obedience and love man ascends to God; so God with man unites. The stair or ladder is a homely symbol of this vital spiritual movement.

After his long and perilous journey through hell and chaos, Satan, as he traverses the outer surface of the dark globe of the universe, is at last cheered by a gleam of dawning light:

> now at last the sacred influence
> Of light appears, and from the walls of Heav'n
> Shoots farr into the bosom of dim Night
> A glimmering dawn.   (II, 1034–37)

By this light he sees in the far distance a most impressive structure "Ascending by degrees magnificent/Up to the wall of Heaven," where appeared

> The work as of a Kingly Palace Gate
> With Frontispiece of Diamond and Gold
> Imbellisht, thick with sparkling orient Gemmes
> The Portal shon, inimitable on Earth
> By Model, or by shading Pencil drawn.   (III, 505–509)

The comparison which follows is especially significant:

> The Stairs were such as whereon *Jacob* saw
> Angels, ascending and descending, bands
> Of Guardians bright, when he from *Esau* fled
> To *Padan-Aram* in the field of *Luz*,
> Dreaming by night under the open Skie,
> And waking cri'd, This is the Gate of Heav'n.   (III, 510–15)

Somewhat cryptically Milton adds,

> Each Stair mysteriously was meant, nor stood
> There alwaies, but drawn up to Heav'n somtimes,
> Viewless.   (III, 516–18)

At this particular time, when Satan drew near,

> The Stairs were then let down, whether to dare
> The Fiend by easie ascent, or aggravate
> His sad exclusion from the dores of Bliss.   (III, 523–25)

Editors observe that the stairs may have been suggested by Jacob's dream; but they and the critics virtually ignore the spiritual meaning of the figure and its intimate relationship to other parts of the epic and particularly to the plan of salvation.

Some meanings of these stairs should be apparent to the most casual reader. They obviously link the universe and heaven; but they are not open to all. All

> who in vain things
> Built thir fond hopes of Glorie or lasting fame,
>
> . . . .
>
> All who have thir reward on Earth, the fruits
> Of painful Superstition and blind Zeal   (III, 448–52)

will never set foot upon these stairs. Obviously this stairway leading to heaven is the counterpart of the broad and firm causeway to hell, which later Sin and Death will speedily construct. These ways are two symbols, the spiritual meaning of which will later become clear. The stairs illustrate or give visual evidence of God's providence and grace, which was to be offered to all men but which man was free to reject, with loss of salvation; but this grace is denied to the fallen angels, who were self-tempted and self-depraved. Obviously the stair or ladder is a most appropriate figure to suggest the degrees of spirituality, the different stages in spiritual development. In both the individual and in society there was a hierarchy of spiritual values, not unrelated to the traditional picture of the physical universe, and marked by stages in devotion and consecration to God's service and in personal spiritual development. This, however, is only a preliminary and cursory view of the meaning of the figure.

To understand its full significance and implications we may divide the examination of the figure and its spiritual meaning into two main periods, the early or Roman Catholic one and the later or Protestant one, without necessarily implying that there was any conflict in meaning or interpretation. As we study the subject, the simple figure that occurs in Jacob's dream expands and grows to include various steps and dogmas in the Christian plan for the soul's development in time by contemplation and self-discipline to attain by God's grace salvation.

The first interpretation of the figure to be noticed occurs in Saint Ambrose's commentary on Genesis 28:11:[3]

Et profectus est Jacob, et dormivit, quod est quieti animi indicium: et

---

[3] Saint Ambrose, "Hexaemeron libri sex . . . De Jacob et vita beata libri duo," *Patrologiae Latinae,* XIV, cols. 620–21. All references to the *Patrologiae Latinae,* . . . ed. by J. P. Migne (Paris, 1844——), will be cited hereafter as *Pat. Lat.*

vidit Angelos Dei ascendentes et descendentes (Gen. xxviii, 11), hoc est, Christum praevidit in terris, ad quem Angelorum caterva descendit atque ascendit, obsequium proprio domino pio praebitura servitio.

Jacob's dream in Ambrose is a prefiguration of Christ, to whom as to their own Lord the angels in pious service offer obedience. This identification of the ladder as Christ or association of the ladder with Christ is, of course, most important. Here Christ is worshiped by the angels, but he is not explicitly, although always potentially, the Redeemer. There are no human beings in this vision, but it must be remembered that the ladder was "set upon the earth." What seems to be required to complete or to implement the figure is to associate it and Christ with a definite plan of salvation, to show how man by contemplation, devotion, and the practice of Christian virtues may ascend this ladder, achieve purity of heart and sanctity of life and ultimately salvation.

In Zeno's "De Somnio Jacob" the ladder means not only Christ but also the Old and the New Testaments:[4]

Igitur Jacob habet imaginem Christi. . . . Scala autem duo testamenta significat, quae et evangelicis intexta praeceptis, credentes homines voluntatemque Dei facientes quasi per quosdam observantiae gradus in coelum levare consueverunt.

Therefore Jacob bears the image of Christ. . . . The ladder, moreover, signifies the two testaments, which . . . have been accustomed as it were to raise to heaven men believing and doing God's will through certain steps of observance.

Philippus Harvengius declares that the ladder prefigures Christ's descent from the cross of the redemption of the human race, which was in Jacob's time being prepared. He says that the ladder consists of two woods, that is the two Testaments, which teach and lead us to the knowledge of divine majesty. Only by fulfilling the commands of the two Testaments can we arrive at the Lord himself.[5]

Bernard speaks of that ladder "quae in typo humilitatis Jacob monstrata est,"—which was shown Jacob as a type of humility, at the top of which is knowledge of truth. Bernard evidently associates this ladder with Benedict's Twelve Steps of Humility, which he mentions.

In St. Benedict's "De Humilitate"[6] the ladder of Jacob's dream is a

---

[4] *Pat. Lat.*, XI, col. 428.
[5] *Pat. Lat.*, CCIII, col. 1.   [6] *Pat. Lat.*, LXVI, col. 371.

means of reaching celestial exaltation through humility or of descending through pride. Benedict says that the ladder "is our life in the world," and that the sides of the ladder are our body and soul. "Scala vero ipsa erecta, nostra est vita in saeculo: quae humilitato corde a Domino erigitur ad coelum. Latera enim ejusdem scalae, dicimus nostrum esse corpus et animam." The chapter on the twelve stairs or steps of humility is, according to Taylor, "the great example of how the precepts of monastic and Christian living, having been gathered and systematized by others, are by Benedict's *regula* made anew into an organic unity fitted to constitute the life of a Christian monk."[7] The twelve steps of humility are listed and described: (1) the continual fear of God and the constant guarding from sins of thought, will, and act, for we and our deeds are always beheld by God and His angels; (2) loving not our own will but the Lord's will; (3) complete submission in all obedience to the Lord; (4) perseverance in obedience in spite of vexations and undeserved injuries; (5) not concealing evil thoughts or sins in confession; (6) being content in spite of deprivations or indignities that are imposed; (7) conviction of personal unworthiness; (8) complete obedience to regulations; (9) preserving silence unless questioned; (10) avoiding laughter; (11) speaking gently and sparingly; (12) showing humility in heart and demeanor. By these steps of humility the monk will reach the perfect love of God which casteth out fear. This ideal of complete humility and obedience could hardly be attained by one living in the world. However, in spite of the cares and allurements of the world, the aim of the true Christian would be similar to the monastic ideal, to overcome bodily lusts, to be obedient to God, to ascend to perfection in a prescribed manner. It would be the Christian's purpose to achieve a character faultless in humility and obedience to God, knowing neither pride nor vanity, nor covetousness nor lust, a personality grave and meditative, with an inner peace and joy, "for whom this world has passed away and the lusts thereof," and whose life is centered in God and the hope of eternal life.

Alardus Gazaeus in a commentary on Cassian[8] supplements Cassian's account of pride with a summary of information culled from Bernard, Benedict, and others on the "Scala Humilitatis et Scala Superbiae" and appends from Bernard the explanation that the ladder is descended in pride and ascended in humility and that the sides of

---

[7] Taylor, *The Classical Heritage of the Middle Ages*, p. 170.
[8] *Pat. Lat.*, XLIX, col. 465.

the ladder are the body and the soul. He then adds a significant comment on the "Scala Superbiae":

Scalam quippe suam invertit et evertit Lucifer superbiae parens, dum naturae et rationis ordine inverso et everso, a suo conditore aversus, ad seipsum autem conversus, et in seipso magis ac magis intumescens.

Indeed Lucifer, author of pride, inverted and overturned that ladder, having turned away from his creator and, having inverted and overturned the order of nature and reason, but having turned to himself, and swelling with pride more and more in himself, fell down to the depths gradually and as if by degrees: and thus by that ladder by which he should have ascended, turning back, he descended into hell.

As proof that Lucifer fell because of pride various opinions are cited, including Jerome's (*Epistle* 45): "Satanas ex archangelico fastigio non aliam ob causam, nisi ob contrariam humilitati superbiam, ruit." It was, of course, a dogma that pride was Satan's sin, that his "Pride/ Had cast him out of Heav'n, with all his Host/Of Rebel Angels." The interesting point here is that Satan *descends* the *ladder* because of pride and that man *ascends* by humility. In *Paradise Lost* Satan and his host fall from the verge of heaven in "universal ruin," and eternal wrath "Burnt after them to the bottomless pit." Chaos heard and saw the numerous host fleeing through Chaos "With *ruin* upon *ruin*, rout on rout,/Confusion worse confounded." There is, of course, no place for a ladder here; but there is *descent*, headlong *fall* "With hideous *ruine* and combustion *down*/To bottomless perdition." Having seduced mankind, Satan then *descends* by that "stupendious Bridge" which Death and Sin, his enchanting daughter, have just finished building, "a broad and beat'n way/Over the dark Abyss," from hell to

> th' utmost Orbe
> Of this frail World; by which the Spirits perverse
> With easie intercourse pass to and fro
> To tempt or punish mortals, except whom
> God or good Angels guard by special grace. (II, 1029–33)

While Death and Sin invade the universe, "Spreading thir bane. . . *Satan* went *down*/The Causey to Hell Gate," to report his triumph. The movement *downward* through *pride* is to be contrasted with the movement *upward* by *humility*. The *bridge* plunges *downward* to *hell* and *perdition*; the *ladder* soars *upward* to *heaven* and *life everlasting*. Thus the contrast between pride and humility, frequently emphasized by the fathers of the church, is in *Paradise Lost* made impressively clear. The ladder is the *scala humilitatis*, the bridge the *scala superbiae.* These are symbols of contrasted movement: the one Christian, spiritual, virtuous, tending *upward* through humility and obedience to God and salvation; the other pagan, physical, sinful, leading *downward* through pride to hell and damnation. These fateful ways meet in "this frail World" for man under grace freely to choose. "Take away free-will and there remaineth nothing to be saved, take away grace and there is no means whereby it can be saved. . . . Accordingly free-will is said to cooperate with the grace which worketh salvation. . . ." Where there is will there is freedom, which Milton sums up, for angels and men:

> Freely they stood who stood, and fell who fell.
>
> . . . .
>
> I formed them free, and free they must remain,
> Till they enthrall themselves.

Under grace this freedom was the basis and the condition of Christian discipline.

An excellent illustration of the pattern of gradual spiritual development, of the soul's progress toward perfection is found in St. Augustine's *De Quantitate Animae.* As explained by Rand,[9] Augustine distinguishes seven steps or degrees by which the soul climbs to perfection. The first is *animatio,* physical life, which the soul shares with trees and other living things. The second is *sensus* or feelings, which animals also have. The third is reason, which is peculiar to man alone and which manifests itself in memory, art, agriculture, language, military and civil government, philosophical thought, and so forth. The fourth degree is attained when the soul becomes good, abstracts itself from the flesh and whatever defiles, applies the Golden Rule, follows wisdom, and believes in God. In the fifth degree the soul, purged and fixed in virtue, contemplates the truth, which is in God. In the sixth stage the soul enjoys the beatific vision of the things that really are, the supreme truth. In the seventh and final stage the soul reaches an abiding place of "delight and the enjoyment of the highest and true good." As Rand says, if you climb "with St. Augustine step by step, you will attain a region where beauty is truth, truth beauty," but there is no implication that beauty is all we know on earth and all we need to know. As a happy pilgrim the soul, moving along "the sweet, quiet, yearning ways of the Christian *vita contemplativa,*" ascends by gradual steps and unremitting effort the ladder of perfec-

[9] Edward K. Rand, *Founders of the Middle Ages* (Cambridge [Mass.], 1928), pp. 259–63.

tion, so that it becomes finally "a fit receptacle for the holy spirit and grace of God." This is a matter far different from indulgence in the delights of sensual beauty. St. Augustine's ideal is not that of the romantic dreamer but that of the devout Christian, strong in faith and humility and always obedient to God, the source and sanction of life. The goal is perfection; and although perfection is not to be expected in the present life: "It is our duty," Milton says, "to strive after it with earnestness, as the ultimate object of our existence."[10]

In this earnest striving the believing soul has the assurance of salvation, which Milton defines as *"a certain degree or gradation of faith, whereby a man has a firm persuasion and conviction, founded on the testimony of the Spirit, that if he believe and continue in faith and love,"* he will at length most certainly attain to everlasting life. This assurance of salvation naturally produces, Milton says, "a joy unspeakable." This Christian doctrine implies, of course, "a truly regenerate and Christian purity of life, and not a mere outward and philosophical morality." For true believers God has provided many pledges of salvation, which are arranged in an ascending order: election, regeneration, justification, adoption, union, and fellowship with God "conjointly with Christ and the Spirit."[11] This forms a ladder, which seems to be definitely Protestant, with emphasis upon the mystical doctrines of regeneration and salvation rather than upon the life of contemplation and rigorous discipline and the persistent cultivation of specific cardinal virtues, which form the older ladder. But here I anticipate.

A ladder of specific religious virtues is to be found in the "Scala Coeli Minor seu de Gradibus Charitatis Opusculum" of Honorius of Autun, who was also author of the most popular handbook of sermons in the Middle Ages, the *Speculum Ecclesiae.*[12] By this ladder, which is love, the faithful reach heaven: "Haec enim scala est charitas, per quam ad coeli fastigia tendit." The sides of the ladder are the precepts of the twofold love of God and neighbor. The steps of the ladder are the virtues through which the precepts of love are fulfilled. By practicing these virtues he who climbs will see in glory the face of God, who is love. There are fifteen steps because through fifteen branches or ways the celestial things of love are sought after. On this ladder one ascends to the sanctuary of the celestial

---

[10] *The Christian Doctrine* I, xxi.

[11] *Ibid.,* xxv.

[12] *Pat. Lat.,* CLXII, cols. 1239–42; Henry Osborn Taylor, *The Medieval Mind* (4th ed.; Cambridge [Mass.], 1951), II, 76.

temple or Christ. These are the steps: patience, kindness, piety, honesty or candor, humility, contempt of the world, voluntary poverty, peace, goodness, spiritual joy, endurance, faith, hope, long-suffering, and perseverance. By this ladder of love we enter into the inheritance of the Lord: "per charitatem omnia bona perfiamus, ut heriditate Dei sanctuarium possideamus." Honorius' interpretation of the ladder is illustrated in the *Hortus Deliciarum*, which may have been inspired by a Byzantine model. Various temptations, including a bed, baskets of gold, and smiling Luxuria, lure clerk and layman from the ladder, and demons shoot arrows at them; but one woman, probably a nun, arrives at the summit, where a crown is offered to her.[13] A similar subject appears in a mural, probably of the twelfth century, in Chaldon church. Here a ladder reaches from the grave to heaven and the presence of God. The lower half of the picture, which shows the damned, shows a cauldron, a bridge made like a saw, a serpent and tree, and such sins as usury and lust. The upper half shows the weighing of souls, the release of the souls from limbo, and the Lord bestowing His blessing. Two figures, probably Elias and Enoch, ascend the ladder without using the rungs. Somewhat more closely related to Honorius' ladder is "A Ladder to Heaven" by Baccio Baldini, which shows the Lord surrounded by angels at the top. The rungs are *Sapientia, Intellecto, Consigno, Fortessa, Scientia, Pieta, Timor Domini, Fortézza, Temperantia, Prudentia,* and *Humilita*—neither the same number nor the identical virtues of Honorius. This ladder rests on the rock of Faith, Hope, and Charity. Under it a young man bound by a shackle named Cecita is held by a demon but holds a scroll on which is written "Levavi oculos meos."[14] When we associate the ladder with Christ, with humility and love, and with the specific virtues listed and specified by Honorius and others, we have perhaps a key to the assertion "Each Stair mysteriously was meant," and we inevitably recall these lines—God is speaking to His Son:

> because in thee
> Love hath abounded more then Glory abounds,
> Therefore thy Humiliation shall exalt
> With thee thy Manhood also to this Throne;

[13] Émile Mâle, *Religious Art in France XIII Century,* trans. by Dora Nussey (3d ed.; Paris, 1913), pp. 105–106. There is an excellent illustration.

[14] N. H. J. Westlake, *History of Design in Mural Painting from the Earliest Times to the Twelfth Century* (London, 1905), II, 161, 163. The first ladder is illustrated. Cf. Longfellow, "Sandalphon," quoted in Rappoport, *Myth and Legend of Ancient Israel* (London, 1928), I, 53–54. Standing on the ladder of light, Sandalphon presents human prayers to God.

Here shalt thou sit incarnate, here shall Reigne
Both God and Man, Son both of God and Man,
Anointed universal King.   (III, 311–17)

In spite of the title the conception of the ladder is not generally present in Walter Hilton's *Scala Perfectionis,* which is a book of instructions for the anchorite, who renounces worldly riches and honors and gives herself unreservedly body and soul to the service of the Lord. But the notion of ascent occurs. There are degrees in the life of contemplation. The first degree is in knowing God and spiritual things but without spiritual affection and inward favor sealed by the special gift of the Holy Ghost. The second lies in affection, in fervor of love and spiritual sweetness without the light of spiritual understanding. The third lies in both cognition and affection, in the knowledge and the perfect love of God. The means of coming to virtue are classified: first, reading Holy Writ and teaching; second, ghostly meditation; third, busy prayer with devotion. There are three manners of prayer: first, the forms used in the church; second, oral prayers not following set forms; third, silent prayer from the heart. There are two rewards in the bliss of heaven: first, the knowledge and love of God, which is sovereign; second, a special reward for good deeds above what one is bound to do, as for martyrdom, preaching, chastity. There is a general movement toward increasing holiness and spiritual insight through meditation and devotion and especially by virtue of humility and obedience; for then, it has been said, religion was "a school of humility and obedience."[15] With its detailed analysis of the life of contemplation, devotion, and daily discipline in the cardinal virtues, Hilton's *Scala* presents a sharp contrast to the Protestant dogma of salvation through faith.

St. Thomas Aquinas observes that the various degrees of angelic order are presented under the figure of the ladder.[16] "Nota quod diversos gradus angelicorum ordinum sub specie scalae vidit. . . ." Aquinas explains that the angels ascend to share the gifts of God and descend to communicate them to men. The steps also indicate the degrees of rank in the church militant. The angels also signify the saints of the Old and New Testaments, who ascend to God and descend to neighbors, according to the two commandments of twofold love.[17]

With St. Thomas Aquinas one period of the survey may fittingly be

[15] Helen C. Gardner, "Walter Hilton and the Mystical Tradition in England," *Essays and Studies,* XXII (1937), 103–127.

[16] "Expositio in Genesim," *Opera omnia,* XXX, 139.

[17] The reference is, of course, to Matt. 22:37–40.

closed. In this early or Catholic period we observe that the ladder is interpreted so that it has a fundamental meaning in Christian doctrine and conduct. In Jacob's vision Christ is first of all the Mediator between God and man—and this idea remains or persists. The interpretation is expanded to include the Old and New Testaments, the body and the soul, the steps by which the soul through the cultivation of Christian virtues may ascend to heaven, the angels and the officers of the church militant and the saints of the church. The interpretation of the ladder as Christ or *charitas,* the love of God and God's love for man, with angels as its ministers, is probably the one that accords most nearly with both Catholic and Protestant doctrine and with Milton's conception in *Paradise Lost.* The Catholic emphasis upon the monastic virtues in a cloistered life, withdrawn from the temptations and distractions of the world, is, of course, one that never appealed to Protestants and to Milton, who rejected asceticism as a philosophy. But from experience and by religious conviction Milton was persuaded that man, unaided by grace, is a fallible creature, unable by reason to make a proper use of nature or a proper choice of nature's gifts. Woodhouse has argued that, for Milton, nature was "a living whole, a vital scale," and that after *Comus* the role of reason was confirmed and emphasized.[18] The first statement applies to nature *before* the Fall; and it would be nearer the truth to say that in the major poems man's reason is discredited. Certainly *after* the Fall nature is corrupted or infected with evil, and man without grace is utterly lost. Now the spiritual ladder, the ladder of grace is indispensable:

> Man shall not quite be lost, but sav'd who will,
> Yet not of will in him, but grace in me
> Freely voutsaft.   (III, 173–74)

Man cannot rely upon "nature the vital, the abounding" or "nature the ordered, the rational," or "reason the prerogative . . . of the soul." Man's spiritual welfare and his salvation consist in denying nature, in practicing the Christian virtues, especially obedience and love and faith, especially grace, without which salvation is impossible and inconceivable.

Among Protestants John Calvin may have the first place. In his commentary on Genesis Calvin writes that there is nothing ambiguous or doubtful in Jacob's vision. The dream does not, as the Hebrews

[18] A. S. P. Woodhouse, "The Argument of Milton's *Comus,*" *University of Toronto Quarterly,* XI (October, 1941), 46–71.

say, represent the providence of God. It undoubtedly signifies that the Covenant of God was laid upon Christ, through whom God revealed himself to the holy fathers.[19]

Therefore, it is Christ alone which ioyneth heauen and earth together: he onely is the mediatour whiche reacheth from heauen to earth: he is the verie same, by whom the fulnesse of all heauenly graces floweth downe to us, and by whome, in like manner, wee ascende unto God. He being the head of Angels, bringeth to passe, that they minister unto his earthly members.

The ladder of Jacob's vision is a "figure of Christ" because

the similitude of a ladder, doeth verie well agree with the mediatour, by whome the ministerie of Angels, righteousnesse, and life, and all other graces of the Holy Ghost, do come unto us, as it were by steppes. We also, whiche were not onely fastened to the earth, but also whiche were plunged in the deepe pitte of malediction, and of hell it selfe, doe reache and ascende euen unto God. And, the God of hostes sitteth uppon the ladder; bycause the fulnesse of the Godhead dwelleth in Christe. And hereof also it commeth to passe, that it reacheth euen unto Heauen.

God established with His servant Jacob the covenant of eternal salvation in His Son, whom all should worship and before whom every knee should bow.

But withall, his friendly and delectable image is depainted unto us, to the ende we may knowe, that by his comming downe, heauen is opened unto us, and that the Angels are made familiar with us.

Calvin's is the authoritative and accepted interpretation. It occurs in *The Times, Places, and Persons of the Holy Scripture, or The Generall View of the Holy Scriptures* (1607):

This *Ladder* representeth Christ: the foot on the earth, his humanities: and the top reaching to heauen, his deity: the Angels of God ascending and descending, the mediations betwixt God and us: and the Lord standing aboue uppon it, the readinesse of the Father to receiue our prayers.

The ladder represents the whole mediation of Christ. If in the ladder two or three steps are broken, we can neither ascend nor descend; "euen so the whole mediation is so united and knit together, that by despising any one part, we bereaue ourselues of the benefit of the whole."

[19] *A Commentarie of John Calvin upon the first booke of Moses called Genesis:* Transl. out of Latine into English by Thomas Tymme (London, 1578), pp. 595–96.

In the Geneva Bible there is this commentary on the familiar text: "Christ is the ladder whereby God & man are ioined together, & by whom the Angels minister vnto us: all graces by him are giuen vnto us, & we by him ascend into heauen." This commentary in what may be called the Protestant Bible is especially important. It appears that Protestants generally would accept this explanation, which is referred to in another annotation, on John 1:51: "Christ openeth the heauens, that we may haue accesse to God, and maketh us fellowes to the Angels."

In *Certaine Godly and Learned Sermons* . . . (1605) Edward Philips explains that Christ is the ladder of Jacob on which angels ascended and descended.[20] And in *The Art of Prophecying: or, A Treatise Concerning the Sacred and Onely True Manner and Methode of Preaching*,[21] William Perkins, explaining the third method, the comparing of places from Scripture, shows from Genesis 28:12 and John 1:51 that the ladder is Christ, who is the foundation of all our comfort. By his vision of the ladder reaching from earth to heaven Jacob was comforted; "and this Ladder is the Sonne of God made man." In one of Henry Smith's sermons entitled "Jacobs Ladder, or The Way to Heauen,"[22] Smith declares that as there is a heaven so there is a way.

One way Adam came from Paradise, and by another way he must returne to Paradise: the passage is not so stopt, but there is a way, though a straight way: and a doore, though it be a narrow doore, and therefore few doe finde it, only they which are like Iacob, do see a ladder before them, as Iacob did, he had many dreames before & did not see it, at last he dreamed, & behold a ladder which reached from earth to heauen, and all the Angels descended and ascended by it, to shew that no man ascendeth to heauen, but by that Ladder; this Ladder is Christ, which saith, *I am the way*, and therefore he biddeth us to follow him.

Smith tells how Christ went to heaven. He began betimes, at twelve years of age saying that he must go about His Father's business. He made good speed, doing more good things in three and thirty years than could be written. He kept the right way, and none could accuse him of sin. He continued well, at his death praying that His enemies should be forgiven. Therefore the steps of the ladder are called *ma-*

[20] Edward Philips, *Certaine Godly and Learned Sermons* . . . (London, 1605), p. 190.
[21] Written in Latin and translated by Thomas Tuke; *The Workes of* . . . *William Perkins* (London, 1631), II, 643–73.
[22] *The Sermons of Master Henry Smith* (London, 1599), pp. 533–53.

ture, propere, recte, constante; that is, begin betimes, make haste, keep the way, and hold to the end. Seek Christ early; they who seek Him early shall find Him. This is the acceptable time; this is the day of salvation. Keep the way; there is only one right way; there is only one truth. Jacob saw only one ladder, which reached to heaven. The right way is the Word. Do unto others as thou wouldst have others do unto thee; do good works and yet believe that Christ's works will save thee. Pray without doubting; keep within thy calling; bring thy will unto God's will. Every day kill some vice; every week sow some virtue. Love God with all thy heart, with all thy strength, with all thy mind. Persevere unto the end. Be faithful even unto death.

Smith states clearly the Protestant doctrine of salvation:

We see Christ when we heare his Word, and we embrace his saluation, when we beleeue it: they see him that heare him, they embrace him that follow him.

Christ is salvation: "there is no remedy but to come to Christ." The Protestant faith is contrasted with that of the Papists:

The Papists haue found out many saluations, they have found out a saluation by Saints, a saluation by Angels, a saluation by Masses, saluation by Merits, as though Christ had least to doe in his owne office, for they haue other saluations to flie unto: They will haue it, but they will buy it, and what will they giue for it? Why they will fast so many dayes, goe so farre on Pilgrimage, hire a Priest to say so many Masses, build so many Abbeys, and giue so many sums of money to the Monks and Friers.

They do as Nimrod did, heaping stone upon stone and sin upon sin, in the vain attempt to reach heaven. Heaven is not to be reached by works. Christ is the only way.

Then seeing Christ is both our righteousnesse, saluation, and also the way, the truth, and the life, to lead us thereunto: it is as possible for us without Christ to be iustified or glorified, as it is to be wise without wisdome, righteous without righteousnesse, or saued without saluation. . . . Christ is the Fountaine of all wisdome, of all righteousnesse, of all truth, of all knowledge, of all saluation, and briefly of all goodnesse; for there is no other Arke to saue us from the floud, no other ladder to ascend with into heauen, no other *Ioseph* to feed us in the famine, no other *Moses* to lead us thorow the wildernesse.

Salvation is "the sweetest word in all the Scripture," and "Christ is called *Saluation,* because it is impossible to be saued without him."

A few other examples may serve our purpose. In a sermon Hugh

Latimer explains the *scala coeli*. The Bishop of Rome has a *scala coeli*, he says, but that is "a masse matter." Latimer goes on:[23]

But this *Scala Coeli*, that I now speake of, is the true ladder that bringeth a man to heauen: the top of the ladder, or first greese is this: Whosoeuer calleth upon the name of the Lord shall be saued. The second step: How shall they call upon him, in whom they haue not beleeued? The third stayre is this: How shall they beleeue in him, of whom they neuer heard? The fourth steppe: Howe shall they heare without a preacher? Now the nether end of the ladder is: How shall they preach except they be sent? This is the foote of the ladder: so that we may go backward now, and use the schoole argument *A primo ad ultimum*. Take away preaching, take away saluation.

Here faith, preaching, and salvation are joined, and preaching is essential. In another sermon Latimer extolled Christ as "the preacher of all preachers, the patrone and exemplar, that all preachers ought to follow." Christ is indispensable.

It is whole Christ. What with his natiuitie, what with his circumcision, what with hys incarnation, and the whole processe of his life, with hys preaching, what with his ascending, descending, what with hys death, it is all Christ that worketh our saluation.

This insistence upon Christ, the Word, and the preaching of the Word is to be carefully noted. Grace, faith, Christ, the Word, and preaching—these are the essential steps to heaven.

After declaring that the Christian is set free by the passion and obedience of Christ and faith in the promises of the Gospel, Richard Rogers enumerates the means by which this freedom and joy are to be maintained and increased: first, the Word should be heard reverently; second, the Lord's supper is very effectual; third, the Word should be read daily; fourth, the Word should be meditated upon; fifth, the Word must be practiced; sixth, the Christian must pray continually and render thanks to God; seventh, he must patiently submit to affliction and adversity.[24] In his second sermon upon Luke 13 Samuel Wright describes the means by which one may enter heaven: the first means is faith, without which there is no entrance; to faith must be added courage, zeal, and magnanimity; to these must be added pa-

[23] Hugh Latimer, *Fruitfull Sermons* . . . (London, 1584), fol. 38; ed. for the Parker Society by the Rev. George Elwes Corrie (Cambridge, 1884). These sermons were frequently printed. He derived the steps (though not the principle of the ladder) from Rom. 10:11–15.

[24] Richard Rogers, *Certaine Sermons Preached and Penned by R. Rogers* (London, 1612), pp. 208 ff.

tience, for zeal without patience is not permanent; add wisdom, mutual encouragement, and exhortation; to all these we must add continual and incessant prayer. Thus we are to strive and labor to enter heaven.

We return to the theme in Donne's sermon "Preached at Lincolns Inne, preparing them to build their Chappell," on Genesis 28:16–17.[25] Donne said:

> God had revealed to *Jacob,* that vision of the ladder, whose foot stood upon earth,. and whose top reached to heaven, upon which ladder God stood, and Angels went up and down. Now this ladder is for the most part, understood to be *Christ* himselfe; whose foot, that touched the earth, is his *humanity,* and his top that reached to heaven, his *Divinity;* The ladder is Christ, and upon him the Angels, (his Ministers) labour for the edifying of the Church; And in this labour, upon this ladder, God stands above it, governing, and ordering all things, according to his providence in his Church. Now when this was revealed to *Jacob,* now when this is revealed to you, that God hath let fall a ladder, a bridge between heaven, and earth, that Christ, whose divinity departed not from heaven, came down to us into this world, that God the father stands upon this ladder, as the *Originall* hath it, *Nitzab,* that he leanes upon this ladder, as the *vulgar* hath it, *Innixus scalae,* that he rests upon it, as the holy Ghost did, upon the same ladder, that is, upon Christ, in his baptisme, that upon this ladder, which stretches so farre, and is provided so well, the Angels labour, the Ministers of God doe their offices, when this was, when this is manifested, then it became *Jacob,* and now it becomes every Christian, to doe something for the advancing of the outward glory, and worship of God in his Church.

Since Donne was in this sermon mainly interested in building the chapel, he applies the dream and Jacob's awakening to this purpose:

> But yet even from this holy, and religious sleep (which is a departing from the allurements of the world, and a retiring to the onely contemplation of heaven, and heavenly things) *Jacob* may be conceived to have awaked, and we must awake; It is not enough to shut ourselves in a cloister, in a Monastery, to sleep out the tentations of the world, but since the ladder is placed, the Church established, since God, and the Angels are awake in this businesse, in advancing the Church, we also must labour, in our severall vocations, and not content our selves with our own spirituall sleep; the peace of conscience in our selves; for we cannot have that long, if we doe not some good to others.

It is clear that Donne was familiar with some of the earlier exegeses

[25] Number 10 in *The Sermons of John Donne,* ed. by George R. Potter and Evelyn M. Simpson (Berkeley, 1953——), II, 213–34.

of this dream; but his application to the present need is typically direct, practical, and Protestant. The cloistered monastic life is rejected. Donne reminds his audience that upon this ladder the angels were *busy*, ascending and descending, and that "none stood still but God himself." Therefore, though the religious sleep of enjoying and contemplating God "be a heavenly thing," we must, till we come to Him "to sleep an eternall Sabbath in heaven,"—we must "awake even out of this sleep, and contribute our paines, to the building, or furnishing, or serving of God in his Church." This admonition and that which follows would certainly have had Milton's approval:

Beloved, it is not enough to awake out of an ill sleep of sinne, or of ignorance, or out of a good sleep, out of a retirednesse, and take some profession, if you winke, or hide your selves, when you are awake, you shall not see the Ladder, not discern Christ, nor the working of his Angels, that is, the Ministery of the Church, and the comforts therein, you shall not hear the Harmony of the quire of heaven, if you will bear no part in it; an inward acknowledgment of Christ is not enough, if you forbear to professe him, where your testimony might glorify him.

Again and again Donne repeats the call to service:

When Angels and men, Priests and people, the Preacher and the congregation labour together upon this Ladder, study the advancing of his Church (as by the working of Gods gratious Spirit we doe at this time) *Ibi verè est & ibi verè Dominus est*, surely he is in this place, and *surely* he is Lord in this place, he possesses, he fills us all, he governs us all: and as, though we say to him, *Our Father which art in heaven*, yet we beleeve that he is within these walls, so though we say *Adveniat regnum tuum*, thy kingdome come, we beleeve that his kingdome is come, and is amongst us in *grace* now, as it shall be in *glory* hereafter.

As interpreted and applied by Donne the ladder of Jacob's dream becomes a practical and potentially effective instrument for the advancement of the church. The dream and the awakening are then skillfully utilized to provide the utmost spiritual insight. When a man has proceeded so far with Jacob as to sleep, to be at peace with God, to awake, to do something for the good of others, and to speak, to publish his sense of God's presence, and "then to attribute all this onely to the light of God himself, by which light he grows from faith to faith, and from grace to grace," he may then say in all places and in all his actions, "*This is none other but the house of God, and this is the gate of heaven*." As a result he "shall see heaven open, and dwell with him, in all his undertakings: and particularly, and principally in his expressing of a care, and respect, both to Christs Mysticall, and to his materiall body; both to the sustentation of the poor, and to the building up of Gods house."

Donne skillfully made use of the interpretation of Jacob's dream. It is also likely that the identification of the ladder as Christ and Love or *charitas* suggested Donne's observations on charity:

> This vertue then, *Charity,* is it, that conducts us in this life, and accompanies us in the next. In heaven, where we shall *know God,* there may be no use of *faith;* In heaven, where we shall *see God,* there may be no use of *hope;* but in heaven, where God the Father, and the Son, love one another in the Holy Ghost, the bond of charity shall everlastingly unite us together. But *Charitas in patria,* and *Charitas in via,* differ in this, That there we shall love one another because we shall not need one another, for we shall all be full; Here the exercise of our charity is, because we doe stand in need of one another.

Charity testifies to our love of Christ; it is a sure way to salvation. It is a virtue that all may practice: "Every man hath something to give *God:* Money, or labor, or counsail, or prayers: Every man can give; and he gives to God, who gives to them that need it, for his sake." In conclusion, as a good Protestant, relying upon faith, Donne denounces as "shamelesse slanderers" those who "place their salvation in works, and accuse us to avert men from good works." The doctrinal contrast between Protestant and Catholic, between faith and works, is explicit.

In Alexander Ross's "Jacobs Ladder"[26] some pedestrian verses restate the familiar idea:

> Christ is this Ladder, who hath ioyn'd in one,
> The Earth and Heauen by his passion.
> His foote is on the Earth, in Heauen his head,
> Hee's God and man, *Emanuell* indeed.
>
> . . . .
>
> By him from God, Angels to us descend,
> By him to God, Prayers from us ascend.

The ladder of Jacob's dream is a symbol of Christ, who here appears as Mediator. Although His office as Mediator is a familiar one,

---

[26] *Three Decades of Diuine Meditations* (London, 1630), pp. 7–8. John Hall's *Jacob's Ladder: or, The Devout Souls Ascension to Heaven,* a book of private and family devotions with sacred poems, has nothing to our purpose.

it might be instructive to hear some authoritative opinions on that subject from Ussher's *A Body of Divinity*, . . . Christ's office is[27]

To be a Mediatour betwixt God and man: and so discharge all that is requisit for the reconciling of us unto God, and the working of our salvation . . . he is called an Intercessor and an Advocate: because he prayeth for us to the Father, and pleadeth our cause before his Judgement seat . . . he was *anointed with all gifts and graces of the spirit* of God needful for a Mediatour, and that without measure . . . he continually maketh intercession for us to God, and of himselfe alone is able to save us, comming to the Father through him. . . . Iesus Christ our *high Priest* became obedient even unto the death, offering up himselfe once for all, to make a full satisfaction for all our sins; and maketh continuall intercession to the Father in our name: whereby the wrath of God is appeased, his justice is satisfied, and we are reconciled. . . . *Redemption* . . . is a deliverance of us from sin and the punishment thereof, and a restoring of us to a better life then ever *Adam* had. . . . For our Saviour Christ hath *First*, redeemed us from the power of darknesse: . . . namely, that wofull and cursed estate which we had justly brought upon our selves by reason of our sinnes. *Secondly,* translated us into his own kingdome and glory: . . . a far more glorious and excellent estate then ever our first parents had in Paradise.

The doctrine, though familiar, acquires from such statements a certain added force and persuasiveness; and this helps one to realize the vital importance of the Ladder-Christ symbol.

The stairs in *Paradise Lost*, it is clear, embody or represent a fundamental Christian idea or doctrine: the doctrine of redemption and salvation through Christ. The stairs are strategically and appropriately placed in the poem. One may recall that the universe in its perfection had already been created and that Adam and Eve, who in Satan's opinion are but little inferior to heavenly spirits bright, are already in Paradise,

> in the happie Garden plac't,
> Reaping immortal fruits of joy and love,
> Uninterrupted joy, unrivald love
> In blissful solitude

innocent and unaware of approaching danger, unaware of Satan then

[27] James Ussher, *A Body of Divinity, or the Summe and Substance of Christian Religion* (London, 1649), pp. 166 ff. Compare the italicized words with the passages from *Paradise Lost* quoted at the end of this essay.

Coasting the wall of Heav'n on this side Night
In the dun Air sublime, and ready now
To stoop with wearied wings, and willing feet
On the bare outside of this World.

The stairs would suggest that the spiritual structure of the universe has been perfected, that the means of salvation are at hand before the Fall, to be used when and if required.

On reflection it is clear that Milton has suggested and indeed prepared us for the interpretation here offered. In Book III, God and His Son conferred at length with regard to Satan's imminent assault and man's jeopardy. By his foreknowledge the Father knows that man, though created good, will hearken to the Devil's lies and that he will succumb. But man because he is deceived will find grace and mercy. Justice must be satisfied, "But Mercy first and last shall brightest shine." The agent of mercy is, of course, the Son; through Him "Man shall not quite be lost, but sav'd who will." For man's sake the Son will put off his glory and for man He will die. But He will not long lie vanquished under death's gloomy banner. Rising victorious, He will lead death and hell captive and finally re-enter heaven with the multitude of His redeemed. The first of Book III prepares one to recognize Christ as the Redeemer, not as the invincible adversary of Satan and his hosts. In the poem the role of Redeemer of mankind is most important—and the ladder or stairway is the symbol of redemption, the symbol of divine grace, mercy, and love, the symbol of Christ the Redeemer.

The other part or, as Latimer would say, the nether foot of the ladder, the *scala coeli,* designated in language not picturesque or pictorial but abstract, is found after the Fall and almost at the end of the epic, where Adam and Michael together present the Christian ideal. Adam has learned from Michael

> that to obey is best,
> And love with feare the onely God, to walk
> As in his presence, ever to observe
> His providence, and on him sole depend,
>
> . . . .
>
> . . . that suffering for Truths sake
> Is fortitude to highest victorie,
> And to the faithful Death the Gate of life;
> Taught this by his example whom I now
> Acknowledge my *Redeemer* ever blest.   (XII, 561–73)

Adam had just been told of the dark future when true religion would be oppressed by "Wolves"

> Who all the sacred mysteries of Heav'n
> To thir own vile advantages shall turne
> Of lucre and ambition, and the truth
> With superstitions and traditions taint

in a world "To good malignant, to bad men benigne," but he had also been comforted by the knowledge that in the end his Saviour and Lord would come "to dissolve/*Satan* with his perverted World," and that He would raise new Heavens and a new Earth "Founded in righteousness and peace and love,/To bring forth fruits Joy and eternal Bliss." In the meantime Adam (and, of course, all true Christians) should follow Michael's advice:

>   add
> Deeds to thy knowledge answerable, add Faith,
> Add Vertue, Patience, Temperance, add Love,
> By name to come call'd Charitie, the Soul
> Of all the rest: then wilt thou not be loath
> To leave this Paradise, but shalt possess
> A Paradise within thee, happier farr.   (XII, 582–87)

The Paradise within seems almost a reminiscence of Ussher's "a far more glorious and excellent estate then ever our first parents had in Paradise," but, of course, Ussher had in mind heaven and God's kingdom and glory, a "far happier place/Then this of *Eden,* and far happier daies," the home of every true believer who practiced the Christian virtues and persevered in the faith.

Milton has justly been called "the last great exponent of Christian humanism in its historical continuity."[28] But the general impression is that, set beside Chaucer or Shakespeare, he seems "cold, inhuman, an unapproachable Jehovah of poetry," who treats "themes and problems which seem remote and no longer of vital concern to us." If we think only in human terms, the charge against Milton is valid; for, as Housman says cynically, "malt does more than Milton can/To justify God's ways to man." To Christians, however, the subject of this study, redemption and salvation through Christ, is vital; for it is the heart of Christianity. Consider what Bishop Hall says:[29]

[28] Douglas Bush, *The Renaissance and English Humanism* (Toronto, 1939), p. 101.

[29] "The Soules Farewell to Earth, and Approaches to Heaven," *Divers Treatises* ... (London, 1662), pp. 930–31.

But that which may justly challenge thy longer stay, and greater wonder, is the more-then-transcendent work of mans redemption; the mysteries whereof the holy Angels have desired to look into, but could never yet sufficiently conceive or admire: That the Sonne of God, the Lord of Glory, Coeternall, Coequall to his Father, God blessed for ever, should take upon him an estate lower than their own; should cloath his Deity with the rags of our flesh; should stoop to weak and miserable man-hood, and in that low & despicable condition, should submit himself to hunger, thirst, weariness, temptation of Devils, despight of men, to the cruelty of tormentors, to agonies of soul, to the pangs of a bitter, ignominious, cursed death, to the sense of his Fathers wrath for us wretched sinners, that had made ourselves the worst of Creatures, enemies to God, slaves to Satan, is above the reach of all finite apprehension. Oh never-to-be-enough-magnified mercy! Thou didst . . . out of thine infinite love and compassion, vouchsafe, so to abase thy blessed self, as to descend from thy Throne of thy Celestial glory to this dungeon of earth. . . . Thou that art the eternal Son of God, wouldst condescend so low, as to be man; that we who are worms and no men might be advanced to be the Sons of God: thou wouldst be a servant, that we might reign: thou wouldst expose thy self to the shame and disgrace of thy vile Creatures here, that thou mightest raise us up to the height of Heavenly honour with thee our God, and the holy Angels: thou wouldst die for a while, that we might live eternally.

The subject so eloquently presented is one of the greatest moment. "Pause here a while, O my soul," Hall exclaims, "and do not wish to change thy thoughts; neither Earth nor Heaven can yield thee any higher concernment, of greater comfort." For Christians this must be true. In the light of this truth and with this faith Milton should be read. His culture, it is true, is unique in its richness and breadth. But it cannot be doubted that Milton's "simple faith . . . transcended, controlled, and ordered . . . all his learning"[30] and indeed all his art and his life. It may be said that this view of Milton is too narrow, that it ignores the riches, the subtleties, and the ramifications of his thought; that it disregards his humanism and his faith in human reason; that in short it makes his mind appear more simple than it is. There is much truth in these objections. Milton's interests were far-ranging; his mind was rich, his culture broad and genuine. However, religion was the dominant subject in his life, and he was in some respects "the last voice of an essentially medieval tradition." In his major poems the humanist is dominated by the Christian. It has recently been urged

[30] Charles G. Osgood, "Milton," *Poetry as a Means of Grace* (Princeton, 1946), pp. 86–87.

that *Paradise Regained* with its choice of a life of "withdrawal and self-denial" and its rejection of Greek culture, "one of the most powerful influences" in Milton's intellectual and creative life, is an exception,[31] that in *Samson Agonistes* Milton recovered his old interest in Greek poetry. The argument is not very convincing. Bowra, of course, knows that Milton found the subject of *Samson Agonistes* not in Greek myth but in the Bible, and in a footnote he quotes from the anonymous *Life* the statement "And David's Psalms were in esteem with him above all poetry." For Milton religion was, as he says in *The Christian Doctrine*, a "divine revelation disclosed in various ages by Christ," not derived from the schools of philosophers or the laws of man. Milton's address to all the churches of Christ closes with the admonition that they should "live in the faith of our Lord and Saviour Jesus Christ."

The religious and moral values surveyed in this study constitute a segment of the hierarchical order according to which "degrees of value are objectively present in the universe." Happiness, virtue, and salvation itself consist in obeying this hierarchichal order of values, in which the soul rules the body, reason rules passion, and so on. According to Lewis, Milton accepts this hierarchical order, which is the central idea of *Paradise Lost*. Lewis states:[32]

The Hierarchical idea is not merely stuck on to his poem at points where doctrine demands it: it is the indwelling life of the whole work, it foams or burgeons out of it at every moment.

He pictures the life of beatitude as one of order. . . . He pictures his whole universe as one of degrees, from root to stalk, from stalk to flower, from flower to breath, from fruit to human reason. . . .

This is not the writing of a man who embraces the Hierarchical principle with reluctance, but rather of a man enchanted by it.

In this order the spiritual ladder is inevitable and indispensable; for, Milton says, "A man that would climb upon a ladder that is high . . . must go by degrees from one to another." From the Protestant point of view the ladder is Christ, by whose mediation through the grace of God man is redeemed. Adam hears from Michael the fulfillment of the prophecy uttered after the Fall:

[31] C. M. Bowra, *Inspiration and Poetry* (London, 1955), pp. 112–13. Don E. Ray in "Milton and the Elizabethan Tradition of Christian Learning" (doctoral dissertation, The Rice Institute, 1957), undoubtedly presents the true explanation of Christ's rejection of Greek culture.
[32] C. S. Lewis, *A Preface to Paradise Lost* (London, 1946), pp. 78 ff.

> thy punishment
> He shall endure by coming in the Flesh
> To a reproachful life and cursed death,
>
> . . . .
>
> But soon revives, Death over him no power
> Shall long usurp; ere the third morning light
> Returne, the Starres of Morn shall see him rise
> Out of the grave, fresh as the dawning light,
> Thy ransom paid, which Man from death redeems,
> His death for Man, as many as offered Life
> Neglect not, and the benefit imbrace
> By Faith not void of workes.   (XII, 404–27)

In the last days Christ will descend once more, to judge the quick and the dead, to reward the faithful and receive them into bliss.

In Milton's thought this doctrine of redemption and salvation is, Bush thinks, supported by his recognition of the rational and philosophic conscience implanted in all men.[33] In its moral parts the Christian religion as conceived by Milton is, Bush declares, nothing but the law of nature and reason. Like the Cambridge Platonists, Milton emphasized the rational and ethical imitation of Christ. To go against reason is to go against God, for God and nature are one. Milton believed that a "certain remnant, or imperfect illumination" of the law of nature given originally to Adam still dwells in the hearts of all mankind and that in the regenerate under the influence of the Holy Spirit it tends toward a "renewal of its primitive brightness." Thus right reason and the nature of man are in harmony with the Word of God. The sovereignty of right reason and the law of nature is accepted "not as servitude but as the condition of true freedom." Through God's grace and by his own insight and efforts man becomes a "free agent, a self-directing son of God," endowed with a faculty which enables him "within limits, to understand the purposes of a God who is perfect reason as well as perfect justice, goodness, and love." According to Bush, this is the basic religious philosophy of Christian humanism, of which, in seventeenth-century England, Milton was the "greatest exponent."

Although, as explained elsewhere in this study, Bush seems to exaggerate the importance of human reason or the rational element in Milton's religion, his analysis refutes the critics who see in our poet only a bigoted individualist and an arrogant rebel who deified the

---

[33] Douglas Bush, *Paradise Lost in Our Time* (New York, 1948), pp. 29–57.

human will, who was completely emancipated from the true humility of religious faith, who indeed regarded pride "not as a vice but as the mark of a superior nature." The preposterous fantasies of these critics, who would have dethroned Milton to deify the skeptical, sensual, and cynical Donne, are now generally discredited. Among those who know, Milton is—as he has always been—the peerless Christian poet and true humanist, from whose exalted seat are heard only the oracles of virtue and of God.

The intelligent and informed student knows that the man who wrote the great poems was not the confident, aggressive, and optimistic reformer. He had been disillusioned; he had in fact suffered a long series of disillusionments. He had lost some of his faith—in bishops, king, parliament, and people, in the possibility of reform. Although he had fallen on evil days, his faith in God and the soul of man, his faith in the divine regeneration of man's soul "by the Spirit" for the perception of heavenly things and the performance of good works—this faith survived. It was a strenuous and exacting faith in the divine order and individual righteousness. His spiritual insight, which was the heart of his religion, had been sharpened; his understanding of the divine nature had been enriched. His career, which may have begun with some measure of humanistic pride, ended in the repudiation of self-sufficiency. Milton, like Adam, had learned the sum of wisdom:

> Greatly instructed I shall hence depart,
> Greatly in peace of thought, and have my fill
> Of knowledge, what this Vessel can contain;
> Beyond which was my folly to aspire.
> Henceforth I learn, that to obey is best,
> And love with fear the only God, to walk
> As in his presence, ever to observe
> His providence, and on him sole depend, . . .

ending with lines commending the Christian virtues—lines which are, it has been said, a true and deeply felt summary of Christ's teaching.

This is Milton's message, which is founded on orthodox religious doctrine and is not here at least associated with the philosophical identification of God with the law of Nature or right reason. This orthodox faith seems to be the basis of all his major poems, which, generally speaking, present, on the one hand, as an ideal so many illustrations of faith and obedience and the exercise of the Christian virtues, while on the other, they show the sin, misery, and death that are the inevitable consequences of infidelity and disobedience. *Para-*

85

dise Lost reveals that the root of man's (and angels') sin is pride, which leads to "foul distrust, and breach Disloyal on the part of Man, Revolt/And disobedience: . . ." and the endless story of human depravity and iniquity. In *Paradise Regained* Christ, adorned with "Perfections absolute, Graces divine" and invincible in His "filial Vertue," easily repels the temptations of the Devil and shows how by one man's firm obedience paradise may be regained and "*Eden* rais'd in the wast Wilderness." It has recently been said that Samson's sin was pride[34] (though it should be added that his sin was in part due to his lack of judgment and his surrender to passion): his fall "comes from the essence of his being, from the pride which has first made him a great warrior and then grown through success until it ruins him." Through bitter suffering and humiliation Samson of course comes to recognize and deplore his weakness and sin, and he is finally restored to God's favor.

Obviously Milton condemned pride and believed than man's great need is humility.

> The first stair of humility is, if, setting the fear of God continually before our eyes, we never forget His commands, always remembering that those who despise Him go to Hell because of their sins, and that eternal life is prepared for those who fear Him.

Although it may be a pagan virtue, pride is in Christianity the worst of sins. This contrast between humility and pride is represented in the stairway to heaven and the bridge to hell: the one a symbol of divine humility and love, the other a symbol of pride and hate. Henry Osborn Taylor in his summary of Benedict's *regula* says,[35]

> Therefore, brothers, if we wish to touch the summit of complete humility and reach that heavenly exaltation to which we ascend through the humility of the present life, we must by our ascending acts erect those stairs which appeared in Jacob's dream, on which the angels were shown to him descending and ascending. By this we should understand descent through exaltation and ascent through humility. *The upright stairway is our life on earth, which a heart humbled by the Lord raises to heaven.* The sides of this stairway we call our body and soul; in them the divine summons (*evocatio*) sets the stairs of humility or discipline to be ascended.

Although Milton may not always have practiced the virtues of obedience and humility, he was enamored of the hierarchical principle, and devoted to the achievement of moral and spiritual perfection

[34] Bowra, *Inspiration and Poetry*, p. 119.
[35] Taylor, *The Classical Heritage of the Middle Ages*, pp. 170–71. Italics mine.

with a system of religious and ethical values which have a very practical application in life. The fundamental law, the paramount rule of conduct, is obedience to God. True worship of God consists in the performance of good works, in the practice of all the prescribed duties, toward God and man. True wisdom is the knowledge of the will of God and the regulation of all actions by His will, which is revealed by consulting the Holy Scriptures as well as by meditation, prayer, and worship. The general virtues are love and righteousness. The special virtues are temperance, fortitude, patience, charity, and all the others by which the true Christian is governed and directed in his incessant striving for perfection.

The ladder or stairway is thus a fitting symbol of the course or way leading to salvation. It represents and requires the perception of heavenly things and the practice of love and all the virtues. It represents in particular the gradual steps by which,without faltering, we must strive for perfection "as the ultimate object of our existence." The ladder is a symbol of Christian thought and character, of the life of virtue and reason enlightened by faith. It is the means by which, following after "righteousness, godliness, faith, love, patience, meekness," we must try to realize perfection here and to prepare for eternal life hereafter, to lay just hands on that golden key "That ope's the palace of eternity."

IV

The Glassy Sea and the Golden Compasses

A bright sea flowed . . . to circumscribe this universe

The promise of the Christian religion is to free the soul from the sense of irremediable guilt, to promote virtuous conduct in obedience to a spiritual order of righteousness in this life, and to assure the faithful that after death they will live forever in a kingdom of joy, peace, and love. Opposed to worldly interests and on principle devoted to spiritual values, religion, invoking divine grace, operates by worship and prayer, comforting and inspiring the worshiper by doctrines and rituals which offer the hope of salvation and reveal the mysteries of heaven. Although often debased in popular practice, religion in its ideal form is "an imaginative achievement," a symbolic representation of moral and spiritual reality, and it has a vital function in vitalizing the mind and interpreting and transcending experience.[1] In its imaginative quality, in its use of figurative language and symbols, religion is akin to poetry; but it is, of course, more formal than poetry and more traditional. In religion a genuine metaphysic mystery takes the place of a mere figure of speech, expressing in each case "a little miraculous drama" in an orthodox sacred mythology hallowed by tradition.

It is a well known fact that in religion a material object or a physical action may be regarded as the symbol of spiritual truth; and

[1] George Santayana, *The Life of Reason or the Phases of Human Progress* (New York, 1954), pp. 183 ff. Hereafter cited as *The Life of Reason.*

Whitehead is doubtless correct in declaring that the inability of the great majority to read is the "one great reason for the symbolism of religion."[2] There is, to be sure, a great difference between the common and the religious use of words; for in religious doctrine and ritual the word is abstracted from its common and immediate surroundings, and a fixed spiritual value is attached to the idea and the object. In religion the object has no meaning in itself; its significance lies in the spiritual truth which it represents and with which it is identified. Indeed during fifteen centuries of the Christian era the difference between the object and the spiritual idea was frequently ignored. It was felt and believed that there was a "magically wrought presence of the divine and the spiritual" within the spiritual objects and human acts. This is, of course, the case in the sacrament of the Lord's Supper when the bread and the wine are regarded as being converted into the body and blood of Christ. In the sacrament of baptism also the water acquires a mysterious power or virtue. Bishop Ussher says, in *A Body of Divinity,* . . . that the washing of the water represents "the *powerfull* washing of the *bloud* and *spirit* of Christ; . . . and so sealing our *regeneration* or newbirth, our *entrance* into the Covenant of Grace, and our *ingraffing* into Christ, and into the body of Christ, which is his Church."[3] The learned bishop distinguishes between the common and the religious meaning: "The word *Baptisme* signifieth in general any *washing:* but here it is specially taken for that sacramentall washing which sealeth unto those that are within Gods Covenant, their birth in Christ, and enterance into Christianity." The word *entrance* must be emphasized. Observe also Ussher's explanation of the reason for calling baptism the "first Sacrament": "Because Christ gave order to his Apostles, that after they have taught, and men believe, they should baptize them; that so they might be enrolled amongst those of the household of God, and entered into the number of the Citizens and Burgesses of the heavenly *Jerusalem.*"

This sacrament has two essential parts: the outward signs and the inward things signified. The outward signs are the water and the outward sacramental actions performed by it when blessed by the minister and consecrated. As everything is sanctified by the Word of God

---

[2] Henry Osborn Taylor, *The Classical Heritage of the Middle Ages* (3d ed.; New York, 1911), p. 91; Alfred N. Whitehead, *Modes of Thought* (Cambridge, 1938), p. 52.

[3] James Ussher, *A Body of Divinity, or the Summe and Substance of Christian Religion* (London, 1649), p. 411.

and prayer, "so in especiall manner the Sacramentall water in baptisme is blessed and consecrated by the Word of God and prayer." As for the inward part, the water signifies

the bloud of Christ, the Ministers consecrating the water signifies God the Fathers setting apart his Son for the expiation of the sins of the world by his bloud; the Ministers applying the water to the body of the baptized to cleanse it, signifieth Gods applying the bloud of his Son to cleanse the soul for justification and remission of sins: and not onely to signifie, but to seal up unto the believer, that the inward part is effected as well as the outward.

There is a natural fitness and aptness in the outward thing to the inward. The water and the blood of Christ are both necessary, the water to the natural life of man, the blood of Christ to his spiritual life. The water is a comfortable element, and so the thirst of the soul cannot be quenched but by the blood of Christ. The water is a free element, so is the blood of Christ. Water is a common element, so the blood of Christ is offered to all. Water is a copious and plentiful element, so the blood of Christ is "all-sufficient, it can never be drawn dry." And "lastly and especially, water is a cleansing and a purifying element: and it resembles the bloud of Christ fitly in that." The "symbolicalnesse between the Sacramentall action of washing, and the inward grace signified" is also explained. First, nothing is washed but what is unclean; "even so the Sacramentall washing implies our naturall pollution": second, as the application of the water cleanses and cleans, "so it is with the bloud of Christ; it cleanseth not the soul, but by being applied to it, in the merit and efficacy of it, by the sanctifying Spirit."

Baptism is a divine institution, a divine ordinance; what makes the outward signs significant "is Gods Word and appointment," which establishes a sacramental union between them, the one being conveyed and "sealed up by the other." Baptism is the *first* sacrament, the sacramental *washing* sealing the birth in Christ, the *entrance* into Christianity, the *entering* "into the number of the Citizens and Burgesses of the heavenly Jerusalem." Baptism marks "*admission* into the visible body of the Church," and is "but the porch, the shell, and outside" of the church. Besides this, a special grace is required for these to be "spiritually ingraffed into the mysticall body of Christ." Baptism is a "high Ordinance of God" appointed "to communicate Christ and his benefits to our soules." It seals and confirms our right and interest in God's covenant and promise. It is, Ussher says, "not the

90

water that purgeth our sins, but the bloud of the Covenant." Such is Ussher's authoritative interpretation of the first sacrament, the relation of which to a part of *Paradise Lost* may later be made clear.

Whitehead has observed that in the medieval period in Europe "symbolism seemed to dominate men's imaginations" but that with the Reformation a reaction set in, and men tried to dispense with symbols as "fond things, vainly invented."[4] This reaction was doubtless part of the Protestant protest against Roman Catholic modes of thought and specifically the Roman ritual. Some illustrations of the prevalence of symbolism in Roman Catholic thought and ritual of the high Middle Ages may be recalled. It had its source doubtless in the allegorical interpretation of Scripture which dominated the literature and inspired the art of the Middle Ages. An illustration from the twelfth century is to be found in Hugh St. Victor's explanation of creation, which he interprets symbolically and allegorically. In Hugh the severance of light from darkness is the material example of God's dividing the good from the evil. The earth represents the sensual nature of man; the heavens stand for "the purity of his intelligence quickening to immortal life." The material world corresponds to the unseen world. In addition to their material nature, light and water "are essentially symbols." And their symbolism is as much a part of their nature "as the symbolical character of the Eucharist is part of the nature of the consecrated bread and wine."[5] God's entire creation represents in a less perfect way the sacraments, which are among the deepest truths of the Christian faith. And the sacrament itself is symbolical, the corporal or material element signifying from its institution and containing from its sanctification "some invisible and spiritual grace."

In the twelfth and thirteenth centuries the Mass itself was elaborately symbolical. According to Durandus the Mass is devised to contain the major part of what was accomplished by and in Christ from the time he descended from heaven to the time when he ascended to heaven. In the Introit the antiphonal chanting signifies the aspirations and deeds, the prayers and praises of the patriarchs and prophets looking for the coming of Christ. The chorus of the chanting clergy represents the yearning of saints of the Ancient Law. The bishop clad in his vestments and advancing to the altar represents

[4] Alfred N. Whitehead, *Symbolism Its Meaning and Effect* (New York, 1927), p. 1.
[5] Henry Osborn Taylor, *The Medieval Mind* (4th ed.; Cambridge [Mass.], 1951), II, 93 ff.

Christ emerging from the Virgin's womb and entering the world. The seven lights before him are the seven gifts of the Holy Spirit. The two acolytes preceding him are the Law and the Prophets, shown in Moses and Elias. The four who bear the canopy are the four Evangelists. Taking his seat and laying aside his miter, the bishop is silent, as was Christ during His early years. The clergy around him represent the Magi and others. Every word and act of the service is "filled with symbolic import." The reading of the Epistle represents the preaching of John the Baptist. The reading of the Gospel represents the beginning of Christ's preaching. "The Creed follows the Gospel, as faith follows the preaching of the truth." The twelve parts refer to the calling of the twelve apostles. The symbolism of the Mass is extended to the edifice. "The material church signifies the Holy Church built of living stones in heaven, with Christ the corner-stone. . . . The walls . . . are the Jews and Gentiles, who believing come to Christ from the four quarters of the world. The faithful people predestined to life are the stones thereof." In the mortar the lime is fervent love, the sand earthly toil, the water the Spirit, uniting the lime and the sand. The stones are hewn and squared, that is, sanctified and made clean. Again, the four walls of the church represent the four Evangelists. The length is long-suffering, which endures adversity. The breadth is love, which embraces its friends in God and loves its enemies. The foundation is faith, the roof is charity, the door is obedience, the pavement is humility. The four walls are the four virtues, righteousness, fortitude, prudence, and temperance. "The windows are glad hospitality and free-handed pity." The apse signifies the faithful laity; the crypts, the hermits; and the nave signifies Christ, "through whom lies the way to the heavenly Jerusalem." The lofty dome with the cross "signifies how perfect and inviolate should be the preaching and observance of the Catholic Faith." The glass windows are the divine Scriptures, "which repel the wind and the rain, but admit the light of the true son, to wit God, into the church, that is, into the hearts of the faithful." And so on and on, each bit of the church edifice having a spiritual meaning.

In the carving of the Gothic cathedral nature and Scripture are depicted. The Creator is shown contemplating His work or resting from His toil. A lion, sheep, or goat represents the animal creation, and trees represent the vegetable world. The man, the lion, the ox, the eagle stand for the four Evangelists. "The allegorical interpretations of Scripture were an exhaustless source of symbolism for Gothic sculptors"; but some of the carving was sheer fancy. In short the Gothic

92

cathedral as a speculum or *summa* was intended to "include the whole of God's creation, not omitting even the devils who beset men's souls."[6] In the colored glass of Chartres and Bourges may be seen the Passion and the Resurrection of Christ and significant incidents in the life of the Saviour and His virgin mother, with leading personages of the Old Testament. "Everywhere the tendency to symbolize is strong," in scenes of the life of Christ, the parables, the crucifixion, and so on, to the Last Judgment, with "the damnation of the damned and the beatitude of the elect." All these scenes "are full of symbolism, and full of 'historic' reality as well." The nameless men who depicted the sacred drama of man's creation, fall, redemption, and final judgment "rendered it in all its dogmatic symbolism" and created "matchless ideals of symbolism in art." As Taylor said, these artists do not set forth mortal man in his natural strength and beauty, but rather they "seek to show the working of the human spirit within the power and grace of God." They could deftly render earth's beauty in vine, flower, and leaf, and they could present the daily life in shop, field, and market place, the toiling laborer, "the merchant with his stuffs, the scholar with his scrolls." But these scenes were not unconnected with "the drama of creation and redemption mirrored in the cathedral," and even the exquisitely cut leaf and rose might suggest "the grace incarnate in the Virgin and her Son." In these artists "man's mind and spirit are palpably the devout creatures of God's omnipotence, obedient to His will, sustained and redeemed by His power and grace." The humble details of daily routine and of natural life unobtrusively serve the design of the whole which was "a visible symbol of the unseen and divine power." In essence their art is not natural but symbolic: the mortal and the tangible, the carved image or the painted picture is "the realizing symbol of the unseen and eternal Spirit."

For a moment we may now consider the reason for the use of symbolism in religious ritual and art. Man's consciousness of the supernatural ,which is the basis of all religion, is vague and formless unless it can be defined and made intelligible by symbols, which, Dean Inge said, "are as it were the flesh and bones of ideas."[7] The symbol is the means by which the worshiper hopes to "close the cleft between sense and spirit, between the seen and the unseen, between time and eternity."[8] For the religious mind everything in the world is sacramental, symbolizing and expressing something more than itself. According

[6] *Ibid.,* 109.
[7] William Ralph Inge, *Christian Mysticism, . . .* (New York, 1933), p. 5.
[8] William Ralph Inge, *Things New and Old* (London, 1933), p. 30.

to Bernard, the Lord through His grace provided sacraments, of which *baptism is the beginning,* "ut invisibilis gratia signo aliquo visibili praestaretur"—so that invisible grace might be presented in or by some visible sign.[9] Essential in the sacraments, symbols are particularly needed to illustrate the doctine of regeneration and the life beyond the grave. Because Christ's kingdom could not be established in this world, Christians transferred their anxious thoughts and longings to heaven, their Master's home. "These thoughts and longings form the central motives of Christian symbolism."[10] In Scripture, especially in the writings of St. John, visible things are symbols of the invisible. The signs, the works, the miracles of Christ are evidences of His divinity. He is the Bread of Life, the Good Shepherd, the Light of the World. Indeed all things in the world "remind us of Him who made them, and who is their sustaining life."[11]

Contrasted with symbolism at opposite extremes are pagan naturalism or natural magic on the one hand and mysticism on the other. The first is scarcely Christian or even religious; the second is religious in the most abstract and refined form. In pagan naturalism everything participates in divinity; everything is actually, not symbolically, divine. The peasants of Italy are only nominally Christian. Even the ceremonies of the church become pagan rites, celebrating the existence of inanimate things and earthly divinities.[12] On the other hand, mysticism, yearning to commune with divinity, seeks to spiritualize everything. Although it has been defined as "the tendency to approach the Absolute, morally, by means of symbols,"[13] mysticism in its most complete and refined development is emancipated from material things and forms. These along with reason and natural apprehension are but hindrances to the isolated and lonely soul which in the dark night seeks illumination and union with the divine.

Although natural magic and mysticism tend not to rely upon symbols, religion and its symbols are inseparable, the symbol being the visible form of religion. The mystic believes, with William Law, that the temple of God is "within thee, . . . where alone thou canst worship

---

[9] *Patrologiae Latinae,* CLXXXIII, col. 271. All references to the *Patrologiae Latinae,* . . . ed. by J. P. Migne (Paris, 1844——), will be cited hereafter as *Pat. Lat.*

[10] *Encyclopaedia of Religion and Ethics,* ed. by James Hastings (New York, 1922), XII, 134.

[11] Inge, *Christian Mysticism,* . . . p. 59.

[12] Carlo Levi, *Christ Stopped at Eboli* (New York, 1947), pp. 116–47.

[13] Inge, *Christian Mysticism,* . . . p. 250.

God in spirit and in truth" and that thus "wherever thou goest thou wilt have a priest, a church, and an altar along with thee." But the orthodox worshiper must rely upon the outward forms and rites of the church. But here a difficulty arises, for, as Dean Inge said, it is the tendency of all symbols "to petrify or evaporate, and either process is fatal to them." Some symbols endure: falling leaves are a symbol of human mortality; a flowing river is a symbol of the stream of life; a vine and its branches are symbols of the unity of Christ and the church. There are three requisites for the religious symbol to be valid as a sacramental act: the symbol must be appropriate; the thing symbolized must be a spiritual truth; and "there must be the intention to perform the act *as* a sacrament."[14] If the third requisite is lacking, the symbol, though by tradition impressive in its form, loses its real, its spirtiual value and becomes the fossil of a sterile faith.

With the passing of time and the decline of faith, something of this inevitable tendency is felt in the reading and understanding of *Paradise Lost*. The ideas and their symbols have lost much of their original vitality and power. The symbols have been petrified. Even though their original import is understood, the ideas seem old-fashioned, and the symbolism lacks its sacramental value.

"The most striking characteristic of the poetry of Milton," wrote Macaulay, "is the extreme remoteness of the associations by means of which it acts on the reader. Its effect is produced, not so much by what it expresses as by what it suggests, not so much by the ideas which it directly conveys, as by other ideas which are connected with them. He electrifies the mind through conductors." Milton cannot be understood or enjoyed, Macaulay goes on to say, "unless the mind of the reader cooperate with that of the writer." He does not paint a finished picture; he does not play for a "mere passive listener." He sketches and leaves others to fill in the outline. "He strikes the keynote, and expects his hearer to make out the melody."[15] Milton's poetry acts like an incantation. Its merit "lies less in its obvious meaning than in its occult power." Developing his famous comparison between *Paradise Lost* and the *Divine Comedy*, Macaulay declares that the poetry of Milton differs from that of Dante as "the hieroglyphics of Egypt differed from the picture-writing of Mexico." Ignoring the necessary copious annotation of the *Divine Comedy*, Macaulay says that

14 *Ibid.*, p. 255.
15 Thomas B. Macaulay, "Milton," *The Edinburgh Review*, XLII (August, 1825), 314.

the images of Dante "stand simply for what they are"; they speak for themselves. On the other hand, the images of Milton have a meaning "which is often discernible only to the initiated."

We shall now examine principally two of these images or symbols, both of them traditional. The first, in origin part of the church ritual, is strictly sacramental; the other is sacramental only in the sense of Hugh St. Victor, for whom all things in creation are divine. In this inquiry we shall adhere to a main effort of Renaissance thought, which was "to strengthen and purify rather than break with tradition." We desire "not to strike off into strange seas of thought alone, but to restore a primal purity lost in the accretions and distortions of time."[16] We would restore part of the Christian tradition, which is essential to the understanding and appreciation of *Paradise Lost*.

The Glassy Sea occupies a space between the empyrean heaven and the newly created universe. The world is

> From Heaven Gate not farr, founded in view
> On the cleer *Hyaline*, the Glassie Sea.   (VII, 618–19)

Some explain that this sea is the crystalline sphere or ocean, which protects the universe from chaos. Patrick Hume thought that it may be the "Empyrean Heaven," which from its clearness, calmness, and solidity is compared to the crystalline sea. Although the Glassy Sea is here an area in space, the physical meaning is not the only one. The phrase is a theological term and has a meaning and history which commentators have ignored. It is of this sea that Milton writes in another part of the poem. Under the great stairway leading to heaven

> a bright Sea flow'd
> Of Jasper, or of Liquid Pearle, whereon
> Who after came from Earth, sayling arriv'd,
> Wafted by Angels, or flew o'er the Lake
> Rapt in a Chariot drawn by fiery Steeds.   (III, 518–22)

This sea not only bounds the universe but is a passage to heaven. It is in this latter sense that the phrase is most significant: the term "Glassie Sea" and the symbol have a theological background and rich spiritual associations which have a great and not merely occasional interest. How much of the rich spiritual meaning Milton may have intended to suggest we cannot tell, but we can be sure that the symbol carries rich traditional values, which I shall attempt to sketch.

[16] Herschel Baker, *The Wars of Truth* . . . (Cambridge [Mass.], 1952), pp. 2–3.

In origin the symbol is scriptural: "Before the throne was a sea of glass, like unto crystal" (Rev. 4:6). This text was variously interpreted. Ambrose compared this sea to the sea of brass in Solomon's Temple, which represented the Old Testament. This darkens the spiritual intelligence. But as brass when rubbed becomes bright the spiritual intelligence is enlightened by the grace of God. Therefore this sea of glass is the New Testament: "Per mare ergo vitrem atque crystallum non inconvenienter Novum Testamentum intelligitur."[17] Three things are to be noted: the sea signifies history, the glass moral intelligence, the crystal spiritual intelligence. Moral intelligence reveals whatever is vicious in men's minds. Spiritual intelligence explains obscure things in Scripture, enlightens the mind, and kindles love of God and heaven. The phrase is to be spiritually understood: "sed spiritaliter intelligendum est." It may be recalled that Jacob's ladder also stood for the Old Testament and the New. The sea is a symbol of Scripture and of moral and spiritual intelligence.

Ambrose's interpretation recurs in the thirteenth century, when St. Martin explains that the sea, the glass, and the crystal stand respectively for the literal, the moral, and the spiritual intelligence.[18] Centuries earlier and more important is St. Augustine, who explains the text thus: "*In conspectu throni mare vitreum:* mare vitreum, fontem Baptismi; ante thronum dixit, id est, ante judicium."[19] St. Augustine says that there is only one true doctrine: "Doctrina Dei una est, non sunt multae aquae, sed una aqua, sive sacramenti baptismi, sive doctrinae salutaris." The Glassy Sea stands for baptism, the first sacrament, which is regeneration by water. St. Augustine interprets baptism as a kind of memorial to Christ: "All who attain to this grace die thereby to sin" as Christ is said "to have died to sin because he died in the flesh, that is, 'in the likeness of sin'—and they are thereby alive by being born in the baptismal font, just as he rose again from the sepulcher." All, young and old, "die to sin in baptism" and are reborn.[20]

---

[17] *Pat. Lat.*, XVII, col. 801.

[18] *Ibid.*, CCIX, col. 326.

[19] *Ibid.*, XXXV, col. 2422.

[20] *Library of Christian Classics*, VII, *Augustine: Confessions and Enchiridion*, Albert C. Outler, trans. and ed. (London, 1955), 365–66. Gregory of Nyssa also says that in baptism we imitate Christ's experience: as Christ was buried in the earth and on the third day returned to life, so in baptism the person is immersed three times in water, and this produces the grace of resurrection (*Library of Christian Classics*, III, *Christology of the Later Fathers*, 312 ff).

In Cassiodorus the Glassy Sea represents the quality of this world: a sea because it fluctuates, and glassy, that is, fragile.[21] Alcuin's interpretation is like St. Augustine's. The sea of glass represents baptism: "Quid autem per mare vitreum, nisi baptismus figuratur."[22] Baptism is the first of the seven sacraments; it is the door to the church. By baptism one is made a member of Christ. Alcuin defines it as the sacrament of regeneration by water in the word: "per aquam in verbo." It is a symbolic rite, the external washing cleansing an invisible blemish. Alcuin says that the glass represents faith and that crystal represents the faith of the saints made firm by trial: "inter pressuras per incrementa temporum." Anselm explains that baptism is clear with the purity of faith, "sinceritate fidei lucidum," and crystalline because just as a crystal from water hardens into stone, so from the soft and liquid baptism makes solid and invincible.[23] Rupert, who says that the sea represents baptism, adds that it stands beneath the throne because whoever wishes to enter into the kingdom of heaven must cross this sea.[24] In Richard of St. Victor baptism is said to be like a sea because in it the bitterness of iniquity is remitted: "Baptismus namque tamquam mare, quia in ipso amaritudo remittitur iniquitatis." It is glassy because in it the purity and clarity of divine knowledge are conferred. It is like crystal, for through it every elect person is confirmed in the splendor and firmness of righteousness.[25] Baptism is essential but it is only the entrance into the church, not into heaven. Rupert explains that this sea is in the sight of the throne because through the sacrament of baptism, the remission of sins, and the death of Christ the kingdom of heaven is prepared. Donne's distinction is pertinent here. In his sermon on Apocalypse 7:9 he says: "*Stabitis ante Thronum;* you shall stand, and *stand before the Throne;* Here in the *militant Church,* you stand, but you stand in the *porch,* there, in the *triumphant,* you shall stand *in Sancto sanctorum,* in the *Quire,* and the *Altar.*"[26]

The culmination of medieval interpretations is reached in that of St. Thomas Aquinas. Here the threefold sea is the effect of baptism, namely purity from guilt, brightness of innocence, and firmness against vices: "Mare triplex est effectus baptismi, videlicet sinceritas a culpa, claritas innocentiae, et firmitas contra vitia." He adds that

[21] *Pat. Lat.,* LXX, col. 1408. Contrast Victorinus, who says that the sea, which is baptism, is crystalline to signify permanence. (*Pat. Lat.,* V, col. 324.)
[22] *Ibid.,* C, col. 1117.   [23] *Ibid.,* CLXII, col. 1517.
[24] *Ibid.,* CLXIX, col. 910.   [25] *Ibid.,* CXCVI, col. 748–49.
[26] John Donne, *The Sermons of John Donne,* ed. by George R. Potter and Evelyn M. Simpson (Berkeley, 1953——), VI, 165.

through this sea the Scriptures may also be understood, which have the threefold effect mentioned above. For the World of God cleanses, clarifies, and confirms.[27] This may fitly conclude the survey of Roman Catholic interpretations of the symbol. These almost uniformly interpret the symbol to mean baptism, the first of the sacraments, though it must be observed that in Aquinas conditionally and in Ambrose certainly the sea stands for the Scriptures.

An important Protestant work is John Bale's *The Image of bothe Churches after the moste Wonderfull and Heavenly Revelacion of Sainct Iohn* (1549), which asserts that Revelation describes "the true Christen church" from the time of the Apostles to the end of the world. Here the sea of glass means "a plentefull understandinge of the veritie," the Word of God: it is like a crystal "clere, bewtyfull, & pure, without anye corruption of humaine fantasyes." The Word of God was to be the sole basis of faith and conduct in the Reformation. In an apparently authoritative compilation, *A Catholike exposition upon the Revelation of Sainct Iohn* by Augustine Malorate (1574) the sea is the church, "a company of much people, whome the spirit of God enlighteneth." It is delivered from darkness and sin by Christ. Its being before the throne signifies the power of Christ. In *The Revelation of S. Iohn reveled* (1582) James Brochard combines two ideas: the sea is the faithful embracing the everlasting Gospel. It is one church in Christ. In *An Learned Commentarie upon the Revelation of Saint Iohn* (1614) Patrick Forbes says that the sea is a type of the pure Word of God, which is before the throne that we may see His glory. Like water it is refreshing and comforting. In *A Revelation of the Revelation* (1614) Thomas Brightman says that the sea stands for the outward worship of God, which shows the face of God as through a most clear glass. In the Geneva Bible (first published in 1560 and frequently thereafter) this sea is compared to the world, which is like the sea because "of the changes and unstablenesse." Henry Bullinger in *A Hundred Sermons upon the Apocalips* (1561) says that the sea is this frail world, which is always in the sight of God and is unstable, "more brickle than glasse." Whatever things are done in this world shine "as in a glasse before the Throne, so that God seeth them all as it were in a Christall." In all of these works one explanation of the symbol is conspicuously lacking: *it does not mean baptism.*

In John Mayer's *Ecclesiastico Interpretatio . . .* (1627) there are

27 *Opera*, XXXI, 524.

various explanations: the sea is the Word of God; it is baptism; it is this world. Mayer's personal opinion is that it is a sea of pure water in heaven, which prevents anything impure from approaching God's throne. It may be the *coelum crystallinum,* which serves as a perspective glass making all things in the world perfectly clear. In *The Spiritual Navigator Bound for the Holy Land,* a sermon preached at St. Giles without Cripplegate, on Trinity Sunday in 1615, Thomas Adams offers a survey of interpretations in this order. The sea is contemplative men; an abundant understanding of the truth, historical knowledge, moral knowledge, spiritual knowledge; the fullness of those gifts and graces which the church receives from Christ; the *coelum crystallinum,* which is under heaven, where God keeps His court; the Gospel, which is as clear as crystal; baptism—as the children of Israel entered Canaan through the Red Sea, so Christians enter the celestial Canaan through the Glassy Sea; the world. Adams accepts the last, which he ingeniously expounds. Although both Mayer and Adams mention baptism, neither accepts it as an interpretation—but the idea in "Christians entering the celestial Canaan through the Glassy Sea" is like that in *Paradise Lost.*

John Gill's interpretation in his *Exposition of the New Testament* (1809) surveys various meanings. Gill rejects, as meanings of the symbol, heaven, the souls of the blessed there, the holy angels, and the first converts to Christianity in Jerusalem. He mentions as possible the world, like the sea for its multitude of people, like glass in its frailty and transitoriness, like crystal because all things in it are open to the omniscient eye of God, but unlike these because it is disturbed and troubled by winds and tempests. Another meaning is baptism, which is like the sea of glass for its transparency in representing the suffering, death, and resurrection of Christ; it is like crystal for its purity and it is before the throne as being the entrance into "the Gospel church." Still another meaning is the blood of Christ, in allusion to the brazen sea in the tabernacle and the molten sea in the Temple, for the blood of Christ is a fountain to wash away the sin of all those who come into a "Gospel church-state." Gill's personal opinion is that the sea means the Gospel, which is compared to a sea because of the deep things of God and the mysteries of grace in it, to glass because in the Gospel as in a glass we see the glory and righteousness of God, to crystal because the truths contained therein are clear, and to a still and quiet sea because it is the Gospel of "peace, love, grace and mercy." It is before the throne, where the rainbow of the covenant is, "of which the Gospel is a transcript," and where are the four and twenty elders, the seven spirits of God, and His four Ministers.[28] Christina Rossetti believes that this sea is the knowledge of God: it is like a vast permanent mirror which "will convey to the redeemed a perfect knowledge" of God and the saints. "Everything which is very good, all things lovely, the height of the heaven in comparison of the earth, the wide distance of the east from the west, all will be seen and known. For in that day and in fulness the delights of the Uncreated Wisdom shall be with the sons of men."[29] This reminds us of Ambrose's spiritual intelligence. Protestants prefer this meaning and specifically the Gospel, though some take the sea to mean the world. No Protestant, it seems, accepts the Roman Catholic gloss that the sea is baptism, which has been called "the true illumination of the soul."[30]

Our indefatigable pursuit of the various meanings of this symbol should not lead us to ignore the aesthetic values of the poem. But these in Milton are intimately associated with the ethical values and the religious background. In Milton's poetry the symbol or image cannot be taken in its mere aesthetic sense. It should denote all that the poet intends us through his verse to see.[31] It should also denote what can be seen by the reader who is acquainted with the Christian tradition and the theological background. It is true that some of Milton's imagery is easy to understand. These images may have been derived from his own experiences, though it has been said that he shows no familiarity with the "basic processes or tools of everyday life."[32] Binyon does well to cite the perenially fresh and delightful lines from *L'Allegro:*

> While the Plowman neer at hand,
> Whistles ore the Furrow'd Land,
> And the Milkmaid singeth blithe,
> And the Mower whets his sithe,
> And every Shepherd tells his tale
> Under the Hawthorn in the dale.

lines which Eliot had used to show that Milton almost completely

[28] John Gill, *An Exposition of the New Testament* (London, 1809), III, 717–18.

[29] Rossetti, *The Face of the Deep: A Devotional Commentary on the Apocalypse* (5th ed.; London, 1907), p. 156.

[30] James Moffatt, *An Introduction to the Literature of the New Testament* (rev. 3d ed.; Edinburgh, 1949), p. 549.

[31] Laurence Binyon, "A Note on Milton's Imagery and Rhythm," *Seventeenth Century Studies* . . . (Oxford, 1938), pp. 184 ff.

[32] Theodore H. Banks, *Milton's Imagery* (New York, 1950), p. 9.

lacked the visual imagination. Very sensibly Binyon reminds us that Milton is describing figures in a landscape, where we should not see them "as individual persons." The landscape, Binyon continues, has an English character and "all the details of the poem are in keeping, distinct but not obtrusive."

So are the details of *Paradise Lost*. But here the imagery, as the cosmic scope of the poem required, is often vast and impressive, though we should not forget the fact that, to use Banks's words, there are suggestions of familiar domestic scenes, "the spring flowers and gardens of England, the clouds of English skies, the colors of dawn and sunset."[33] However, what is presented in *Paradise Lost* is often viewed from a distance, from a very great distance. In what other poem are there such vast spaces, such lofty prospects, such sublime visions as in *Paradise Lost?* One need recall only a few illustrations: the astounding fall of Satan from heaven—

> Him the Almighty Power
> Hurld headlong flaming from th' Ethereal Skie
> With hideous ruine and combustion down
> To bottomless perdition.   (I, 44–47)

the vast and gloomy reaches of Hell—

> The dismal Situation waste and wilde,
> A Dungeon horrible, on all sides round
> As one great Furnace flam'd, yet from those flames
> No light, but rather darkness visible
> Serv'd only to discover sights of woe,
> Regions of sorrow, doleful shades.   (I, 60–65)

and beyond this a frozen continent,

> dark and wilde, beat with perpetual storms
> Of Whirlwind and dire Hail, which on firm land
> Thaws not, but gathers heap, and ruin seems
> Of ancient pile; all else deep snow and ice, . . . (II, 588–91)

Then the hoary deep,

> a dark
> Illimitable Ocean without bound,
> Without dimension, where length, breadth, and highth
> And time and place are lost; where eldest Night
> And *Chaos*, Ancestors of Nature, hold

[33] *Ibid.*, p. 140.

God with His Compasses

God sits in the midst of the Cosmos in the act of Creation with His great compasses open. In the blue circle of Heaven are sun and moon, . . . Above are twelve angels, winged like winds in poetry as God's speedy messengers. On the right they face in adoration an enthroned central figure . . . and one offers him a crown. . . . On the left other angels turn away in dispute. . . . Below grins Hell's mouth. . . . (The Holkham Bible Picture Book, W. O. Hassall, editor. London, Dropmore Press)

> Eternal *Anarchie,* amidst the noise
> Of endless warrs, and by confusion stand.   (II, 891–97)

and finally heaven and the new-created universe:

> Farr off th' Empyreal Heav'n, . . .
> With Opal Towrs and Battlements adorn'd
> Of living Saphire, once his native Seat;
> And fast by hanging in a golden Chain
> This pendant world, in bigness as a Starr
> Of smallest Magnitude close by the Moon.   (II, 1047–53)

To this distinguished company of indescribably vast and impressive images belongs the Glassy Sea—but it is, as we have seen, a term with hidden meanings. Of Satan it has been said that the impression is "not only of externals but from a superhuman force and fire within." So we may say of this symbol that it has for the initiated a rich inner content, a spiritual meaning far transcending the physical. Critics have said that Milton has had no adequate illustrator. Perhaps the best was Blake, whose ideas, however, were naturally Gothic, with unassimilated borrowings from Michelangelo. In spite of his eighteenth-century mannerisms, Blake succeeded at times in communicating something of his own "flame-like intensity" in his drawings of the demons and the angels. But in truth no artist can adequately portray the vastness and the sublimity of the poet's imagery. Certainly none can convey by line and color the spiritual meaning of such a symbol as the Glassy Sea, though one might suggest the sea of jasper or of liquid pearl under the throne. Only the human mind with some knowledge of tradition can hope to acquire some dim notion of this symbol with its vast "momentum of intellectual energy" inherent in its theological history. Unless we are resolved to strip the term of all its spiritual meaning, we must admit that the Glassy Sea is more than an area in space, more than a splendid part of an antiquated cosmos.

In the epic, where the term is taken out of its traditional context, it, of course, could not mean the world, which besides, was at that time perfect and free from sin; and it could not mean the church, which did not then exist. But as a body of pure water through which Christians pass to heaven it might suggest baptism. And as pure glass before the throne of God it might suggest spiritual intelligence, the kind of vision which the angel Raphael enjoys when from heaven's gate he views earth and paradise, "Earth and the Gard'n of God, with Cedars crownd/Above all Hills." Even though Raphael had what an early commentator called "Angelick optics," the Glassy Sea may have been an aid to his celestial vision. As the symbol of spiritual intelligence this sea might also suggest, not recorded Scripture, of course, or the Gospel specifically—the favorite Protestant gloss—but in its clarity the pure Word of God, a revelation of the divine mind and will. This sense and that of baptism would seem most obvious to those who are acquainted with the meaning of the symbol. Indeed it is clear that in the seventeenth century such orthodox interpretations would have been not only possible but probable and even inevitable. They were almost certainly known to Milton, who was familiar with Biblical exegesis. The position of the sea in the poem might be slightly distracting. But only the ignorant and those whose narrow vision is restricted to a mere physical region, to a quaint portion of an outmoded cosmic system, would venture to exclude the spiritual meaning. For such obtuse readers, however, Milton, who implored his muse to find "fit audience . . . though few," did not write.

Like many other images in *Paradise Lost*, the Glassy Sea has an appearance of substantial and material reality. But, as this study shows, this sea suggests or implies far more important spiritual values, —which the reader should understand and appreciate. The task of understanding is, however, not an easy one; for unfortunately symbols, even religious symbols, tend to petrify and evaporate, to repudiate their mystical origin, and forthwith to lose their religious content. If in the present state of formalism, materialism, and skepticism the meaning of the old symbols is exhausted, it can probably never be restored even by a genuine revival of spiritual life. A symbol is, in Coleridge's words, characterized by "a translucence . . . of the general in the special . . . above all, by the translucence of the eternal through and in the temporal." It is extremely difficult now to know what is eternal. In the midst of a civilization devoted to the worship of material things, generally oblivious of Scripture and the Christian tradition, and cultivating the church mainly for its commercial and social advantages,—in such a society only the dedicated few may hope to catch in this symbol of the Glassy Sea some glimpse, however fleeting, of the meaning and the spiritual truth once fondly believed to be eternal.

The need of understanding and appreciation is no less with respect to another Biblical symbol, the "golden Compasses" used in creation. The figure is essentially that of a device used to bound or circumscribe space. The Bible says that Wisdom was with the Lord in the beginning: "I was set up from everlasting, from the beginning, or ever the earth was. . . . When he prepared the heavens, I was there:

104

when he set a compass upon the face of the depth." (Prov. 8:27). In orthodox accounts of creation the compass is not mentioned. Creation was, of course, the act of God. According to Ussher, "Creation is a work which God only is able to doe," and he adds that "All things indeed that were made, were made by the Son the second Person of the Trinity,"[34] who was "from all eternity." The orthodox doctrine, of course, was that the world was made of nothing, that is, as Ussher says, "of no matter which was before creation." The "rude masse or matter of the world . . . wherein all things were confounded and mingled one in another" was made the first night of creation. After this, creation proceeded in order, according to God's plan, which was "as it were a shaddow and a common draught" of the world. This draught did not include any circumscribing of this rude mass, which was in the beginning without form or figure. In this orthodox account the compass is not mentioned.

In *Paradise Lost* the Son goes forth at God's command to create another world. He rides far into the "immeasurable Abyss" of chaos and then as his first act circumscribes the bounds of the universe:

> in his hand
> He took the golden Compasses, prepar'd
> In Gods Eternal store, to circumscribe
> This Universe, and all created things:
> One foot he center'd, and the other turn'd
> Round through the vast profunditie obscure,
> And said, thus farr extend, thus farr thy bounds,
> This be thy just Circumference, O World.   (VII, 224–31)

The matter of creation existed before the universe was created. This does not mean that matter was independent of God. In *The Christian Doctrine* Milton emphatically says, "That matter should have been always independent of God (seeing that it is only a passive principle, dependent on the Deity, and subservient to him . . .) that matter, I say, should have existed of itself from all eternity, is inconceivable." In fact "all things are of God," and original matter is "not to be looked upon as an evil or trivial thing, but as intrinsically good, and the chief productive stock of every subsequent good." Creation is mainly a matter of organizing original matter, of shaping and endowing with life individual forms, in a limited but vast region of order and harmony,

[34] James Ussher, *A Body of Divinity, or the Summe and Substance of Christian Religion*, p. 94. Writing about 1614, Ussher asserts that God created the world "Four thousand years before the birth of our Saviour Christ: and so about 5614 yeares before this time."

which is separated from the great chaos, where original matter still exists in a state of great disorder, as

> a dark
> Illimitable Ocean without bound,
> Without dimension, where length, breadth, and highth
> And time and place are lost; where eldest Night
> And *Chaos*, Ancestors of Nature, hold
> Eternal *Anarchie,* amidst the noise
> Of endless warrs, and by confusion stand.   (II, 891–97)

It is philosophically most significant that this ordered universe, created by God, was separated from the

> vast immeasurable Abyss
> Outrageous as a Sea, dark, wasteful, wilde,
> Up from the bottom turn'd by furious windes
> And surging waves, as Mountains to assault
> Heav'ns highth, and with the Center mix the Pole.
>   (VII, 211–15)

In the created universe divinely imposed order and harmony should prevail,—and would have prevailed forever but for man's fatal disobedience. The order, the peace, and the clearness of the created universe, of which the Glassy Sea is a symbol, is contrasted with the wild disorder and the darkness of this ocean, this turbulent sea of chaos, whose "dark Pavilion" is spread "Wide on the wasteful Deep." In creation the realm of divine order, with which, as Lewis says, Milton was enchanted, is marked off by God's "golden Compasses" from the "wilde Abyss," which Milton tersely calls "The Womb of nature and perhaps her Grave." Between these antagonistic realms, of primaeval chaos and divine order, there is a borderland, a dim region, where is felt the sacred influence of light, which from the walls of heaven

> Shoots farr into the bosom of dim Night
> A glimmering dawn; here Nature first begins
> Her fardest verge, and *Chaos* to retire
> As from her outmost works a brok'n foe
> With tumult less and with less hostile din.

Here pausing after his laborious and perilous journey, Satan reconnoiters, at leisure beholding

> Farr off th' Empyreal Heav'n, extended wide
> In circuit, undetermined square or round,

106

> With Opal Towrs and Battlements adorn'd
> Of living Saphire, once his native Seat;
> And fast by hanging in a golden Chain
> This pendant world, in bigness as a Starr
> Of smallest Magnitude close by the Moon.

It is God's will that this divinely created and ordered universe, set apart from chaos, shall ultimately, through man's obedience, become a part of heaven: "And Earth be chang'd to Heavn, & Heav'n to Earth,/One Kingdom, Joy and Union without end."—lines which unmistakably indicate that Milton had in mind not a physical but a spiritual universe.

For the sake of comparing them with Milton's version, we shall now examine some of the scriptural texts and the commentaries. In Jerome's *Liber Proverbiorum* the text reads as follows: "Quando praeparabat coelos, aderam: quando certa lege, et gyro vallabat abyssos," which may be translated: When he prepared the heavens, I was there: when by a certain law, he surrounded the depths with a circle.[35] In *The Holy Scriptures According to the Masoretic Text* the last part of Proverbs 8:27 reads: "When He set a circle upon the face of the deep." In the Authorized Version the word "compass" in the text "when he set a compass upon the face of the depth" carries in the margin the gloss "Or, a circle," and the phrase "set a compass" is explained: "Lit. 'in tracing a circle,' that is, when the Creator traced the curved line or horizon which the surface of the sea presents."[36] The phrasing of the Authorized Version is like that of the Geneva version: "when hee set the compasse upon the deepe." The Holy Bible (1576) is unambiguous: "when he compassed the depths about." In all these versions *compass* means *circle* or to *surround* or *encircle;* it does not designate the instrument for describing a circle.[37]

Orthodox accounts of creation avoid details and do not mention the compass, the instrument. In his *Hexaemeron* Ambrose thinks of creation as being the effect of "the immediate working of God's inscrutable will." God did not fix the earth's stability "as an artisan would, with compass and level, but as the Omnipotent, by the might of His

[35] *Pat. Lat.*, XXVIII, col. 1251. The same phrasing is found in *Biblia Sacra* (1679).
[36] *The Old Testament According to the Authorised Version with a Brief Commentary by Various Authors* (1888).
[37] Grant McColley, "Milton's Golden Compasses," *Notes and Queries*, CLXXVI (February, 1939), 97–98. McColley is mistaken in saying that the figure in *Paradise Lost* is supported "by the Authorised Version of Scripture."

command."³⁸ The world stands in the midst not as if suspended by an equal balance but because God constrains it by the law of His will: "Voluntate igitur Dei immobilis et stat in saeculum terra. . . ." God is, of course, omnipotent. Ambrose does not explain creation; as Taylor says, he gazes "beyond the works of Creation to another world."

In his commentary on Job 38, St. Thomas Aquinas declares that human intelligence does not suffice to understand God's acts in creation: "Cognoscere rationem fundationis terrae non potes. . . ." The foundations of the world are compared to those of a building, which is made according to the plans of the builder; but there is a difference: "fundatio terrae est facta secundum providentiam divinam, quam humana intelligentia comprehendere non valet. . . ."³⁹ To speculate is in vain. Man is unable to understand divine reason and the world, which is the work of God.

In searching out and setting forth the creation of the world and its parts, the "diligence of all wise men hath been set on work," says Henry Bullinger; and there will always be "witty men" occupied and evermore exercised in searching out and setting forth the secrets of nature and of creation. Bullinger briefly states the faith of the reformed church: "But we do simply by faith conceive, that the worlds were made of nothing, and of no heap of matter, of God through the Word of God; and that it doth consist by the power of the Holy Ghost, or Spirit of God."⁴⁰ To supplement this brief statement he then quotes from *De Trinitate*, Tertullian's "lively" history of creation, which has nothing to our purpose.

About 1585 the doctrine of the Church of England was simply that the world and all things both visible and invisible therein were made and are preserved by the almighty and only power of God: "all things were created by him, and for him; by his Son he made the worlds."⁴¹ This doctrine, then acknowledged by all churches, "primitive and modern," has not a word to say about stages in creation or about the compass.

Even the learned and verbose Du Bartas is apparently ignorant of

³⁸ *Pat. Lat.*, XIV, col. 134; Ann Mary Gossman, "Man Plac't in a Paradise: A Comparative Study of Milton, St. Ambrose, and Hugh St. Victor" (unpublished master's thesis, The Rice Institute, Houston, 1954), pp. 78–79; Taylor, *The Medieval Mind*, II, 72 ff.

³⁹ *Opera*, XVIII, 196.

⁴⁰ *The Decades of Henry Bullinger. The Fourth Decade*, ed. for the Parker Society by the Rev. Thomas Harding (Cambridge, 1851), p. 174.

⁴¹ Thomas Rogers, *The Catholic Doctrine of the Church of England* (Cambridge, 1854), p. 39.

some details. In Sylvester's famous translation he is made to say that only "he that weares the spectacles of Faith" can understand creation, comprehend "th' Arch-moover of all Motions," and behold "Th' Orb from his Birth, in's Ages manifold." Creation was instantaneous:[42]

> The Power and Will, th' affection and effect,
> The Work and Project of this Architect,
> March all at once.

But God needed no plan, and the universe was not circumscribed.

In one point the following commentary of John Gill resembles slightly Milton's account:[43]

When he set a compass upon the face of the depth; or *compassed the waters with bounds,* as Job says, ch. xxvi.10 or made the earth with the sea globular, which makes one terraqueous globe: or *made a circle;* all around it, called the circle of the earth, on which he sits, Isa. xl. 22. this compass may design the vast expanse of firmament of heaven, which is stretched and drawn around the terraqueous globe as a canopy or curtain.

This great compass or circle, indicating the expanse of the firmament of heaven, suggests the vast circle which the Son of God draws with the "golden Compasses" through the immense profundity of chaos, commanding "This be thy just Circumference, O World."

In the orthodox fashion Gill has, of course, no thought of the compass as an instrument for drawing a circle and he has no conception of matter outside the created universe in boundless space, where darkness, confusion, and discord reign. The texts of Scripture and the commentaries show that the compass as an instrument is not only not commonplace but also not scriptural and not orthodox. One might recall here Donne's subtle distinctions regarding creation. Donne explains that God made heaven and earth as matter without form "*sine sermone,* without speaking"; that He made specific forms, "Light and Firmament, Land and Sea, Plants and Beasts, and Fishes and Fowls," by his word, "*in sermone*"; that He made man in consultation, "*faciamus hominem.*"[44] So it may be said that God compassed the deep: *in gyro,* not with compasses. The compass is doubtless somewhat incongruous in a supernatural and mysterious creation, one that defies explanation and is conceived as being the effect of God's omnipotent and inscrutable will. On the most orthodox grounds objections to such a rational or geometrical method of creation might

[42] *Du Bartas His Diuine Weekes and Workes* . . . (London, 1633), p. 3.
[43] *An Exposition of the Old Testament* (London, 1810), IV, 384.
[44] *The Sermons of John Donne,* ed. by Potter and Simpson, I, 289.

109

be justified—and were, as we shall see. On the other hand, many images and symbols derived from Scripture and sanctioned by tradition were indispensable in ritual, painting, poetry, and in art generally.

During the centuries when the church was the dominant force in society, religious art, in the form of sculpture, painting, and "storied Windows richly dight," was naturally at home in the church. This was a time when reading and writing were the accomplishments of only the few, when many of the priests themselves did not understand Latin—the language of religion—and when preaching was generally neglected. For the unlearned and the poor there was the appeal to the eye by painting, sculpture, and windows. The churches were the Bibles of the poor, and the church thoroughly understood the truth that men are often more stirred by sight than by hearing or reading. Images served two purposes: they were ordained "to stir man's affection and his heart to devotion," and they were ordained "to be a token and a book to the lewd people that they may read in imagery and painture that clerks read in a book." There was a warning:[45]

So that thou kneel if thou wilt before the image, but not to the image. Do worship afore the image not to the image. Make thy prayer before the image but not to the image. For it seeth thee not, heareth thee not, understandeth thee not . . . for if thou do it for the image or to the image thou dost idolatry.

Unfortunately the church allowed a multiplicity of images, which served not merely to remind the people of Christ's passion and the saints' and "not to warm up their morality with pictorial preaching" but to gratify the love of splendor and the love of mystery and to enrich the church. In the end the images became objects of worship, and this idolatry led ultimately to the destruction of the images and much of the art in English churches—an irreparable loss.

In the Middle Ages subjects for illustration were drawn much more from the New Testament than from the Old. In the surviving mural paintings in English churches there are from the Old Testament only twenty-one, a meager showing, indicating conclusively that the Old Testament subjects were not popular, although the Middle Ages were especially interested in the fall and redemption of man. Kendon says that there is only one Creation to be found in all England.

[45] Frank Kendon, *Mural Paintings in English Churches during the Middle Ages* (London, 1923), pp. 165–66.

110

This Creation is at Exeter Cathedral, where it is the first of a series of panels on the organ screen. The others are Adam and Eve in the Garden, the Deluge, the Children of Israel crossing the Red Sea, the destruction of Solomon's Temple, the angel appearing to Zacharias, the Nativity, the Baptism of Christ, the Deposition, the Resurrection, the Ascension, and the Day of Judgment. From the point of view of the church these were the main events in history. Mistakenly assuming that there was no reason why Puritans should destroy representations of Creation, Kendon concludes that this subject was never common. Considering the wholesale destruction of ecclesiastical art in England, one cannot be sure. Besides the one in Exeter, there was another Creation, which from our point of view is most interesting; but this one, as we know from the records of a famous trial, was destroyed because it was regarded as idolatrous.

The facts are stated at length in the "Proceedings in the Star-Chamber against Henry Sherfield, esq. Recorder of Salisbury, for breaking a painted Glass-Window in the Church of St. Edmonds in the said City: 8 Charles I. A.D. 1632."[46] Sherfield, an inhabitant of the parish of St. Edmonds in the city of New-Sarum, was "an ancient bencher of Lincoln's-Inn," an aged man "with grey hairs upon him"; he was a respected and influential citizen. The charge against him was that he and "some factious persons" had conspired to deface "an ancient and fair Window, containing a description of the Creation" in the church of St. Edmonds in New-Sarum. Obtaining the keys, he had entered the church, locked the doors to prevent interruption, and had then "beat down the said Window, and utterly defaced it; and when he had thus done, he bid boast and glory that he had so done, and reported that himself was a Defacer of Idolatry."[47]

Sherfield's defense was that the said church was exempt from the jurisdiction of the bishop of Sarum, that the vestrymen had "time out of mind" the right to make repairs and alterations in the church without any orders from the bishop, and that the history of creation as illustrated in the window was unscriptural, unlawful, and idolatrous:[48]

That it is no true relation or story of the Creation, in that true manner

[46] *Cobbett's . . . State Trials* (London, 1809), III, 519–62; hereafter cited as *State Trials.* Rushworth's *Collections* (London, 1721), II, 152–56; Joseph Crouch, *Puritanism and Art* (London, 1910), pp. 124–29; John A. Knowles, *Essays in the History of the York School of Glass-Painting* (London, 1936), pp. 174–75.

[47] *State Trials*, III, 519.   [48] *Ibid.*, p. 522. Italics mine.

as it is set down in the book of Moses; but there are made and committed by the workmen divers falsities and absurdities in the painting of the same Window, as that he hath put the form of a little old man in a blue and red coat, for God the Father, and hath made seven such pictures; whereas God is but one Deity: and in his order of placing the several days works of God in the Creation, he hath placed them preposterously, the fourth before the third; and that to be done on the fifth, which was done on the sixth day; and in one place he hath represented God the Father creating the Sun and Moon *with a pair of compasses in his hand, as if he had done it according to some geometrical rules.*

Sherfield declared that for many years past he "had been settled and resolved" in his judgment; he insisted that it is "utterly unlawful to make any such Representations of God the Father" and he mentioned authorities set out and declared in the time of Elizabeth and otherwise "for the taking down and abolishing superstitious Images and Pictures, especially in the Churches."

He was "rather emboldened" to take away the said window "because it had been a cause of Idolatry plainly to some ignorant people." Sherfield said:

That this Window, and the painting therein, was not a true Representation of the Creation; for that it contained divers forms of little old men in blue and red coats, and *naked in the heads,* feet and hands, for the picture of God the Father; and in one place he is set forth *with a pair of compasses* in his hands, laying them upon the Sun and Moon; and the painter hath set him forth creating of the birds on the third day, and hath placed the picture of beasts and man and woman, the man a naked man, and the woman naked in some part, as much as from the knees upwards, rising out of the man; and the seventh day he therein hath represented the like image of God, sitting down, taking his rest: whereas this Defendant conceiveth this to be false, for there is but one God, and this representeth seven Gods; and the Sun and the Moon were not made on the third day, but on the fourth day; nor the trees and herbs on the fourth day, but on the third day; nor the fowls on the third day, but on the fifth: and man was not created on the fifth, but on the sixth day; nor did the Lord God so create a woman as rising out of man, but he took a rib of the man, when he was in a deep sleep, and thereof made he the woman, in all which the workman was mistaken.

Sherfield, believing it "altogether unlawful" to make any representation "of the true God in any church, or wall, or window," hoped to make this appear "by the Scripture, by orthodox Writers, Councils,

112

and Decrees of Emperors, and by a certain Book of the now bishop of Sarum (Dr. John Davenant) written on one of St. Paul's Epistles, in the 97th and 98th pages;[49] king James's Book, intitled 'Premonition to all Christian kings and Princes,' and the Book of Homilies, set forth by authority, and therein the Homily against Idolatry in particular. . . ." Deeming this so false a representation and "so profane a setting down of the image of God the Father seven times," Sherfield, a parishioner "in all his actions . . . conformable to the canons and constitutions ecclesiastical, the Rites and Ceremonies of the Church of England," had been troubled in conscience "by the space of twenty years," for "he could not come into the church, but he must see it, sitting right opposite to it." Finally, "seeing the dishonour done to God thereby" and "fearing that others might offend in Idolatry," he did take down "some little quarrels of the Window" but only in such places of the glass "as the Representation of the Deity so falsified was." It should be emphasized that Sherfield acted by the authority of the vestry, which, on January 16, 1629, ordered that the window should be taken down "for the darkness caused by it, and for that it was superstitious." Five of the vestrymen were justices of the peace in New-Sarum.

As to the age of the defaced window, the solicitor general, Sir Richard Skelton, said that the "painter" of it died "100 years ago," but the Archbishop of York said, "Nay, it hath been there these 300 years." For the defendant, Peter Thatcher testified:

That he saw Emma Browne bowing to the Window aforesaid, on which occasion (this Deponent coming in the mean while) he asked what was the cause she so bowed. To which she answered, I do it to my Lord God. Why, said this Deponent, where is he? Said the said Emma Browne, In the Window, is he not?

With regard to the spirit of the time, Sir Richard Skelton declared:

I undertake there are some spirits now, that if they had been alive in Solomon's time, would have gone nigh to have done violence to the Cherubims; God knoweth what would have become of them!

With regard to reformation of the church, the attorney general, William Noy, said:[50]

Reformation ought to be made always by the supreme power, not by

[49] *Ibid.*, p. 523. In Rushworth, *Collections*, II, 155, the title of the Lord Bishop's book is given: *Exposition on the Epistle to the Colossians.*
[50] *State Trials*, III, 538.

private men: but when private persons, or a vestry, will take upon them reformation, I make bold to say, it is the highway to pull all out of order with their reformation. . . . Nay, some hold our church is idolatrous and unclean, because Common Prayers are said in them, and Masses have heretofore been said in them; and therefore these reformers would at the next bout take away our churches also; this must be next.

According to the attorney general, the meaning of the injunctions and articles was

that all relics of idolatry and superstition should be taken away; but every memorial, or story of a saint or prophet, is not a relic of idolatry or superstition. Any monument of superstition, or of feigned or false miracles, may be taken down; but monuments, or pictures for memorials of saints or prophets, are not idolatrous or superstitious. If they should be so, because some men conceive them so, and then they may pull them down of their own heads, why then, many might, and I doubt not but some fiery spirits would, take upon them the boldness, to pull down all cathedral churches, because they are made in form of a cross, which some of the precise sort cannot abide.

It was concluded that Sherfield's action was "a great offence, an offence of great scandal and presumption." He was committed to the Fleet, fined 500 pounds, and ordered to repair to the lord bishop of his diocese to make acknowledgment of his offense and contempt—all because "with his staff" he "brake divers holes in the said painted Window, wherein was described the Creation of the World."[51]

In partial justification of Sherfield, it should be said that some of the judges approved of his sentiments—but not of his actions. The Lord Chief Justice, Sir Thomas Richardson, said, "There was cause, I am satisfied, that this Window should be removed." The picture of God the Father was idolatrous and their bowing to it was "conceived to be idolatry." Secretary Cooke also thought the pictures in the window idolatrous, and he said that "our Church doth not allow any adoration to be given to any image or picture whatsoever, nor the image of God the Father to be in the Church." The taking away of such a picture is, he said, "no offence; but in the manner of doing it, is the greatness of the offence. Reformation in a private man, is deformation." Cooke commended Sherfield's "zeal" but he emphatically declared that "private men are not to make batteries against glass

---

[51] My statement in the note "The Golden Compasses in *Paradise Lost*," *Notes and Queries* (April 24, 1937), p. 295, that Sherfield "had the window destroyed" is incorrect. The records show that he himself destroyed the window.

windows in Churches at their pleasure, upon pretence of reformation." Much of the prevailing sentiment against paintings in churches
is neatly stated in the words of the Earl of Manchester, Lord Privy
Seal: "The painted picture inciteth the ignorant to idolatry." Although in Laud's mind there was a great difference between an image
and an idol, the Bishop of London also thought it unlawful "to make
the Picture of God the Father," though it is lawful, he said, to make
the picture of Christ; "for the Deity cannot be pourtrayed or pictured, though the Humanity may."[52] In Laud's opinion, however, the
question certainly was not whether the defaced picture had been idolatrous or superstitious. Laud was firmly convinced that Sherfield had
acted "in contempt" of the authority of the Church and the King, and
he was firmly resolved that the accused should be severely punished.
The Earl of Dorset, on the other hand, thought it were a good work
if "all unlawful pictures and images were utterly taken out of the
churches"; for "at the best they are but vanities and teachers of lies."
Indeed, he wished that "there were no image of the Father, neither in
the Church, nor out of the Church." There can be no doubt that something of this stern disapprobation of pictures and images of God the
Father is reflected in the angelic symphony of sacred song:

> Thee Father first they sung Omnipotent,
> Immutable, Immortal, Infinite,
> Eternal King; thee Author of all being,
> Fountain of Light, thy self invisible
> Amidst the glorious brightness where thou sit'st
> Thron'd inaccessible, but when thou shad'st
> The full blaze of thy beams, and through a cloud
> Drawn round about thee like a radiant Shrine,
> Dark with excessive bright thy skirts appeer,
> Yet dazle Heav'n that brightest Seraphim
> Approach not, but with both wings veil thir eyes.
> (III, 375–82)

In scenes of majesty God and the Holy Spirit were represented
only symbolically in early religious art, God as a hand coming out of
a cloud: "Le Père et le Saint-Esprit ne sont jamais représentés dans
les scènes de majesté que d'une manière symbolique, le Père par la
main sortant d'un nuage et souvent bénissante, l'Esprit sous la forme

[52] *State Trials*, III, 542–50.

d'une colombe."[53] The hand emerging from the cloud might hold a pair of compasses, the sign of "Him who fixed the earth and sky, and measured out the firmament."[54] It is said that the two points of the compass represent spirit and matter, life and form—which are the source of the complex, ever changing life within the circle of God's universe. In illustrating Genesis the artists represented God in the terrestrial Paradise—but here they borrowed the figure of Christ, almost always framed or encircled in a cloud, to represent God.

It is in the light of this tradition that we should consider the doctrine, not only Puritan but also Anglican, that God, the infinite and omnipotent, could not lawfully be represented in the church, by image or picture. Besides, the belief or the fact that God as Creator of the world was represented in the window at New-Sarum runs counter to an ancient theological doctrine, which Milton followed. This is the traditional doctrine: the world was created by the Father through the Son of God. From the beginning the world was in the thought of God, who created the world—"but He created through His Word, that is, through His Son. The thought of the Father was realized in the Son through whom it passed from potentiality to act, and thus the Son is the true Creator."[55] This doctrine was observed by the artists: "The artists of the Middle Ages, imbued with this doctrine, almost invariably represent the Creator in the likeness of Jesus Christ."[56]

Milton strictly followed this tradition. The Son is He in whose face the invisible becomes visible:

> Son in whose face invisible is beheld
> Visibly, what by Deitie I am,

and, what is more, the Son is the Word of God:

> And thou my Word, begotten Son, by thee
> This I perform, speak thou, and be it don.

Accompanied by the Holy Spirit, attended by a glorious retinue,

> Girt with Omnipotence, with Radiance crown'd

[53] Louis Bréhier, *L'Art Chrétien* . . . (Paris, 1918), p. 87.

[54] Harold Bayley, *The Lost Language of Symbolism* (New York, 1951), I, 73–74. The hand with the compasses forms the central part of the trade-mark of Christopher Plantin, the great printer.

[55] Émile Mâle, *Religious Art in France XIII Century,* trans. by Dora Nussey (3d ed.; Paris, 1913), p. 29.

[56] *Ibid.*

116

> Of Majestie Divine, Sapience and Love
> Immense,

the Son rides into chaos—and creates the world:

> So spake th' Almightie, and to what he spake
> His Word, the Filial Godhead, gave effect.

This was theologically the correct way to create the world. It was theologically sound in the thirteenth century; and this doctrine was accepted in the fourteenth and fifteenth centuries—and much later, as we know. But there was a significant change. The artists substituted God for Christ as Creator.[57]

On sait que le XIIIᵉ siècle, quand il represente la création, donne toujours à Dieu les traits de Jésus-Christ. Les théologiens, en effet, enseignaient que Dieu avait créé le monde par son Verbe. Telle était bien encore la doctrine de l'École au XIVᵉ et au XVᵉ siècle, mais elle n'arrivait plus jusqu'aux artistes: dès temps de Charles V, ils l'ignoraient profondément. Rien n'est plus curieux que d'étudier le type du Createur dans les Bibles historiales de la Bibliothèque nationale, qui vont des premières années du XIVᵉ siècle jusqu'au XVᵉ, et forment une suite ininterrompue. Jusque vers 1350, c'est le Verbe, c'est Jésus-Christ, qui crée le monde. Mais alors on voit soudain apparaître un grand vieillard qui mesure la terre avec un compas et lance dans le ciel le soleil et les étoiles. Certes, ce Dieu aux cheveux blancs, à la longue barbe blanche, a sa grandeur; il est l'Ancien des jours; les siècles ont passé en laissant sur sa tête un peu de cendre. Déjà on pressent le formidable du plafond de la Chapelle Sixtine. Mais n'est-il pas vrai que les artistes qui l'ont imaginé avaient perdu toute intelligence de l'ancienne théologie?

This deity, with the white hair and the long white beard, is unmistakably God. And the compass must not be overlooked. Was this a common figure? One recalls that the "little old men in blue and red coats" in the window at New-Sarum lacked white hair; their heads were naked. Is it not likely that Milton had seen just such a Creator?

A unique illustration of the Creator with compasses appears in *The Holkham Bible Picture Book.* This work, a fine example of the early English art of the fourteenth century, is "a pictorial representation of the Creation and Fall ánd the need of a Redemption." Described as "one of the most lively graphic products of the Middle Ages," this book presents in numerous scenes "the story of Paradise Lost and

[57] Émile Mâle, *L'Art Religieux de la Fin du Moyen Age en France* (Paris, 1908), pp. 237–38.

Paradise Regained." There are four illustrations of creation. The scene (folio 2) entitled "God with His Compasses" is described thus:[58]

God sits in the midst of the Cosmos in the act of Creation with His great compasses open. In the blue circle of heaven are sun and moon, not darkened as at the Crucifixion. One is higher than the other, perhaps to suggest rotation.

Above are twelve angels, winged like winds in poetry as God's speedy messengers. On the right they face in adoration an enthroned central figure who points to himself, and one offers him a crown just as in the Caedmon manuscript a bad angel offers a crown to handsome Lucifer on high shortly before he is cast headlong with his throne to hell. On the left other angels turn away in dispute, as in the Towneley *Creatio* a good angel disputes with a bad angel who has been praising Lucifer. Below grins Hell's mouth.

The Aelfric manuscript in the British Museum has a dramatic scene of the fall of the angels and in *Queen Mary's Psalter* Hell's mouth is shown below *the Creator with His compasses.*

The Creator has a cruciform halo as he often does. God and Compasses, a symbol familiar to Freemasons and recalled in the tavern sign 'Goat and Compasses' occurs in Anglo-Saxon art of about 1000, in the *Bible Moralisee*, *Queen Mary's Psalter* and the *Carew Poyntz Horae* as well as in the poetry of Milton and the painting of Blake. The compasses do not appear in English churches before the fifteenth century, despite their attractiveness for the producer of a Creation play. By the later middle ages they had come to signify Science and Philosophy in general.

If, as seems quite probable, Milton had seen such pictures of God as creator with compasses, it is the more remarkable that, retaining the compasses as appropriate for even a divine architect, he should have returned to the theologically sound doctrine of the Son as creator of the universe.

We have here in Milton an apparent fusion of orthodox doctrine with science, the latter represented by the instrument traditionally associated with geometry, sometimes portrayed as a figure clad in a robe embroidered with stars and holding in the right hand a pair of compasses, in the left a globe. But in a real sense Milton's picture is, of course, not scientific. It is a survival of the thought and the art of the Middle Ages.[59]

L'art de la fin du moyen âge enseigne d'abord à l'homme quelle est sa

[58] *The Holkham Bible Picture Book.* Introduction and Commentary by W. O. Hassall (London, 1954), pp. 56–59.
[59] Mâle, *L'Art Religieux de la Fin du Moyen Age en France*, p. 316.

place dans le monde. On connaît la fresque du Campo Santo de Pise: Dieu porte l'universe entre ses bras; la terre est au centre, et les sept planètes décrivent leurs cercles autour de leur reine immobile; le soleil se tient à son rang, comme un modeste vassal; au delà des orbes des planètes commence le monde invisible et la hiérarchie des anges.

As Mâle says, nothing could be more reassuring. How solid was the ground under the feet of the old generations!

This was a trim universe, circumscribed by compasses, limited, precisely ordered and regulated, created by God and always obedient to Him, and not unfriendly to man who knew his place and duty in the divine scheme of things. It is essentially the universe of *Paradise Lost,* where, however, the size of the universe from within seems immense, though this "pendant world" is like a star of smallest magnitude in comparison with the inconceivable vastness of external space. It is the divine plan that the race of men, most favorably placed on earth and highly favored by God, should by their own effort "open to themselves at length" the way to heaven. It is God's purpose that "under long obedience tri'd" earth should be changed to heaven and heaven to earth, "One Kingdom, Joy and Union without end." Unfortunately man's fatal disobedience temporarily frustrates God's perfect plan. Satan exultantly declares that through his exploit "Hell and this World" are made "One Realm, one Continent/Of easie thorough-fare." The Fiend may exaggerate, but there is some truth in what he says. Urged on by Satan, Sin and Death invade the fair universe, Death devoting himself first to the plants and animals, "No homely morsels," and Sin directing her attention to man, to infect his thoughts, looks, words, and actions, seasoning him for Death's "last and sweetest prey."

It is truly a sad prospect, which prompts Adam to exclaim,

> O miserable of happie! is this the end
> Of this new glorious World, and mee so late
> The Glory of that Glory.   (X, 720–23)

And the prospect becomes still more discouraging when one contemplates the long course of human history illustrating the violence and oppression, the disease and suffering, the unending triumph of wickedness—all directly due to Adam's original crime. But the future though dark is not without hope. For, as the Father says,

> Man shall not quite be lost, but sav'd who will,
> Yet not of will in him, but grace in me
> Freely voutsaft; once more I will renew

119

His lapsed powers, though forfeit and enthrall'd
By sin to foul exorbitant desires;
Upheld by me, yet once more he shall stand
On even ground against his mortal foe,
By me upheld, that he may know how frail
His fall'n condition is, and to me ow
All his deliv'rance, and to none but me. (III, 173–82)

God will not be deaf or blind "To prayer, repentance, and obedience due," but it is, of course, to the Son of God that man will really owe his salvation. As the Son had created the world, so He would for man's sake freely put off His glory, die for man's sin, and rising victorious disarm Death of his mortal sting. Finally He will re-enter heaven with the multitude of His redeemed, there to reign forever over

New Heav'n and Earth, wherein the just shall dwell
And after all thir tribulations long
See golden days, fruitful of golden deeds,
With Joy and Love triumphing, and fair Truth.

In view of Milton's exquisite artistry, it is not improbable that by design the *golden* compasses of Creation are complemented by the *golden* days of *golden* deeds in the "New Heav'n and Earth, wherein the just shall dwell." But, of course, the salvation of man does not come unearned. He also has his obligations and duties to perform. By faith, by prayer, repentance, and obedience due, by the practice of Christian virtues and by the aid of the sacraments of the church, man must individually win his salvation "And one bad act with many deeds well done" redeem.

Although religious doctrine has survived the universe which it created, the doctrine itself has been eroded by time, discredited in practice, weakened by skepticism. Still nominally accepted by millions, the doctrine is scarcely a vital force in a church now devoted largely to social and worldly programs. With the decay of vital faith the symbols have lost much of their religious content, their supernatural power. Thus in spite of vigorous religious activity, it can hardly be denied that many have lost a living faith not only in particular dogmas and their outward symbols but also in the essential religious spirit, the "vision, basic to all religion, of an ordered plan and purpose of the world," in the traditional doctrine that the universe, created and ruled by a fatherly God, is a friendly habitation to man. The opinion of science, on the contrary, seems to be that we are surrounded by an immense spiritual desert, a universe purposeless and void of meaning.[60]

Blind to good and evil, reckless of destruction, omnipotent matter rolls on its relentless way; for man, condemned today to lose his dearest, to-morrow himself to pass through the gate of darkness, it remains only to cherish, ere yet the blow falls, the lofty thoughts that ennoble his little day; . . . to sustain alone, . . . the world that his own ideals have fashioned despite the trampling march of unconscious power.

What has apparently happened is that which Carlyle, in his evangelical style, calls the most brutal error, the most lamentable of conclusions, a kind of original sin that vitiates all other conclusions: God has vanished out of men's conception of the universe. According to Carlyle, this sinful error produces a spiritual paralysis, in which everything that is "noble, divine, inspired" drops out of life. What Carlyle calls a delusion seems now to be a scientific truth.

In such an intellectual milieu the traditional religious doctrines which underlie the symbols here studied must seem as obsolete as the orthodox universe. To speak plainly, this world is no longer thought of as a spiritual universe, a universe created by God through His Son, ordered and governed by God, always obedient to His omnipotent will, and forever compassed by His providential care, which embraces every individual being, for whose salvation God has personally provided through the life, the sacrificial death, and the triumphant resurrection of His Son Jesus Christ. This change in our conception of the universe, this rejection of traditional religious ideas concerning the relationship of the earth and the cosmos to God, this pervasive modern skepticism has inevitably rendered orthodox doctrine and its symbols less convincing if not completely obsolete. Milton was not confronted by any such dire dilemma as we face today. For him and his time poetry was not forced to counteract skepticism; it confirmed faith. As a Christian rationalist, he did not surrender to the flux of material objects, and of course he did not seek refuge in any castle of art. He controlled and ordered his material and ideas, which were essentially traditional. For these ideas, which were generally orthodox, he provided a form and structure, and by the most sophisticated or artistic methods he fused them into the most complete unity. In his grievous affliction, deprived of "that one Talent which is death to hide," isolated from the cheerful ways of men, from "sight of vernal

---

[60] Bertrand Russell, "A Free Man's Worship," *Mysticism and Logic* (London, 1913), pp. 56–57.

bloom, or Summers Rose,/Or flocks, or herds, or human face divine"; cut off from the book of knowledge fair, and with "wisdome at one entrance quite shut out," Milton prayed for celestial guidance, that he might see and tell "Of things invisible to mortal sight." He appealed to spiritual values which transcend this world of matter and this brief moment of time and reveal "a higher realm and reality beyond the finite daily level" of routine and ephemeral animal existence. Conscious of his lofty purpose, he invoked the divine and holy Spirit, the sacred Muse, which should be the "intercessional factor in this our sensuous world, unifying and transcending the competing and frustrating trends of human desire."[61]

Finally, it may be asked, what is the value of Milton's vision? In Milton's day when, generally speaking, the religious doctrines of the Middle Ages still prevailed and when religion was a main concern of greater multitudes of people than in any period before or since, it was far easier to "assert Eternal Providence,/And justify the wayes of God to men" than it is today. Appreciation of religious poetry is not a matter of mere aesthetics, of responding to sonorous cadences and vivid or sublime images. True appreciation demands thoughtful consideration of religious doctrine and spiritual values. Is this possible now that the traditional religious account of the universe is obsolete, now that there is no shelter from the icy winds, the cosmic darkness of the universe, in one small corner of which, to borrow a phrase from Carlyle, we are left to gyrate alone? In this age of scientific progress, when we seem to hear only the melancholy long withdrawing roar of the sea of faith, is it possible to consider *Paradise Lost* not as a monument to dead ideas but as a significant spiritual masterpiece?

The approach may be made in one of two ways or by both: by a renaissance of the ethical-religious spirit or by a zealous effort to understand the past. The first is illustrated by Albert Schweitzer's principle that society must be ethically transformed, that individuals must maintain themselves in the community as ethical personalities, that the church must be transformed "toward the ideal of a religious community."[62] The world offers no basis for an ethical-religious life. "We can discover in the world no trace of any purposive development which might lend significance to our actions." Our view of life depends not upon the world-view but upon our volition, our will-to-live.

---

[61] Martin Foss, *Symbol and Metaphor in Human Experience* (Princeton, 1949), p. 117. In this statement Foss is thinking not of Milton but of art in general.

[62] Schweitzer, *Civilization and Ethics* (London, 1923), pp. 275–90.

This must be in essence a reverence for life, from which both ethics and religion develop. Schweitzer writes: "I live my life in God, in the mysterious ethical divine personality which I cannot discover in the world, but only experience in myself as a mysterious impulse." Thus his thought, born in the stillness of the African forest, ends in mysticism that should have practical results. He calls for a renaissance of faith which will be like a burning firebrand in the gloomy darkness of our time. This ethical and religious transformation will proclaim and should establish the "sacred rights of humanity; not those which political bigwigs extol at banquets, and trample under foot in the sphere of real action, but the true and genuine rights."[63] This is Schweitzer's message designed to counteract the "spiritual decadence" and skepticism of mankind.[64] Founded upon reverence for life, this renaissance of faith will make man a true human being, and "out of the universe of errors in which he now forlornly gropes, blinded with the darkness that results from knowledge and the pride of power," it will lead him home. This ethical mysticism is linked with the eternal will, the will-to-live on the highest level. Reverence for life becomes life in God. "The ethic of Reverence for Life is the ethic of Love widened into universality. It is the ethic of Jesus, now recognized as a logical consequence of thought." Recently he has urged that the kingdom of God is the only alternative to destruction; he declares "that nothing remains but to long for the realization, somehow or other, of the Kingdom of God on earth."[65] Through a "living ethic" we should thus return to a vital Christian faith.

The other approach, which, of course, does not exclude the first, is historical and philosophical. This academic approach presupposes an understanding of the past, of the poet's character, and more particularly of the relationship of the ideas to the images and symbols in the poem. Religious symbols, unlike the scientific variety, are based upon some intrinsic relationship between the sign and the thing signified. In religion the symbol or image is not a formal term but an expression of transcendental realities, moral, spiritual, and philosophical. Coleridge has said that a symbol is characterized by the translucence . . . of the general in the special . . . above all, by the translucence of the eternal through and in the temporal." Persistently re-

[63] *Ibid.*, p. 276.
[64] Albert Schweitzer, *Out of My Life and Thought* . . . (New York, 1949), pp. 170 ff.
[65] Albert Schweitzer, "How Can We Attain the Kingdom of God?" *The Christian Century*, LXXII (September 7, 1955), 1021–22.

curring, in life and art, the image takes on a general sense and becomes part of an intellectual system, a social structure, a theological order, which is implied and must be understood. Every memorable work of art embodies the creator's vision, which by its very nature cannot systematically expound the underlying ideas. One must be prepared to understand the general truth or doctrine implied or suggested by image or symbol in the poem.

The current vigorous resurgence of religious activity shows little promise of reviving the genuine religious doctrine and the zeal of the sevententh century, an age when, as has been said, "God and Satan, heaven and hell, were radiant or lurid realities," when there was a "sincere and insatiable demand for devotional and hortatory works," a demand motivated not by selfish desires of worldly success and by political expediency but by the sincere hope of salvation. And even in that age, when he had "fall'n on evil dayes . . . and evil tongues," Milton was moved, we recall, to implore his Muse to find "fit audience, though few" and to "drive farr off the barbarous dissonance/ Of *Bacchus* and his Revellers." Although it must be admitted that Milton's political and social environment in his later years was unfortunate and even distressing, we can be sure that his potential audience existed and that it was infinitely larger than it is today. It included not only the cultured few, who could detect the classical allusions and were enchanted by the sublime images and the subtle harmonies of the verse, but also a far more numerous company of devout Christians, who may not have been particularly affected by the superb poetry but who liked the subject matter, apprehended the doctrine, and implicitly believed the story. For these devout believers numerous editions of the epic, most of them unannotated, were published. They understood. The doctrine, the symbols, even the language apparently required very little commentary. The Glassy Sea, the golden compasses, and all the rest, which these studies have endeavored to explain, were doubtless readily understood and appreciated by a public brought up to read and heed the Word of God, to see in religious truth the highest wisdom, to interpret signs and symbols, which Thomas Adams says in *The Spiritual Navigator Bound for the Holy Land* have their own language: "*Signa habent, si intelligantur, linguam suam*, Signes have their language, if they could be rightly understood." In our radically different world, preoccupied with the discoveries of science and with urgent secular interests, it seems necessary to explain the symbols, to point out their intimate relation to Christian doctrine; for these comparatively minor images have become obscure or formal; they do not, like the cross of Christ, tower o'er the wrecks of time, nor do the lights of sacred story gather round their heads sublime. Besides, it seems to me, scholars have neglected them, or misunderstood them, or learnedly traced them to the most improbable sources—the compasses, for example, solely to rabbinical commentaries. It must be insisted that these images were not recondite. On the contrary, they belonged to a religious system of thought intimately related to the familiar and venerated Word of God and profoundly influenced by theological tradition. In some concrete forms they stirred the emotions and even excited controversy. For example, the doctors of the church had long ago decided that God had created the world through His Son, who was the actual Creator; but the artists would go on showing the Father with His compasses performing this miracle; and perhaps in storied windows the Father would appear as a little old man wearing a red and blue coat; and the painter might not follow the right order of Genesis but would show the sun and moon created on the fourth day and man on the fifth. And when Puritans objected to these grievous errors and on principle condemned and defaced as idolatrous such decoration in the church, they would be prosecuted by Laud in the Court of the Star Chamber and very severely punished. Today we deplore such destruction in the churches as the work of fanaticism. We have grown much more tolerant but at the same time more indifferent to religion. Wherever they occur, the old images, one suspects, seem rather quaint. They are probably no cause for idolatry, for they excite only a tepid interest; they arouse no religious fervor. The old symbols have lost much of their power. Because of the great change in environment and the awakening of a critical consciousness "the Biblical claim to absolute authority is jeopardized; . . . the Biblical stories become ancient legends, and the doctrine they had contained, now dissevered from them, becomes a disembodied image."[66]

Imagery is needed in religion and poetry. People are unable to go far beyond imagery, which is "the reduction of the infinite to the finite." The ineffable, the divine, however, can never be given concrete shape and form. God is a "hidden God," and every attribute ascribed to Him robs Him a little of His divinity. In the Middle Ages,

[66] Erich Auerbach, *Mimesis The Representation of Reality in Western Literature.* Translated from the German by Willard R. Trask (Princeton, 1953), pp. 15–16.

it has been said, "All that was thinkable had taken image-shape: conception had become almost entirely dependent on imagination."[67] To know the nature of a thing, the medieval mind looked not at the object but up to heaven, "where it shines as an idea." This, Huizinga says, was the result of their profound idealism, their imperious need to see "the general sense, the connection with the absolute, the moral ideality, the ultimate significance of a thing . . . in a vast hierarchic system of ideas."

Milton shared this idealism and was enchanted by the hierarchic system of values. An idealist by nature, Milton was under a double obligation to present his subject and to clothe his thoughts in images. It would have been unorthodox and irreverent to reduce God to a visible form. But Milton could not avoid treating his conceptions and other abstractions, including angels, as somewhat substantial realities, in the manner of the classical epics. This material presentation of ethical and spiritual abstractions is the basis of much criticism of the poem. Given the subject and the conventions of the epic, there was, however, no other way than to materialize the spiritual and abstract. As a Christian rationalist and a humanist Milton would make the Christian life as reasonable as possible. In conformity with the soundest theological opinion, Adam would be created free, and free he would remain until he himself enthralled. After the Fall the divine plan would require voluntary obedience and would provide free grace for the salvation of all except those who neglect and scorn God's long-sufferance and His day of grace.

Within the limits of Christian doctrine this is an eminently sane and rational plan for a Christian life, with the emphasis upon salvation. This limitation is overlooked or minimized by some who emphasize in Milton the rational humanist. Asserting that Milton has a passionate belief in the freedom of the will, Bush has declared that Milton interprets "the regenerate state in humanistic, that is, in rational and ethical terms."[68] It cannot, however, be maintained that the Milton of *Paradise Lost* is predominantly a humanist or that, with the Gnostics, he would "reconcile the gospel with the science and philosophy" of his time or that he interprets Christianity as merely or mainly "a religious and philosophic system, regarded as the best and only true one."[69] Though by training a genuine humanist, Milton was

[67] J. Huizinga, *The Waning of the Middle Ages* (New York, 1954), p. 214.
[68] Douglas Bush, *The Renaissance and English Humanism* (Toronto, 1939), pp. 114–15.
[69] Helmut R. Niebuhr, *Christ and Culture* (New York, 1951), pp. 86–87.

certainly not selective in his attitude toward Christ. For Milton, Christ was not a Messiah of Culture or a "wise man teaching a secular wisdom, or a reformer concerned with the reconstruction of social institutions." For him Christ was simply the Saviour, and Christianity was "a faith governing all life." But history and the future, as visualized in *Paradise Lost*, offered, it seems, no real hope of the amelioration of social, political, or ecclesiastical institutions.

In his vision of the future Milton was no doubt much influenced by the Biblical conception of nature and life: by the Jewish view that the world is God's, "shaped by His wisdom and obeying His law," but also a place of darkness and cruelty in which "the righteous does not always flourish and his seed seems sometimes to be forsaken"; by the Saviour's recognition of "the perversity and distortion" of the world and the "folly and wickedness of mankind."[70] The earth is a place where "evil beasts devour and ravage; evil thoughts and passions, deeds of violence and fraud, deliberate rebellion against God, deliberate cruelty towards men defile and destroy humanity." Jesus himself ascribes this evil not only to human sin but also to a "personified power of evil, Satan, the devil, the adversary, whose influence is manifest in the imperfection of the natural order and the disease and malice of mankind." To evil His life was a sacrifice, and the cross became a universal symbol of Christendom.

The bleak truth is that evil seems to be invincible; for the world will go on its accustomed way,

> To good malignant, to bad men benigne,
> Under her own waight groaning, till the day
> Appeer of respiration to the just,
> And vengeance to the wicked.

There is no hope that society will be reformed to correspond to the Christian ideal. In fact those who persevere in true worship will be heavily persecuted; religion will be satisfied by the observance of mere outward rites and specious forms; truth will retire bestuck "with slandrous darts"; and works of faith will rarely be found. In this grim picture it is difficult to discover any outline of a regenerate state in this world. The humanistic philosophy seems to be dwarfed by the vision of mankind's inveterate wickedness and the world's dire destiny. Although Milton's humanistic learning undoubtedly gave sub-

---

[70] Charles E. Raven, *Natural Religion and Christian Theology*. The Gifford Lectures 1951. First Series: *Science and Religion* (Cambridge, 1953), pp. 25, 32.

stance and scope to his religious philosophy, it seems clear that his vision of the future is medieval or Biblical.

The effect of the poem is, however, not merely negative. If there is no hope for the general amelioration of society, if Milton could not have said that with "the assistance of God's indwelling Spirit the creation gropes its way forward in hope," if he did not share the optimism of the scientist that life on the earth is capable of further and almost infinite progress in the ages that lie ahead,—there is, nevertheless, Milton would say, hope for the individual who knows, obeys, and loves God. The entire poem has one main purpose: to make clear the saying of Jesus Christ, "This is life eternal, that they might know thee the only true God, and Jesus Christ, whom thou hast sent." To know and to love God, to walk as in His presence, "to observe His providence and on him sole depend,"—this is surely the highest wisdom. To this knowledge must be added deeds to correspond with faith, patience, temperance, and love, the soul of all the virtues. With these virtues and this knowledge the true Christian can make real progress toward a real goal.

In the form of *Paradise Lost*, in the structure, the control of the imagery, in the incomparable style, we find indisputable evidence of Milton the rational humanist, the rare poet indebted to and transcending a rich and invaluable cultural tradition. In the story, the theology and doctrine for the most part, the religious imagery and the symbols, we see the Christian poet, indebted to Holy Scripture, singing of hell, of Paradise, of creation, of the divine order of the world, and of man's fall,

> That brought into this World a world of woe,
> Sinne and her shadow Death, and Miserie
> Deaths Harbinger: . . .

This is the poet's sad task, the argument of his heroic song. But he also sang of man's redemption through Christ, who is the Word, the Spirit, the indwelling spark or seed of deity, the evidence of reason, of divine guidance and purpose in man, manifested in good works and in the joy, peace, and fortitude which are "His fruits." Throughout the epic the Christian and the humanist may be said to have worked in harmony; but at the end, when the erring but penitent human pair is forced to leave Paradise, it is not Reason but Providence who is their guide to that paradise within which is to be their recompense for the one by disobedience lost.

128

V

Paradise Lost, Protestantism, and the Retreat from Christianity

Fair patrimony that I leave ye, sons

It has been said that Milton was the master of all learning, ancient and modern. His mind ranged over the entire realm of knowledge and speculation. He was familiar with classical literature and philosophy, contemporary literature, Biblical and patristic writings, Reformation theology, and the philosophical and political issues of his day, from all of which his own independent system of thought was derived. Overawed by the vastness and complexity of the subject, scholars have hitherto wisely not ventured to deal comprehensively with the sources and elements of his thought.[1] Partial and tentative but relevant contributions may be attempted. I have assumed that Protestantism and its relation to Milton's poetry should be a fruitful area of investigation.

Since it is a compact repository of Protestant thought, if not a source of Protestant doctrine, we may first turn our attention to the Geneva Bible and especially its famous commentary, which seems to preserve the essence of Protestant interpretation of Scripture. After its publication, in 1560, this Bible was frequently reprinted. For more

[1] Harris F. Fletcher's *The Intellectual Development of John Milton.* Volume I: *The Institution to 1625* (1956) appeared too late to be used in my studies.

129

than half a century it was the most popular and accessible Bible in the English tongue. It has been called the "household Bible of the English-speaking nations."[2] Although it was never officially adopted for use in English churches, this Bible was a general favorite with the people; and there can be no doubt that it and its celebrated commentary had a very great influence. It has been established that Milton used in his prose the Authorized Version, which he quotes. It may also be established, I think, that the Genevan commentary and *Paradise Lost* frequently coincide in their interpretation of Scripture. Granted that some of these points are commonplace and conventional, one may say, however, that this agreement stamps both the commentary and the poem as essentially Protestant in ideas and in spirit. In the statement of God's relationship to man, in some fundamental points of theology, in some significant minor details, Milton's interpretation of Scripture and that of the commentary agree, as indeed might be expected.

Of course I do not maintain that Protestant ideas are to be found only in the Geneva Bible, and I shall include some material from other sources. The points emphasized in this study must have been preached and believed in churches and homes throughout England and Scotland.[3] I consider the Geneva Bible first as an unimpeachable and influential Protestant document with a succinct statement of Protestant thought. In the commentary a fundamental point seems to be that the relationship between God and man is or should be an intimate individual relationship. This seems to imply a living faith and in man personal responsibility; it doubtless implies a rebellion against ceremonial forms and, in some degree, a distaste for institutional discipline. In general I shall attempt to classify the inquiry under the headings of divine power and grace, the creation, the nature of man, Satan and wicked spirits, the Fall and its consequences, and the plan of redemption. There will be found striking similarities between the commentary and the poem, as indeed one might expect in the treatment of ideas that are partly conventional. There are also differences, which will be indicated; but the similarities, which are not generally verbal, seem important and significant.

[2] Brooke F. Westcott, *A General View of the History of the English Bible*, rev. by William Aldis Wright (3d ed.; London, 1905), pp. 93 ff.

[3] I understand Protestant to mean "in essence a repudiation of authority" and especially "the Papacy and Papal power in any shape" and, more generally, to indicate freedom of thought in religion, with an appeal to Scripture and the individual conscience. See James P. Whitney, *The History of the Reformation*, pp. 77 ff.

130

With regard to divine power and grace, it is reassuring to read in the Geneva Bible that "God determined and ordayned before the beginning of the worlde to bestowe his grace upon us by his sonne." This is the commentary on II Timothy 1:9: "Who hath saved us, and called us with an holy calling, not according to our workes, but according to his own purpose and grace, which was given to us through Christ Jesus before the world was." And with reference to Ephesians 1: 4–6 it is declared that "God purposed of his onely pure good wil to adopt us for his children by Jesus Christ, and to raise us from death to life, to the ende hee might be glorified for so great grace bestowed upon us." In the poem also God's grace is freely bestowed upon man. In *Paradise Lost* when Satan, bent on desperate revenge, approaches the "new created World,/And Man there plac't," intending to destroy him by force or pervert him by guile, God speaks to His only Son and declares that Satan will succeed, that man by his own choice will fall, but that man, because he was deceived by Satan, shall find grace: "Man shall not quite be lost, but sav'd who will." This is according to God's "Eternal purpose," which precedes the creation of the world. This divine grace is free, "Freely voutsaft"; and man is saved, not by his merit, but solely by God's grace.[4] God's justice, however, must be satisfied. Having disobeyed, man has nothing left to expiate his treason; he is dead in sin and lost. The Son, who is immortal love, therefore offers Himself to save the world from utter loss: "Behold mee then, mee for him, life for life/I offer, on mee let thine anger fall." Thus the Son effects God's eternal purpose of salvation. The Geneva Bible says, "By the ritch grace of God wee are delivered and redeemed from sinne, and made cleane by Jesus Christ." For "God purposed by his onely pure good wil to adopt us for his children by Jesus Christ, and to raise us up from death to life, to the ende hee might be glorified for so great grace bestowed upon us." As Milton says, man's fallen condition is frail, and he owes to God alone "All his deliv'rance." Thus man is saved by God's grace, not by his own works. The Geneva version explains: "We are saved not by works but by grace in Jesus Christ." The grace of God is "the onely cause of salvation." In Ephesians 2:8–9 we read "For by grace are yee saved through faith, and that not of your selves: it is the gift of God, Not of workes." This Protestant doctrine Milton accepts. Man's salvation depends on his voluntary acceptance of God's free grace, and upon prayer, repentance, and obedience. Obeying God's umpire, conscience, man may attain light,

4 *Paradise Lost*, III, 173.

"And to the end persisting, safe arrive." But those who refuse God's grace are excluded from His mercy. Salvation is by faith and grace—not by works, but works may of course exemplify grace. In the poem, the Almighty states that Adam's sin makes guilty all his sons; but Christ's merit

> Imputed shall absolve them who renounce
> Thir own both righteous and unrighteous deeds,
> And live in thee transplanted, and from thee
> Receive new life.   (III, 291–94)

Only the elect believe and have true faith, and election proceeds from the grace of God, not from man's works. In the Geneva Bible and in *Paradise Lost* the doctrine of grace is essential. But in the Geneva version grace is *limited to the elect,* those predestined by God to be saved. In *Paradise Lost,* on the contrary, grace is *for all men,* who are free to accept or reject it; and only those who reject God's grace will be damned. This is a fundamental difference, which those who condemn Milton's God may have ignored.

In his story of the creation of the sun, the moon, and the stars, Milton may have made use of an idea stated in the commentary, the idea that the sun and the moon were created "as instruments appointed . . . *to serve to mans use.*"[5] Observe that Milton wrote,[6] "And God made two great Lights, *great for thir use/To man, . . .* (VII, 346–47).

In the commentary and the poem *firmament* and *heaven* mean an expanse of air or the region above us. The commentary defines *firmament* as "spreading over, and aire" and *heaven* as "the region of the aire and all that is above us." Milton describes the *firmament* as an

> expanse of liquid, pure,
> Transparent, Elemental Air, diffus'd
> In circuit to the uttermost convex
> Of this great Round.   (VII, 264–67)

Concluding this account, Raphael explains, "And Heav'n he nam'd the Firmament." In the text "Let the waters bring forth in abundance every creeping thing," the phrase "every creeping thing" has this marginal commentary: "As fish and wormes which slide, swimme or creepe"; and Milton has a vivid passage describing the innumerable swarms and shoals of fish with fins and shining scales, gliding under

---

[5] Gen. 1:16, note *o*. Taken from my personal copy of the 1580 edition. Italics supplied.

[6] Italics mine.

the green wave, straying through groves of coral, and showing to the sun "thir wav'd coats dropt with Gold." And so on.

The creation of man deserves particular attention. In the commentary the text "in our image according to our likeness" is explained in note *t*: the words "likeness" and "image" indicate that man "was created after God in righteousness and true holines, meaning by these two wordes all perfection, as wisedome, trueth, innocencie, power, &c.," with a reference to Ephesians 4:24. Milton's picture of Adam and Eve in Paradise is a richly elaborated expression of this idea. Satan sees

> Two of far nobler shape erect and tall,
> Godlike erect, with native Honour clad
> In naked Majestie seemd Lords of all,
> And worthie seemd, for in their looks Divine
> The image of thir glorious Maker shon,
> Truth, Wisedome, Sanctitude severe and pure,
>
> . . . .
>
> Simplicitie and spotless innocence.   (IV, 288 ff.)

Similarly in the Geneva version the note on the text "And God said, Beholde, I have given unto you every herbe, which is upon the earth" emphasizes God's great liberality: "Gods great liberalitie to man taketh away all excuse of his ingratitude." Milton's account of the profusion of the material riches of Paradise, the sapphire fount, the brooks "Rowling on Orient Pearl and sands of Gold," flowers worthy of paradise on hill and plain, "Flours of all hue, and without Thorn the Rose," nectarine fruit on compliant boughs—all this and more illustrates God's boundless generosity and man's incomparable good fortune. Adam remarks to Eve that the Power which made them and for them this ample world must be infinitely good[7] "and of his good/ As *liberal* and *free* as infinite" (IV, 414–15). In the commentary and the poem God's boundless liberality is emphasized. Man in Paradise enjoys free leave and choice "Unlimited of manifold delights," and there is for them merely "One easie prohibition."

This perfect state of man includes freedom, or the state is perfect because man is free. In the poem God says (III, 98–99), "I made him just and right,/Sufficient to have stood, though free to fall." Men were made free, God says; and free they must remain "Till they enthrall themselves." This principle of freedom is emphatically stated in the Geneva Bible. In the Argument of Genesis it is said that man, endued

[7] Italics mine.

with infinite graces, "fell willingly from God through disobedience." Perfectly good and innocent, man was free to persevere in this state of blessedness. But by his own choice, "without least impulse or shadow of Fate," as Milton writes, he fell. The Geneva version states that man made "in all perfection," in wisdom, truth, and innocence, "might sinne, or not sinne, liue or die at his pleasure." Milton agrees. Like the angels, Adam and Eve were free. "Freely they stood who stood, and fell who fell." Milton declares that without freedom there had been no proof of true allegiance, constant faith, and love. The Geneva Bible refers to Ecclesiasticus 15:17: "Before man is life and death, good and euill: what him liketh shalbe giuen him." In this important respect commentary and poem agree. God says in *Paradise Lost,* His decree, "Unchangeable, Eternal," ordained "Thir freedom, they themselves ordain'd thir fall."

Before considering more important matters, we may notice a few proper names. In the first table of the Geneva Bible *Auen* is said to be in Greek "Heliopolis the citie of the sun," which "is otherwise called Thebae." This may account for Milton's lines on the phoenix, to which Raphael is compared:

> as that sole Bird
> When to enshrine his reliques in the Sun's
> Bright Temple, to *Aegyptian Theb's* he flies.   (V, 272–74)

Babel, and Babylon, interpreted to mean confusion, is a city "scituate in Chaldea, in the field of Shinar." It was the principal city of the kingdom of the Chaldeans, "ouer the whiche Nimrod the tirant first usurped the gouernement." Nimrod is defined as "a rebell, or rebellious." And two notes on Genesis 10: 8–9 explain that Nimrod was a "cruel oppressor and tyrant," and that his "tyrannie came into a prouerbe as hated both of God and man: for he passed not to commit crueltie euen in Gods presence." One should compare with this Milton's account of the first tyranny after the flood, a ruthless dominion which quite dispossessed "Concord and law of Nature from the Earth" (XII, 24 ff.). Milton particularly remarks that Nimrod "from Rebellion shall derive his name,/Though of Rebellion others he accuse" (XII, 36–37). Uriel is "an Angels name," with reference to II Esdras 4:1; and here Uriel declares that he will show Esdras *"the way, that thou desirest to see."* Uriel performs a similar service for the disguised Satan in *Paradise Lost*. Asmodeus, a destroyer, is an evil spirit, of whom one may read in the book of Tobit. Milton alludes to him (IV, 168 ff.). Azotus or Ashdod (both forms are given) is a famous city in the land of Palestine. Compare (I, 464–65) "Rear'd in *Azotus*, dreaded through the Coast/Of *Palestine,* . . ." Baal and Baalim: "The name of the idol of the Sidonians, or a generall name to all idols." In *Paradise Lost* Baalim is a "general" name of male idols in Syria and Assyria (I, 421–22). Tammuz, it is said, was a prophet of the idols, "who after his death was once a yeare mourned for in the night only of women: S. Jerome taketh it for Adonis, Venus lover." The reference is to Ezekiel 8:14. Milton sketches the story (I, 446 ff.). Tophet or Topheth is defined: "A place in the valley of the sonnes of Hinnom, whiche is in the suburbes of Jerusalem, where parentes were wont to offer their children, half burned in fire to the devill Molech." The reference is to II Kings 23:10 and Isaiah 30:33. The note on II Kings 23:10 adds the information that the worshipers of Molech "smote on the tabret while their children were burning that their crie should not be heard." The note on Leviticus 18:21 describes Molech, "an idole of the Ammonites":

This seemed to be the chiefe and principall of all idoles: and as the Iewes write, was of a great stature, and holowe within, having seven places or chambers within him: one was to receive meale that was offred: an other turtle doves: the third a sheepe: the fourth a ramme: the fifth a calfe: the sixt an oxe: the seventh a childe. This idoles face was like a calfe: his handes ever stretched out to receive giftes.

This information would have been useful to Milton in his description of the worship of Moloch, first in his catalogue:

> horrid King besmear'd with blood
> Of human sacrifice, and parents tears,
> Though for the noyse of Drums and Timbrels loud
> Their childrens cries unheard, that past through fire
> To his grim Idol.   (I, 392–96)

These lines, one might argue, state most effectively the information found in the Geneva version.

Leviathan is the "name of a fish called Whale." References are given, including Isaiah 27:1, where it is said that the Lord with his great and mighty sword "shall visite Liviathan." And the commentary explains: "Hee prophecieth here of the destruction of Satan and his kingdom under the name Liviathan." Lying prostrate on the lake of fire, Satan is compared to that sea beast "*Leviathan*, which God of all his works/Created hugest that swim th' Ocean stream" (I, 201–202).

I do not argue that all of these ideas and names are derived solely from the Geneva verson. There is in *Paradise Lost* a great wealth of material—there is, of course, much that is unmistakably Milton's. But it is proper, I think, to show that often the interpretation of Scripture in this version coincides with Milton's or that directly or indirectly the poem betrays the influence of Protestant thought as expressed in the Geneva Bible.

The commandment not to eat of the tree of knowledge carries in Scripture the threat of dire punishment: "for in the day that thou eatest thereof, thou shalt die the death." In the commentary of the Geneva Bible death is interpreted: "By this death he meaneth the separation of man from God, who is our life and chiefe felicitie: and also that our disobedience is the cause therof." In *Paradise Lost* death is similarly interpreted. Original sin is punished, not by immediate death, but by loss of innocence, by the knowledge of evil, by separation from God. Good is lost and evil got. Adam and Eve are destitute of honor, faith, and purity. Adam suspects that the death that was threatened will be "but endless miserie/From this day onward" (X, 810–11), which he will bequeath as a "Fair Patrimonie" to posterity. Death, he perceives, "Will prove no sudden, but a slow-pac't evill." The immediate results of original sin are not death but shame, anger, discord in the universe, "growing miseries," which are seemingly incurable, as Adam and Eve are inconsolable.

In the temptation of Eve, the decisive point is Eve's doubting God's commandment: "Ye shal not eat of it, neither shall ye touch it, lest ye die." The commentary tersely indicates Eve's fatal weakness or failure: "In doubting Gods threatening, she yelded to Satan." Another note is as follows: "This is Satans chiefest subtilty, to cause us not to feare Gods threatnings." In *Paradise Lost*, Eve, persuaded by Satan's specious reasoning, ignored God's command; she doubted God. She even declared that God's forbidding commended the forbidden fruit. Concluding

> What fear I then, rather what know to feare
> Under this ignorance of Good and Evil,
> Of God or death, of Law or Penaltie? (IX, 773–75)

she reached for and devoured "this Fruit Divine." Her fatal error was to doubt God.

Immediately after their mortal sin Adam and Eve realized that they were naked. The commentary explains: "They began to feele their miserie, but they sought not to God for remedy." This is the situation in *Paradise Lost*, where the consciousness of their physical nakedness is only a minor consideration. Their spiritual nakedness is paramount.

136

They are overwhelmed with misery and despair. Void of honor, faith, and purity, they spend their time in bitter recrimination. In utter despair, in the dark and dreadful night, tormented by his conscience, Adam curses his creation and denounces Eve, "his life so late and sole delight," but now the cause of his ruin. "O fleeting joyes/Of Paradise, deere bought with lasting woes!" They are miserable "Beyond all past example and future," and they long for death. They experience bitter and hopeless misery, but they seek not "to God for remedy."

In both poem and commentary the enmity between the serpent and the woman is of course interpreted as the conflict between Satan and Christ. When God says, "I will also put enmitie between thee and the serpent," the note in the Geneva Bible explains: "He chiefly meaneth Satan." The note on the prophecy "He shal breake thine head" (Gen. 3:15) reads: "The Lorde comforteth Adam by the promes of the blessed seed," that is, Christ, not the Virgin, as the Roman Catholics interpret it. The prophecy "thou shalt bruise his heele" means that "Satan shal sting Christ and his members, but not overcome them." So in the poem Adam realizes that the promise "thy Seed shall bruise our Foe" is the assurance "that the bitterness of death/Is past, and we shall live."[8] And Jesus, rising from the grave, leads captivity captive and treads Satan under his feet. The sin of Adam and Eve will inexorably be punished, but the spirit shall live in faith through Christ. Thus is revealed the hope and the plan of salvation. As the Argument of Genesis in the Geneva version says, God restored man to life and "confirmed him in the same by the promise of Christ to come, by whome he should overcome Satan, death and Hell." The commentary restates the orthodox doctrine of redemption and the final defeat of Satan.

The interpretation of events between the Fall and the Flood is similar in the commentary and the poem. I realize, of course, that the ideas expressed in the commentary may have been traditional and may have been generally accepted. The first example is the Lord's rejecting Cain's sacrifice. The text "But unto Kain & his offering he had no regard . . ." carries the following explanation in the margin: "Because he was an hypocrite and offred onely for an outward shew without sinceritie of heart." Milton writes that Cain's offering was rejected," "for he was not sincere" (XI, 443). This idea is repeated in another note, on Cain's answer to the question, "Where is Habel thy brother?" The note reads: "This is the nature of the reprobate when they are reproued of their hypocrisie, euen to neglect God and despite him." Of course, the text in Scripture says nothing about Cain's hypocrisy—and God's action there seems to be merely arbitrary. The commentary and the poem offer the same reason for the rejection of Cain's sacrifice. This similarity, in addition to the others previously mentioned, seems especially noteworthy. It seems to indicate a specific, not a general relationship—a definite agreement, not merely traditional.

The poem and the commentary agree in the account of the outrageous conditions preceding the Flood. After the invention of metal tools, the new order was evil. Apparently just and grave men descended from the hills and, attracted by a bevy of fair women, gave rein to their lusts. These were the "sonnes of God" or, as the commentary explains, "children of the godly which began to degenerate." The fair women were those that "came of wicked parents, as of Kain." Milton wrote:

> that fair femal Troop thou sawst, that seemd
> Of Goddesses, so blithe, so smooth, so gay,
> Yet empty of all good wherein consists
> Womans domestic honour and chief praise;
> Bred onely and completed to the taste
> Of lustful appetence, to sing, to dance,
> To dress, and troule the Tongue, and roule the Eye.
> (XI, 610–16)

These sirens come from those tents "Of wickedness, wherein shall dwell his Race/Who slew his Brother." I think that there can be little doubt that Milton used the ideas expressed in the commentary, ideas that explain the origin of the corrupt society before the Flood.

Milton's picture of the giants, who trusted in might alone, and for whom heroic virtue was aggressive and ruthless war,

> To overcome in Battel, and subdue
> Nations, and bring home spoils with infinite
> Man-slaughter, . . .   (XI, 691–93)

who were not patrons of mankind but "Destroyers rightlier call'd and Plagues of men,"—this picture seems to be an elaboration of this note in the Geneva Bible: "Which usurped autoritie ouer others, & degenerate from that simplicitie wherein their fathers liued." Milton's account of the broils preceding the Flood, of "Concours of Arms, fierce Faces threatning Warr," of military bands pillaging the country, and of the ensuing bloody battles and sieges— all this seems related to the commentary: "Which usurped autoritie ouer others." One statement in the text is "the earth was filled with crueltie." The commentary runs: "Meaning that all were giuen to the contempt of God, & oppression of their neighbours." *Usurpation of authority* and *oppression* are specific interpretations of the scriptural words *wickedness* and *cruelty.* The commentary and the poem agree. After the Flood tyranny reappeared, as mentioned above. Milton's picture of Nimrod as an ambitious and arrogant autocrat is traditional, as suggested by the Genevan commentary: Nimrod's reputation as "a cruel oppressor and tyrant," the note explains, "came into a prouerbe as hated both of God and man."

As I have said, the commentary and the poem reveal the plan of redemption *in connection with the Fall.* The text in Genesis sets forth God's power in creation, man's fatal error or sin, and God's stern justice. The commentary and the poem add the plan of salvation through Christ, which is not in the text of Genesis. Such statements as the following are often found in the commentary: "The worlde shall recouer by thy seede, which is Christ, the blessing which they lost in Adam"; the blessing of Rebecca's seed is "fully accomplished in Jesus Christ"; in Jacob's vision "Christ is the ladder whereby God and man are ioined together, & by whom Angels minister unto us: all graces by him are giuen unto us, & we by him ascend into heauen." And so on. This introduction of Christ into the story of Genesis, this revelation of the plan of redemption in connection with the Fall, occurs also in *Paradise Lost.* Man's sin must be severely punished. But God is not inexorable. His will is that man shall find grace. The grace is supplied by Christ. "Mercy first and last shall brightest shine." The sum of Adam's knowledge is that man must ever obey and love God. All this is, of course, traditional; it is fundamental Christian doctrine. I merely wish to emphasize the fact that the poem and the commentary *bring together* the Fall and the plan of salvation.

The commentary in the Geneva Bible and Milton in *Paradise Lost* interpret the ancient story in the light of Protestant doctrine. Both emphasize faith, individual responsibility, implicit obedience, trust in God's providence. The statements, "God reiecteth none estate of people in their miseries. . . . The favour of God is the fountaine of all prosperitie. . . . The onely way to overcome all tentations is to rest upon Gods providence. . . . Gods providence always watcheth to direct the waies of his children . . ." and others in the commentary may be illustrated in *Paradise Lost.* The note "True faith renounceth all natural affections to obey Gods commandments" discloses the fundamental reason for the fall of Adam and Eve, whose natural affections led them to disobey God. One should particularly note in commentary and poem the shift of emphasis from Law to Grace. It is a familiar and orthodox principle. Milton says, "Law can discover sin, but not remove" (XII, 290). Therefore in commentary and poem a better covenant, from flesh to spirit, from the imposition of strict law to the free acceptance of liberal grace, from "works of Law to works of Faith," is promised. The new order is established in Christ, who fulfills the law through love and who by his ministry and ascension brings back "Through the worlds wilderness long wanderd man/Safe to Eternal Paradise of rest" (XII, 313–14).

The agreement or harmony in thought between *Paradise Lost* and the commentary in the Geneva Bible suggests a way or pattern of Reformation thinking. Both, it seems, offer a fundamentally Protestant interpretation of Scripture.

A few other minor points may be noticed. The seat of Milton's Muse,

> *Sion* Hill
> . . . and *Siloa's* Brook that flow'd
> Fast by the Oracle of God, . . .   (I, 10–12)

may be explained by the note on Genesis 15:17, "the mountaine of thine inheritance, which is the place that thou hast prepared, O Lord, for to dwell in, even the sanctuarie, O Lorde, which thine handes shall establish." This is the note: "Which was Mount Zion, where afterward the Temple was built." Milton's statement that great military heroes are styled "great Conquerours,/Patrons of Mankind . . . and Sons of Gods" (XI, 691–92) may be glossed by the following quotation from the Geneva Bible, Exodus 15:1: "Who is like unto thee, O Lorde, among the gods, . . ." with this note in the commentary, explaining "gods": "For so, oftentimes the scripture calleth the mightie men of the world." These are the men who achieve worldly fame, but "what most merits fame" is in silence hid. The idea of the true prophet, as stated in a note on Genesis 41:33, is Milton's: "The office of a true prophet is not only to show the evils to come, but also the remedies for the same." This is an apt statement of the theme and purpose of the last two books of *Paradise Lost,* when Adam is dismayed by the vision and the relation of "evils to come," the effects wrought by his "original crime" on those

> who never touch'd
> Th' excepted Tree, nor with the Snake conspir'd,

> Nor sinn'd thy sin, yet from that sin derive
> Corruption to bring forth more violent deeds.   (XI, 425–28)

Other illustrations might be cited. But let us now return to the consideration of other ideas and analogies, perhaps more important.

The sum of wisdom which Adam learns from his divine instructor and guide is to obey and love God:

> Henceforth I learne, that to obey is best,
> And love with feare the onely God, to walk
> As in his presence, ever to observe
> His providence, and on him sole depend.   (XII, 561–64)

This idea, stated in Deuteronomy 5:33, "But walke in all the wayes which the Lord your God hath commanded you, that ye may live, and that it may go well with you . . ." is emphasized in the accompanying note: "As by obedience God giveth us all felicitie: so of disobeying God, proceede all our miseries." The thought is reiterated in a note on Deuteronomy 6:2, "That thou mightest feare the Lord thy God, and keepe all his ordinances, and his commandements." The note: "A reverent feare and love of God, is the first beginning to keepe Gods commandements." In Deuteronomy 6:25 we read: "Moreover, this shalbe our righteousnes before the Lord our God, if we take heed to keep all these commandements, as he hath commanded us." But the note explains that man unaided is unable to satisfy the law: "But because none could fully obey the law, we must have recourse to Christ to be justified by faith." The same idea is expressed in *Paradise Lost*. By fulfilling that which man did not, obedience to the law of God, Christ by obedience and by love alone fulfills the law, and his obedience "Imputed becomes theirs by Faith, his merits/To save them, not thir own" (XII, 409–11). Christ's "God-like Act" annuls man's doom, defeats Satan, Sin, and Death, and to those who believe offers the only hope of immortality, in a paradise which shall include all the earth. Again we observe that in commentary and poem the twofold theme, the loss of Paradise and the redemption of man, emerges.

Indeed, Milton says, Moses is a prophet of Christ to come:

> whose high Office now
> *Moses* in figure beares, to introduce
> One greater, of whose day he shall foretell,
> And all the Prophets in thir Age, the times
> Of great *Messiah* shall sing.   (XII, 240–44)

These lines are explained by Deuteronomy 18:15: "The Lord thy God

141

wil raise up unto thee a Prophet like unto me, from among you, even of thy brethren: unto him ye shal hearken," with the accompanying note: "Meaning a continuall succession of Prophets, till Christ the end of all Prophets come." Later, when we read that "the Lorde thy God shall keepe with thee the covenant, & the mercie which he sware unto thy fathers" (Deut. 5:12), a note explains: "This covenant is grounded upon his free grace: therefore in recompensing their obedience he hath respect to his mercie & not to their merites." As we have seen, this doctrine of free and unmerited grace is Milton's. It is the cause of Adam's exclaiming "O goodness infinite, goodness immense!" For Michael is also a prophet of glad tidings: through Christ good shall spring from evil, grace shall abound over wrath. Satan and his perverted world shall finally be destroyed. And in its place will rise

> New Heav'ns, new Earth, Ages of endless date
> Founded in righteousness and peace and love,
> To bring forth fruits Joy and eternal Bliss.   (XII, 549–51)

This new covenant is the basis of man's hope.

It must be repeated, however, that this blessed state will be attained only by those who believe and are obedient. The note on Deuteronomy 30:16 explains, "So that to love and obey God, is onely life and felicitie." But this obedience is not in man's power, for "Gods Spirit onely worketh it in his elect." As we know, in Milton, election followed or depended upon grace, but it included all who would believe. Man must live in Christ and from Him receive new life. Then after long tribulations the just will "See golden days, fruitful of golden deeds,/With Joy and Love triumphing, and fair Truth" (III, 337–38). This will be the paradise of the future, far happier than that Assyrian garden, for it is wholly spiritual and it will be eternal.

The basis of the dramatic power and lasting appeal of *Paradise Lost* is man's freedom. Before the Fall he was free to choose, to obey or to disobey. We read in Deuteronomy 30:19, "I haue set before you life and death, blessing and cursing. therefore chuse life, that both thou and thy seede may live." Having chosen the way of sin and death, man is graciously granted a second chance. He will not "quite be lost, but sav'd who will." But now, after the Fall, he cannot save himself. He must be regenerated and sustained by God's grace, which with His Spirit worketh in man obedience and love. Again in Deuteronomy (30:6) we read, "the Lord thy God wil circumcise thine heart," and in the commentary this is interpreted: "God wil purge all thy wicked affections which thing is not in thine owne power to do." This spiritual

142

regeneration of the individual, "built by Faith" and unconstrained by "carnal power," is the essence of Protestantism. This doctrine is stated repeatedly in the Geneva Bible, and it is fundamental in Milton's assertion of eternal Providence and his justification of God.

Consider also this illustration. Milton writes that Moses, although of God highly beloved, shall not lead his people into Canaan;

> But *Joshua* whom the Gentiles *Jesus* call,
> His Name and Office bearing, who shall quell
> The adversarie Serpent, and bring back
> Through the worlds wilderness long wanderd man
> Safe to eternal Paradise of rest.   (XII, 310–14)

Compare with this the following statement from the Argument of the Book of Joshua:

This historie doeth represent Iesus Christ the true Joshua, who leadeth us into eternall felicitie, which is signified unto us by this land of Canaan.

The similarity is obvious. Moses was the minister of the Law. Joshua, the ruler and governor of his people, was the type of Christ, and Canaan the symbol of eternal life and felicity. Later, Joshua 5:13–14, we read that at Jericho a captain of the host of the Lord appeared before Joshua, and that Joshua fell on his face to the earth and did worship him. The commentary explains: "In that Ioshua worshipeth him, he acknowledged him to be God: and in that he calleth him selfe the Lordes captaine, he declareth him selfe to be Christ." Perhaps the commentary in the Geneva version influenced Milton to treat Joshua as the type of Christ or rather to merge the two.

From the almost innumerable items in the commentary on the Geneva Bible I cull a few more examples which should be of interest:

For before sinne entred, all things were honest and comely (Gen. 2:13). If the concupiscence & wicked affections overcome reason, we must not marveile though men be blinded, and like unto beasts (Matt. 6:23). Albeit God detest sinne, yet he turneth mans wickedness to his glorie (Gen. 45:8). The devill desireth ever to do harme, but hee can doe no more then God doth appoint (Matt. 8:31). The word of God is the sword of the Spirit, wherewith Satan is overcome (Matt. 4:11). Locusts are false teachers, heretikes, and worldly subtile Prelates, with Monkes, Friers, Cardinals, . . . Archbishops, Bishops, Doctors . . . which forsake Christ to maintaine false doctrine (Rev. 9:3). We may boldly by Christs admonition reiect and contemne all erroneous doctrine and mans inventions and ought onely to cleave to the word of God (Matt. 16:12). The true way to amend abuses, is to returne to the institution of thinges, and to try them by Gods word (Mark 10:10). Then without Christ there is but death: for his word onely leadeth us to life (John 6:68). The power of Satan is beaten downe by the preaching of the Gospel (Luke 10:18). Christ bringeth us from heaven the Spirit of Life (I Cor. 15:45). Where Christ is not, there death reigneth (John 8:44). Men may not teach their owne doctrine, but whatsoever Christ hath taught them: for he reserveth this authoritie to himselfe, to be the onely teacher and the author of the doctrine (Matt. 28:20). We must seeke Gods glory first and above all things (Matt. 6:9). Those that cleave to God shal live, whereas those that follow idols shall perishe (Deut. 4:4). The worlde shall recover by thy seede, which is Christ, the blessing which they lost in Adam (Gen. 12:2). The onely way to overcome all tentations is to rest upon Gods providence (Gen. 22:8). The godly are plagued many times with the wicked: therefore their company is daungerous (Gen. 14:12). His wickedness and lack of true repentance appeareth in this, that he burdeneth God with his fault, because he had given him a wife (Gen. 3:12). We see that there is ever some seede of the knowledge of God in the heartes of the wicked (Gen. 31:55). The holy Ghost covereth not mens fautes, as do vaine writers which make vice vertue (Gen. 37:18). An evill conscience is never fully at rest (Gen. 49:15). The wicked shalbe burned in continuall fire, that never shalbe extinguished (Rev. 19:3). The devill and all his power which burneth with fury, and is red with the blood of the faithful (Rev. 12:3). Meaning the Gospel of Christ, which AntiChrist cannot hide, seeing Christ bringeth it open in his hand (Rev. 10:2). He setteth not his felicitie in the pleasures of this world, but in the feare & service of God (Ps. 23:6). He sheweth that peace and joy of conscience in the holy Ghost is the fruite of faith (Ps. 32:11).

This is a small sampling of the marginal commentary in the Geneva Bible. There are thousands more, many of them relevant. Many of these statements confirm or illustrate ideas in *Paradise Lost*. One generalization may safely be made: only in the interpretation of the elect does Milton differ fundamentally from this commentary. Elsewhere there seems to be complete agreement between the Protestant Bible and the Protestant epic; for each shows "that no evill can come unto man, except he offend God by disobedience."

Conscientious readers of *Paradise Lost* will recognize the relationship between these quotations from the commentary and the ideas of the poem and may be encouraged to explore the subject. Comparison in detail is here not possible or necessary. One will realize the vital importance of the Word of God, the Word free from erroneous doctrines and man's inventions. The Protestant believed that Christ and His Word, enlightened by the Holy Spirit, would defeat the Devil, the Prince of this World. Before all things one must love and obey

144

God, whose grace and mercy are the fountains of peace and felicity and who alone bestows true understanding and wisdom. No duty or love can be preferred to God's service. Man's reason must be enlightened by divine reason. When concupiscence and wicked affections overcome reason, man is like unto the beasts. "All naturall affections must give place to Gods honour." That Adam should be guided by reason and not give place to his affections—this is the essence of Raphael's instruction. This is the heart of Milton's doctrine. Generally speaking, it may be said that the commentary and the poem emphasize obedience, faith, devotion to spiritual truth. The commentary stresses the conflict between the world and the spirit. "Those things which are contemptible to the world, are esteemed and preferred of God: and those things which the world preferreth, God abhorreth" (John 1:46). The commentary declares, "To live in the flesh, is to live in this brittle body till we be called to live everlastingly: but to live according to the flesh, or to be in the flesh, signifie to be destitute of the Spirit, and to be plunged in the filthie concupiscences of the flesh" (Phil. 1:22). The ideal Christian life is one in complete harmony with the will of God: "Then is a man fully sanctified and perfect, when his minde thinketh nothing, his soule, that is his understanding, and will, covet nothing, neither his body doth execute any thing contrary to the will of God" (I Thess. 5:23). After their fall Adam and Eve were for some time subject to the filthy concupiscences of the flesh, and the race of man was cursed by their sin. Ultimately they made their peace with God and strove to live in harmony with his will.

The antithesis of God's kingdom is, of course, the kingdom of Satan, the embodiment or incarnation of all evil, of the flesh and the world. It is established in pride; it is based on greed, craft, ambition,—on all the lusts of the flesh. It is the kingdom of Antichrist, of the "Romish prelates & marchants of soules," whose dumb ceremonies and sacraments true Protestants abhorred.[9]

Judge their penance, pilgrimages, pardons, purgatory, praying to posts, dumb blessings, dumb absolutions, their dumb pattering, and howling, their dumb strange holy gestures, with all their dumb disguisings, their satisfactions and justifyings. . . . Mark at last the practice of our fleshly spirituality and their ways, by which they have walked above eight hundred years; how they stablish their lies, first, with falsifying scripture; then

---

[9] William Tyndale, *An Answer to Sir Thomas More's Dialogue,* . . . ed. for the Parker Society by the Rev. Henry Walter (Cambridge, 1850), p. 9.

through corrupting with their riches, whereof they have infinite treasure in store; and last of all, with the sword.

In the fullness of time this kingdom of evil will be destroyed and Christ will reign over all—but in the meantime it was the duty of every wayfaring Christian to fight the good fight, to keep the faith, to walk humbly before God.

This conflict of good and evil is, of course, not merely Protestant. It is the essence of the Christian religion. But as the conflict is presented in the Geneva Bible and in *Paradise Lost* there is an unmistakable Protestant spirit, a quality of intense sincerity, an almost intimate relationship between the individual and God, a devout longing to serve God's will, a yearning for holiness. The ideal of perfect obedience and complete consecration is expressed in the prayer containing "the duetie of every Christian" in the Geneva Bible:

Poure upon me (O Lorde) thy holy spirite of wisedome and grace: Governe and lead me by thy holie worde, that it may be a lanterne unto my feete, & a light unto my steppes. Shew thy mercie upon me, & so lighten the natural blindnesse and darkness of my heart through thy grace, that I may daily be renewed by the same spirite and grace: By the which (O Lorde) purge the grossenesse of my hearing & understanding, that I may profitably reade, heare, and understand thy word and heavenly wil, beleeve, and practise the same in my life and conversation, and evermore hold fast the blessed hope of everlasting life. . . . And forasmuch as in this world I must alwaies be at warre and strife, not with one sort of enemies, but with an infinite nombre, not onely with flesh and bloud, but with the Divell which is the Prince of darkenesse, & with wicked men executors of his most damnable will: grant mee therefore thy grace, that being armed with thy defence, I may stand in this battell with an invincible constancie against all corruption, which I am compassed with on every side, until such time as having ended the combate, which during this life I must sustaine, in the end I may attaine to thy heavenly rest, which is prepared for me and all thine elect, through Christ our Lord and onely saviour. Amen.

In the directness and obvious sincerity of the plea, in the avowal of man's spiritual blindness and impotence, in the trust in God's Word and the willingness to obey it implicitly, and especially in the conception of life as a never ending mortal conflict with evil, with wicked spirits and wicked men,—in all this and more we find, I believe, a true expression of the real Protestant character, which, as Michael says, is not satisfied by a religion of "outward Rites and specious formes" (XII, 534), which would "never swarve from the trueth taught in holy scripture" but would love the Word fervently, read it diligently, understand it truly, and live it effectually, which would be "truly religious without hypocrisie, lowly in heart without faining, faithful . . . without deceit," serving God in spirit and in truth. For Milton, as we know from *Paradise Lost,* true religion rests upon the individual conscience illuminated by the Holy Spirit, by truth and grace. In religion there is no place for the forms and ceremonies imposed by carnal power:

> for on Earth
> Who against Faith and Conscience can be heard
> Infallible?   (XII, 528–30)

Truth is free to all believers, to every Christian, "built by Faith to stand,/Thir own Faith not anothers" (XII, 527–28). Firm in this living faith and fearing no foe with God at hand to bless, the faithful Christian would go on, conquering and to conquer, withstanding all the assaults of evil, and like Christ vanquishing "sinne, death, the world, the divel, and all the kingdom of hell." With the hope of attaining a spiritual paradise founded upon obedience, wisdom, patience, temperance, and love, "the soul/Of all the rest," it is in this faith that Adam and Eve left Paradise and hand in hand "Through *Eden* took their solitarie way."

It would, of course, not be difficult to find in other Protestant works material that would illustrate and illuminate passages in *Paradise Lost.* One might take, for example, the famous lines describing the worship of Moloch and Chemos:

> First *Moloch,* horrid King besmear'd with blood
> Of human sacrifice, and parents tears,
>
> .   .   .   .
> . . . the wisest heart
> Of *Solomon* he led by fraud to build
> His Temple right against the Temple of God
> On that opprobious Hill, and made his Grove
> The pleasant Vally of *Hinnom, Tophet* thence
> And black *Gehenna* call'd, the Type of Hell.
> Next *Chemos,* th' obscene dread of *Moabs* Sons,
>
> .   .   .   .
> *Peor* his other Name, when he entic'd
> *Israel* in *Sittim* on their march from *Nile*
> To do him wanton rites, which cost them woe.
> Yet thence his lustful Orgies he enlarg'd
> Even to that Hill of scandal, by the Grove

> Of *Moloch* homicide, lust hard by hate;
> Till good *Josiah* drove them thence to Hell.   (I, 392–18)

For comparison here is Coverdale's account of "good *Josiah*," whom he associates with Henry VIII as a reformer and destroyer of idolatry. Coverdale has just said that "blindness" came into the world only because "the light of God's Word" was extinct.[10]

How could men, I say, have been so far from the true service of God and from the due obedience of their prince, had not the law of God been clean shut up, depressed, cast aside, and put out of remembrance? as it was afore the time of that noble king Josias, and as it hath been also among us unto your grace's time, by whose most righteous administration, through the merciful goodness of God, it is now found again, as it was in the days of that most virtuous king Josias.

Coverdale goes on to declare that he may righteously compare the King of England to "that noble and gracious king, that lantern of light among princes, that fervent protector and defender of the laws of God," who commanded that the law of God should be read and taught unto all the people, who "destroyed idolatry and false idols; put down all evil customs and abusions; set up the true honour of God." He exclaims, "O what felicity was among the people of Jerusalem in his days!"

It is plain that Protestants held Josiah in high esteem as a reformer and a destroyer of idolatry and that idolatry in Palestine implied popish idolatry. After reading Coverdale, who would fail to see in Milton's lines a hint of this double meaning of idolatry? Would not idolatry in Palestine suggest to Milton's Protestant readers the idolatry near at hand, perhaps in the Church itself? Corrupted by errors and lies, the greater part of mankind had forsaken their Creator, and their gay religions were "full of Pomp and Gold." Opposed to all this idolatry stood Joshua, "a true defender of the faith": he put down "the houses of idolatry"; he maintained the laws of God; he rooted out wickedness.

One might also recall Coverdale's description of the pains of hell, which in the Holy Scriptures are, he says, suggested by "outward and corporal things." Coverdale writes of "the outward darkness," which suggests terrible sorrow and trouble, of the cold and the continual fire, of the "horror, mourning, weeping, and lamentation of the

[10] From his dedication of his translation of the Bible (1535), *Remains of Myles Coverdale*, ed. for the Parker Society by the Rev. George Pearson (Cambridge, 1846), p. 9.

damned." Isaiah says that hell is in the depth and is "deep and wide." Whoever sinks into it "shall come no more thereout." It is great and wide enough; "for touching wideness, it shall be able to hold all damned persons." Here in "great thick and perpetual darkness" the ungodly shall suffer eternal pain and damnation. Here in the company of most foul spirits, in confusion and loathsome and great torments "they shall all burn together for eternity." Here the Lord's breath, as a river of brimstone, "doth kindle, and as a bellows blow the fire, quickening it, and ever renewing it to burn evermore."[11] This is of course not exactly Milton's hell, but it is composed of some of the same elements; and it is horrible—in a sense more horrible than Milton's for here human beings suffer eternal torments.

Students know that in *Paradise Lost*, the Protestant epic, there is no purgatory. Do they know why Protestants rejected purgatory? The theological reasons for the rejection are stated clearly and briefly by Archbishop Sandys, in a sermon "Made in Paul's" on the text from Job 14:14: "All the days of this my warfare do I wait, till my changing come." Preaching on the customs and causes of funerals and declaring that death "bringeth with it our particular judgment," the good Archbishop admonished his audience: "let us live as we will die, and die as they that hope to rise again and live with Christ hereafter." He unequivocally declares: "After this life there is no help remaining to the dead: to the living, there is mercy offered, to the dead there remaineth only judgment." He then proceeds:[12]

Vain therefore and dangerous is the opinion of purgatory. Vain, because it hath no foundation at all in God's word. Moses, prescribing all kinds of sacrifices in the old law, maketh no mention of sacrificing or praying for the dead. Paul, instructing the Thessalonians what they ought to do in funerals, neither doth remember unto them sacrifice, nor prayer. Just Simeon never dreamed of purgatory, when he said, "Lord, now lettest thou thy servant depart in peace according to thy word." Small peace there is in purgatory, as papists report. It never came into St. Paul's mind when he said, "I desire to depart hence, and to be with Christ." It was not revealed to the angel when he said, "Blessed are the dead which die in the Lord: they rest from their labours." There is no rest but intolerable pain imagined in purgatory,

---

[11] "Hope of the Faithful," *Remains of Myles Coverdale*, pp. 206–207. Of the numerous recent studies of Milton's hell, Joseph E. Duncan's ("Milton's Four-in-One Hell," *The Huntington Library Quarterly*, XX [February, 1957], 127–36) is the most unpretentious and enlightening. Incidentally, Duncan demolishes the strictures of Eliot, Waldock, and Leavis.

[12] *The Sermons of Edwin Sandys . . . Archbishop of York*, ed. for the Parker Society by the Rev. John Ayre (Cambridge, 1842), pp. 162–63.

even to them which die in the Lord. Neither Lazarus, nor the rich man, were acquainted with it: the one was immediately carried into heaven, the other cast into hell. He which said to the thief, "This day thou shalt be with me in paradise," knew only two ways, the strait way to heaven, the broad way to hell: he who knew all things, was ignorant of this third way: for there is no such way to know. This opinion is perilous. The hope of help in purgatory hath sent many deceived souls into hell. This opinion is injurious to the blood of Christ. For if any sin remain to be purged by these after-pains, then the "blood of Christ doth" not "cleanse us from all sin;" and then we make God a liar. It destroyeth repentance; without which there is no remission of sins here. . . . There cometh nothing to the spirits of them that be dead, but that which they wrought while they were alive. "Work thou righteousness before thy death:" for in the grave it is too late.

"We lay," the Archbishop declared in another sermon, "no one stone but only upon the foundation of the prophets and apostles, whereupon whoever is builded, groweth into an holy temple of the Lord—a temple, which no wind, no waves, no storm, no tempest is able to overthrow. The foundation of our religion is the written word, the scriptures of God, the undoubted records of the Holy Ghost." This is the basic doctrine of Protestants, including Milton, who insists that Christian doctrine is derived, not from the schools of philosophers nor from the laws of man, "but from the Holy Scriptures alone, under the guidance of the Holy Spirit." In the epic Michael declares that the truth is "Left onely in those written Records pure,/Though not but by the Spirit understood" (XII, 513–14).

Protestant veneration of Scripture and rejection of Roman Catholic practices based on traditions are effectively and eloquently stated by Archbishop Sandys in another sermon "Made in Paul's, on the Day of Christ's Nativity," on the text from Isaiah 55:1–3. The Archbishop said:[13]

The scriptures have prescribed an holy communion: they upon their foundation have reared a blasphemous mass. The scripture maketh baptism the consecrated seal of man's salvation; they upon their foundation have builded the baptism of bells and ships. The scripture saith, Christ was offered up but once: they upon their foundation have erected an altar, whereupon he is daily offered up. The scripture will have the scriptures to be read of all men, prayer to be made with understanding, Christ to be a full satisfaction for sin, worship to be done unto God alone: they upon their foundation have builded a doctrine that forbiddeth God's people to

[13] *Ibid.*, pp. 19–20.

read his word, that teacheth them to pour out their prayer in a tongue which they cannot understand, that hath found out a way to satisfy the wrath of Almighty God in this life by penance, and after this life by endurance in purgatory; a doctrine that commandeth them to call upon saints and souls departed, to worship the work of their own hands, to say to a piece of bread, "My Lord and my God." If these doctrines of theirs did not contain, as they do, most manifest impiety, yet all religion builded upon such grounds must needs be vain and frivolous. For, although we offer up never so many sacrifices; though we keep all the days in the year holy; though we pray, and give thanks, and do alms; yet, except we know that herein we shew obedience to the laws and statutes of our God, we do but tire ourselves in vain. . . . Doubtless they worship him but in vain, which either teach or practice the precepts of men for the laws of God.

With this Protestant doctrine, here so tersely and comprehensively stated, Milton must have been in complete agreement, as might be demonstrated by quotations from *The Christian Doctrine* and the epic—but this proof is hardly necessary. Certainly the basic doctrine stated in another paragraph of this sermon was Milton's also:[14]

This grace of God which saveth, hath appeared to *all men*: this heavenly food, Christ Jesus, by preaching the gospel is *offered to all,* as manna the heavenly bread, by faith to feed upon; and as a lively fountain to drink of to everlasting life. *All are of mercy, grace, and favour freely called; all may come and freely feed, without penny or penny-worth. The grace of God is free—freely granted, freely given without money.* "The price of our redemption is neither gold nor silver: *Through grace ye are freely saved.*" For "it cannot be grace any way, which is not *every way free,*" saith St Augustine.

Christ offers his heavenly treasures, "remission of sins, justification, sanctification, mercy, grace, and salvation, freely." Milton could scarcely be more definite and emphatic. In *The Christian Doctrine* he declares that God rejects "none but the disobedient and unbelieving" and that "he undoubtedly gives grace to all, if not in equal measure, at least sufficient for attaining knowledge of the truth and final salvation." In the epic it is God's will that after the Fall man should find grace, which through Christ

to all
Comes unprevented, unimplor'd, unsought,
Happie for man, so coming; he her aide
Can never seek, once dead in sins and lost.   (III, 230–33)

and God decrees:

14 *Ibid.,* p. 11. Italics added.

> Man shall not quite be lost, but sav'd who will,
> Yet not of will in him, but grace in me
> Freely voutsaft.   (III, 173–75)

It is to God that fallen man owes "All his deliv'rance, and to none but me." The Archbishop puts it simply and beautifully, with less emphasis on the power and magnanimity of God,

Christ is the fresh fountain, whereof whoso drinketh shall never thirst. Christ is that bread which descended from heaven. He that eateth that bread, which is his flesh, shall live for ever. Christ is that wine which maketh merry the heart of man, and quieteth the troubled conscience. Christ is that milk which nourisheth and feedeth us, that we may grow to a perfect man . . . "Come all that are thirsty." God's mercy is great and general; he hath no partial respect unto any person. . . . He calleth Jew and Gentile, young and aged, rich and needy, bond and free, man and woman . . . Christ himself crieth, in general words, "Come to me all that labour." Be thy sins never so great, fear not to come; for he that calleth thee hath stretched out his arms of mercy at length; they are wide open to embrace thee: mercy is ready to all that will receive it; and to them that need it most, most ready. A comfortable lesson to all sinners.

One is left, I fear, with the distinct impression that the Archbishop's God is less conscious of man's sin than is Milton's, that He is somewhat more merciful and that His grace is just as free.

As a matter of fact, the Archbishop and the poet agree in their view of human nature, as one might expect. Sandys said:

Wherefore, touching ourselves, we teach with the blessed apostles and prophets, "that by nature we are the children of wrath;" that corruption is bred and settled within our bones; that we are both born and begotten in it; that with it all the powers and faculties of our nature are infected; that still it cleaveth fast unto our souls, and, although the deadly sting be taken from it, yet there it sticketh as long as life doth endure, so irksome and so grievous, that it forceth the most upright and perfect to cry, "Miserable man, who shall deliver me?"

Milton's opinion, conventional and theologically correct, is that by Adam's sin man's nature is corrupted and that there is a "general depravity" of the human mind. "All have committed sin in Adam; therefore all are born servants of sin." Milton assures us that "some remnants of the divine image still exist in us, not wholly extinguished by this spiritual death," and that the liberty of the will is not wholly destroyed. Although not wholly inefficient in respect of good works, or at any rate of good endeavors, at least "after the grace of God has

152

called us," the power of the will is "so small and insignificant, as merely to deprive us of all excuse for inaction, without affording any subject of boasting." In the epic, man's state after the Fall is too well known to need rehearsal here. According to the Archbishop, man's will is quite corrupt and impotent. "By this inbred corruption our understanding is so darkened, that naturally we cannot perceive the things that are of God; . . . our will is in such thraldom and slavery unto sin, that it cannot like of any thing spiritual and heavenly, but is wholly carried unto fleshly desires." Therefore, he concludes, we acknowledge willingly and unfeignedly that the good we do is His, not ours; "our beginning to do, and our continuance in doing well, proceedeth only and wholly from him." He declares, "We neither rise when we are fallen, nor stand when we are risen, by our own strength." Milton had somewhat more faith in human nature. He would not say with the Archbishop, "The loathsomest things that can be imagined, the clothes that be most unclean, are not so foul as our very righteousness is unrighteous." But he might say that whatsoever we receive by way of reward at God's hand, either in this life or in the life to come, we receive "as a thing freely given by him, without any merit or desert of ours." Thus, being "naked and utterly destitute" in ourselves, we seek all things in Christ Jesus, who is "our wisdom, our sanctification, our justification, our priest, our sacrifice, our king, our head, our mediator, our physician, our way, our truth, our life."[15]

One point more in this connection. According to the Archbishop, the church of Rome will not acknowledge man's poverty and nakedness, the filthy garments of corruption and sin "wherein Adam hath wrapped his posterity." In the pride of their hearts they dissemble and make light of this; "they pare and lessen this corruption." On the other hand, they brag "of the freedom of their will; as if sin had not utterly bereaved us thereof." They declare that men are not violently drawn to good or evil. The Archbishop replies that we do not say that the freedom of the will is taken away by the eternal decree of God:[16]

but this we say, and all that have the truth do say the same—that the will of man, being free unto natural and civil actions, hath of itself no freedom to desire things heavenly and spiritual; not because the eternal purpose, but because the corruption of our nature, hath addicted us only to evil. We

[15] The doctrine of the total depravity of the world and the radical antithesis of nature and grace is now said to be a perversion of Scripture. (Charles E. Raven, *Natural Religion and Christian Theology*. The Gifford Lectures 1951. First Series: *Science and Religion* (Cambridge, 1953), pp. 21 ff.).
[16] *Ibid.*, p. 24.

do not teach, or ever did, that any man is the servant either of sin or of righteousness by constraint; for whether we obey the one unto death and condemnation, or unto life and salvation the other, our obedience is always voluntary; it is not wrested from us against our wills. But the question being, how we are made willing unto that which is good, this is the difference between our answer and theirs: We say, only by the grace of God; they say, partly by grace, but principally by the power and strength of their own nature.

This is "to make nature the principal cause of our well being." But the truth is that "without the special motion of God's Spirit, and that in every particular action," we are not able to walk in the ways which God commanded. Without the help of the Spirit we "drag and are not able of ourselves to set one foot before another." But "these men," little considering "of what frail metal" they are made and not perceiving how sin hath weakened the faculties of the soul, "vaunt of freedom, of strength, of inward power, and make their own will the chiefest cause of their well doing."

On this important point it is helpful to have the views of a leading Protestant. Some students may see more clearly than before the difference between the Reformers and the church of Rome. In this setting some may understand more clearly Milton's doctrine of the limited freedom of the will. The essential point seems to be that the Reformers, the Protestants, emphasized true humility and that the church of Rome encouraged pride and trust in good works. Obviously Milton shares with Protestantism a genuine sense of humility, at least in this respect. Milton repudiated in religion and religious service the outward pomp and the forms which, as he thought, were false to Scripture and to the spirit of grace and truth, which were free.

Finally, I cannot resist quoting from another sermon—Archbishop Sandys' eloquent statement of the purpose or the mission of the Church. The tone of the whole is rather more sanguine than that of Milton throughout the epic, which no doubt reflected his sense of the failure of the Reformation whereas the Archbishop seemed supremely confident of its success.

Touching ourselves, as the mark which we shoot at is to set up the kingdom of Christ Jesus, a kingdom which is not of the world; so the means which herein we use are not worldly, but altogether heavenly and spiritual. What the proceedings of the gospel have been, ye are not ignorant: ye know very well, how without force, without cruelty, without treachery and deceit, without all wisdom of flesh and blood, in naked simplicity, in truth uncoloured, and, as the apostle speaketh, in foolishness of preaching, we have laboured to prepare you for one husband; to present you as a pure virgin to Christ, not outwardly arrayed in purple and scarlet, gilded with gold, precious stones, and pearl, like the strumpet that sitteth upon many waters; but, like the spouse of Solomon, glorious within, full of Christ, rich in faith and in good works, fulfilled with knowledge of his will in all wisdom and spiritual understanding, strengthened mightily in the inward man, rooted and grounded in sincere love, enabled to comprehend with all saints what is the breadth and length and depth and height of the love of Christ, strengthened with all patience and long-suffering, blessed with all spiritual blessings in heavenly things.

Milton would agree that such is the purpose and the end of true religion, but in his vision of the future he could see no hope of its realization in this world. The purpose of the last three books of the epic is, of course, to show the corruption of human nature and the dire consequences of Adam's original sin along with Christ's coming and the salvation of those who believe in Him and who inherit "that kingdom which he hath prepared for as many as are his." It is good news that Christ "hath delivered all his out of the captivity of Satan and sin, . . . out of that prison of Romish servitude." He has delivered us "from Egyptiacal servitude, that we may serve him henceforward in freedom of conscience." He has led us "out of a marvellous darkness into a marvellous light," by the star of his shining Gospel. Now that Christ "hath opened our blinded eyes, and hath poured understanding into our hearts," let us as the children of light "walk in the light honestly, as becometh men in so clear noon-day." This was the Archbishop's plea. Milton discovered that men willingly served Satan and loved darkness, that the world was "To good malignant, to bad men benigne," and that here Truth is crucified. Man will find a refuge only in the paradise within his own soul.

Except for the passages already noted and others that might be cited, such as the lines describing Satan's entrance into Paradise, "So clomb this first grand Thief into Gods Fould:/So since into his Church lewd Hirelings climbe"—except for these there is in *Paradise Lost* nothing that might be construed as an attack on Roman catholicism. There is nothing to match, for example, the directness of Tyndale's attack in the following passage:[17]

A proper similitude to describe our holy Father
And to see how our holy father came up, mark the ensample of an ivy

[17] "The Practice of Prelates," *Expositions and Notes on Sundry Portions of the Holy Scriptures, together with The Practice of Prelates,* ed. for the Parker Society by the Rev. Henry Walter (Cambridge, 1849), p. 270.

tree: first it springeth out of the earth, and then awhile creepeth along by the ground till it find a great tree. Then it joineth itself beneath alow unto the body of the tree, and creepeth up a little and a little, fair and softly. And at the beginning, while it is yet thin and small, that the burden is not perceived, it seemeth glorious to garnish the tree in winter, and to bear off the tempests of the weather. But in the mean season it thrusteth roots into the bark of the tree, to hold fast withal; and ceaseth not to climb up, till it be at the top and above all. And then it sendeth his branches along by the branches of the tree, and overgroweth all, and waxeth great, heavy, and thick; and sucketh the moisture so sore out of the tree and his branches, that it choaketh and stifleth them. And then the foul stinking ivy waxeth mighty in the stump of the tree, and becometh a seat and a nest for all unclean birds, and for blind owls, which hawk in the dark, and dare not come at the light.

"Even so," says Tyndale, "the bishop of Rome, now called the pope, at the beginning crope along upon the earth," and even so he crept up and "fastened his roots into the heart of the emperor" and "with his sword clamb up above all his fellow-bishops" and finally by subtlety and guile "he clamb above the emperor, and made him stoop unto his feet and kiss them another while." I am, of course, not suggesting that Milton should have attempted to rival this denunciation of the pope by a master of English prose, who is at heart a poet. Milton was wise to exclude from his epic such direct denunciation, which would have in a sense degraded his poem or at least limited it, depriving it of its universal and permanent significance. What a shock it would be to come across in the epic such material as this in Tyndale:

And thus the pope, the father of all hypocrites, hath with falsehood and guile perverted the order of the world, and turned the roots of the trees upward, and hath put down the kingdom of Christ, and set up the kingdom of the devil, whose vicar he is; and hath put down the ministers of Christ, and hath set up the ministers of Satan, disguised yet in names and garments like unto the angels of light.

As a true poet Milton might imply but could not state specifically such ideas. Satan and his angels embody all evil; they are rebels against the divine order. Satan is not merely Antichrist or an agent of Roman catholicism. He is the incarnation of pride and ambition. In the evil to which he dedicates himself, "Evil be thou my good," all evils of whatever description are comprehended.

In view of the evidence, it would be foolish to maintain—and of course I do not maintain—that a single work, even such an important

156

work as the Geneva Bible, exerted directly a decisive influence upon a poem composed of many elements, an epic which Hanford calls a "repository of theological, moral, and political doctrine" but which may more properly be described as an artistic synthesis of varied material. I have not the slightest intention of placing limits upon the range of Milton's reading and learning. The Geneva Bible is not to be thought of as a source of *Paradise Lost* but rather as an important and influential and authoritative Protestant commentary on Scripture. It has been admitted that the poem and this Bible differ on one point of doctrine: *Paradise Lost* is Arminian, the Geneva Bible is Calvinistic. Milton asserts the principle of the freedom of the human will and emphasizes the moral responsibility of the individual. As a rule Milton voices orthodox Protestant doctrines, which are succinctly stated in the commentary of the Geneva Bible—the Bible which for many years was "the household Bible of the English-speaking nations" and which must have had an incalculable influence in spreading Protestant thought. Born and bred a Protestant, albeit an enlightened and cultured one, Milton inevitably and with conviction presented the Protestant code or pattern of religion based upon Scripture. His purpose, the assertion of God's power and providence and the justification of His ways, has a Protestant character: the vindication of God, the loathing of sin, and the love of righteousness.[18] It is at least possible that the Geneva Bible played an important part in fostering the spirit and the character, the climate of religious opinion, which shaped Milton's life and attained full poetic flowering in *Paradise Lost.*

The reader may consider this issue as it is expressed in the later books of the poem. Fallen but not irretrievably lost, environed by evil but sustained and enlightened by the Word of God, man with faith, humility, and obedience to God must stand steadfast in the never ending battle against sin. Subduing carnal lusts and base affections, he must serve God in holiness and truth, with assurance

> that suffering for Truths sake
> Is fortitude to highest victorie,
> And to the faithful Death the Gate of life.　(XII, 569–71)

This is the Protestant ideal. It has been observed that contrast, be-

---

[18] Some think that "in terms of human morality or even of human reason" any such justification is meaningless and unconvincing; for the nature of things is profoundly inequitable. See Aldous Huxley, "Grace, Predestination and Salvation," *The Hibbert Journal,* L (July, 1952), 359–64.

tween hell and heaven for example, is a fundamental aspect of the method of the poem.[19] The crucial contrast, between the state of Adam and Eve before and after the Fall, turns on their failure to obey reason and God, to live up to the Protestant standard or ideal. They were overcome by carnal affections and ruined by disobedience. Part of the commentary on Job 3:11 is pertinent: "when man giveth place to his passions, hee is not able to stay or keepe measure, but runneth headlong into all evil, except God call him backe." Having sinned against God, man can only hope to be reconciled to God through Christ and to serve Him, adding to knowledge faith

> Vertue, Patience, Temperance, . . . Love,
> By name to come call'd Charitie, the soul
> Of all the rest.

This is the Christian ideal, and it was Milton's ideal. In spite of grievous disappointments and afflictions he was sustained by a strong and disciplined faith, the faith that by his own efforts and by God's mercy and grace man might be righteous. In him there was no despair, no surrender. This is an ideal far too lofty for mortals to achieve, but it is one that might create a new heaven and a new earth "Founded in righteousness and peace and love,/To bring forth fruits Joy and eternal Bliss" (XII, 550–51). Milton's mature religion was not "attached to and partly dependent upon dreams of a new age, but founded only upon God and the soul of individual man."[20] Actually the new order of which Milton dreamed, in his apocalyptic vision, was to be established not in time but in eternity. Milton the aggressive and sanguine reformer had been disillusioned; he had arrived at the realization not only that "in His will is our peace" but also that the kingdom of Christ is not of this world. This resignation, born of harsh experience, and this vision of a new kingdom of righteousness and peace and love, born of faith, was for Milton, as it may have been for many of his devout contemporaries, the sum of wisdom.

It seems vain to declare, as Bush apparently does, that this wisdom is accepted today as valid truth. Many intelligent readers reject the sacred story even as a basis for spiritual doctrine, though some of the ethical doctrine may be salvaged. Many do not now believe the orthodox dogmas of original sin, divine mediation, and spiritual re-

[19] Milton Miller, "*Paradise Lost:* the Double Standard," *The University of Toronto Quarterly*, XX (January, 1951), 186 ff.; and, in part, Merritt Y. Hughes, "Myself Am Hell," *Modern Philology*, LIV (November, 1956), 80–94.
[20] Douglas Bush, *Paradise Lost in Our Time* (New York, 1948), p. 55.

demption through divine power. Many rely upon their own intelligence and natural talents which may be trained to find rational solutions for their problems. Although the old faith is still professed in churches and by some individuals, it is ignored in daily life, in trade, in business, in the professions, in politics, where it may sometimes be paid a revolting kind of lip service. The "typical academic man," that is, the typical don, is, we are told, "an unbeliever," for only the unbeliever has "that undistracted zeal for knowledge which is the heart of academic virtue."[21] Though outwardly, formally, and strenuously religious, our age is in truth profoundly skeptical. Even Tennyson's vague faith "that good shall fall/At last—far off—at last, to all" is foreign to the modern temper.

It has been said that the "liberal and humanitarian ideals that inspired the civilization of the last two centuries" are dead or dying, that the "process of secularization" has worked itself out and can go no further. It is confidently asserted that, on the other hand, the real forces that rule the world are spiritual and that Christianity as the hope of the world is "ripe for renewal."[22] It is urged that we must turn from "the emptiness of modern civilization and progress to the vision of spiritual reality which stands all the time looking down on our ephemeral activities like the snow mountains above the jazz and gigolos of a jerry-built hotel." Before World War II we were assured that the Christian tradition contains "an infinite depth of resources" but that these possibilities can only be realized and actualized in a Christian culture "by the dynamic activity of individual Christians." In its emphasis on the responsibility of the individual to be the agent in the vitalizing and diffusion of Christian culture this vision of a potential spiritual renaissance supplements the fundamental principle of Milton, the center of whose theology was the soul's relation and obligation to God. The spirit of grace, as Michael says, is free, and the spiritual life of every Christian is sacred and inviolable:

> for on Earth
> Who against Faith and Conscience can be heard
> Infallible?

Though political leaders find it expedient to profess their devotion

[21] Austin Farrer, "The Queen of Sciences," *The Twentieth Century*, CLVII (June, 1955), 491.

[22] Christopher Dawson, *Religion and the Modern State* (New York, 1938), pp. 152 ff.

to Christian principles, religion and politics are divorced in the modern state.[23] Apart from democratic theory and demagoguery, the average citizen is politically incompetent or impotent. The enlightenment and government of the people, by the people, and for the people have brought only frustration and disillusionment.

The people have been raised to a level of bare literacy which exposes them to the new techniques of mass appeal. Minds are debauched rather than informed, and unscrupulous propaganda has outrun education. The events of recent years have given new force to the Miltonic concept of humanity's ordeal:

> "And Man there placed, with purpose to assay
> If him by force he can destroy, or, worse,
> By some false guile pervert."[24]

Puritanism, which stressed the natural sinfulness and corruption of man after the Fall, seems thus to have a surer basis in fact and to be more realistic than democracy, which tends to emphasize and idealize man's inherent wisdom and virtue. Both Puritanism and democracy are, however, in some degree allied, for both are individualistic in theory and both affirm the Christian code of justice, compassion, and personal dignity.

Intelligent and sensitive minds cannot but be repelled and dismayed by the vulgarity, the materialism, the cynicism, and the hypocrisy which pervade vast areas of public and private life. To this state the "progress" of two hundred and fifty years has brought us—an epoch in which "the ideal of a merely and negatively secular and irreligious way of life has been more sedulously cultivated, than perhaps in any other known to history."[25] This is the perfect flowering of the cultivation of empirical, experimental science and of the cult of nationalism, which began in the Renaissance; of the development of a new theological system or structure "in which biblical theology became in effect the whole of theology," for which the Reformation is responsible; and of the worship of rationalism, which is "a typically eighteenth-century product."[26] This is the modern era of enlightenment, with barbarism and superstition finally discarded and man's

---

[23] This is, of course, not a recent development. It began in the sixteenth century if not before, and Machiavelli was "an observer rather than a pioneer, a symptom more than a cause." See T. M. Parker, *Christianity and the State in the Light of History*. The Bampton Lectures (London, 1955), pp. 144 ff.

[24] Ralph Barton Perry, *Puritanism and Democracy* (New York, 1944), p. 621.

[25] J. V. Langmead Casserley, *The Retreat from Christianity in the Modern World* (London, 1952), p. 8. Hereafter cited as *The Retreat from Christianity*.

[26] *Ibid.*, pp. 10–11.

reason finally enthroned. This is the day of miracles in medicine and surgery, of electronic marvels, of "Speed, to describe whose swiftness Number failes." This is the age of science, of the new idolatry,—and of the atomic and hydrogen bombs and guided missiles with all their thrilling possibilities. In our very time the intellectual sophistication, the "confident and complacent rationalism of the eighteenth century" has obviously attained its logical development and complete consummation.

For the maladies and miseries of our age I would not presume to suggest a cure. It might be insinuated that the quest of the atheist humanist for a kingdom without God, a kingdom in which he will attain physical and metaphysical liberty and satisfaction, is doomed to frustration. It might be realized that the divorce between religion and philosophy turns philosophy into an abstruse irrelevance and religion into an incoherent and irrational cult. It should be obvious that bourgeois Christianity, with its blend of crazy sectarianism, unbridled enthusiasm, and dull conformity, is on the whole a disaster and a disgrace to Christianity. It had better be understood that science by definition, aim, and practice repudiates human values and does not present and can never present a true picture of reality.[27] It should not be necessary to say that true Christianity stands not for the impoverishment of man and his enslavement to the Deity but rather for man's moral health, harmonious development, and spiritual welfare. It should be obvious that the religious spirit in man will inevitably find expression in some channel and that the only remedy for bad religion is good religion. Finally it cannot be denied that evil is one of the plainest and most incontestable of realities. Evil cannot be localized in one individual or one group or one race or one nation and certainly not in the nature or the stars of our political enemies, though that is the sole purpose of the current mythology. Evil is in ourselves. In the consciousness of the reality and the universality of evil, some religious thinkers discover a "tremendous opportunity" to restate prophetically the orthodox concept of original sin and to reassert the doctrine that "ours is a world which cries out, not merely for relatively futile and pettifogging reforms, but for all that the word 'redemption' once meant and must mean again."

It is clear that Christianity, the product of a remote and simple society and age, is in retreat. It has of course never been actually practiced except by rare individuals and groups, and it has never

[27] For some of these ideas and even their phrasing I am indebted to Casserley's invaluable *The Retreat from Christianity.*

dominated secular life. The medieval period, which seems to romantically-minded modern men to have been an "age of faith," was not so. Medieval writers themselves were for the most part "haunted by a consciousness of spiritual crisis, of being surrounded everywhere by lurking dangers and threats to the integrity of an insecure Christianity."[28] They thought that they were threatened by "the subtle and sinister seeping of manichean heresies into the hidden lives of the common people," by the secret survival of Germanic and Mediterranean paganism, by the challenge of Islam and Judaism, by the materialism and immoralism of the new universities, by the rise of sects within the church itself. During the dark and early Middle Ages Christianity failed to live up to its "posthumous reputation" as the great age of faith. The retreat from Christianity into systems of total irreligion seems now to have run its course. The retreat from Christianity into religion may be still more terrible and menacing, because it revives superstitions and mythologies and gives "new life to paganisms and idolatries" which recklessly sacrifice human life and energy. The new idolatry may be refined and intellectualized. We normally think of idols as visible objects painted on canvas, carved in wood and stone, cast in molten metal. But there is a more sophisticated form of idolatry:[29]

Philosophers may construct a god out of a set of concepts, and holy and wise religious teachers may piece together an object of worship out of a few spiritual experiences and ethical refinements. The laziest form of idolatry does not bother to create any idol at all, but simply turns to some finite and secular reality, some facet of the drama of everyday existence, and treats it as though it had the supremacy of God—nation, class or party, family, business or profession, even oneself, any one of these may function as a god. All of them, indeed, frequently do.

This kind of idolatry, to which our age is addicted, is especially repulsive when it wears Christianity as a mask to conceal its real nature, its essential secularism.

Although there is undeniably abundant and vigorous religious activity, there is today, I am sorry to say, not much evidence of a genuine renaissance of Christianity. As Arnold, in his melancholy *Dover Beach* long ago observed, the sea of faith is still receding, retreating

> to the breath
> Of the night-wind, down the vast edges drear
> And naked shingles of the world.

[28] *Ibid.*, p. 2.   [29] *Ibid.*, p. 7.

There seems to be less emphasis upon the theological or Christian virtues, faith, hope, charity. Truth has lost something of its supernatural and dogmatic character which it had derived mainly from the infallible Church and the infallible Book. The infallible Church, which claims obedience as a divine institution, has, it is said, a detestable political record; the infallible Book has, it is said, no longer any adherents except in the Protestant underworld and in American fundamentalism.[30] Of course, no one can predict how much of the supernatural, how much of traditional theology will survive in the religion of the future. The religion of Christ, broadly interpreted, may serve as a bridge from "the world of things to the world of values, from time to eternity, from appearance to reality." There is always a challenge and the possibility of a renaissance. In the words of William Temple, late Archibishop of Canterbury:[31]

In every generation, but in a very peculiar sense in ours, the question has to be answered, What is to be built? There have been few moments in the history of mankind when the issue has been so naked as it is in ours. Which city is to be built? Babylon the Great, which has tumbled down so often, and will always tumble down again, or the City which you cannot build yourselves, but which God can build through you, if unitedly you give yourselves to be used by Him as its builders? . . .

And, remember, the supreme wonder of the history of the Christian Church is that always in the moments when it has seemed most dead, out of its own body there has sprung up new life; so that in age after age it has renewed itself, and age after age by its renewal has carried the world forward into new stages of progress, as it will do for us in our day, if only we give ourselves in devotion to its Lord and take our place in its service.

The message of our poet is, of course, fused with the Christian theology and the scriptural fable of his epic. As the years pass the theology and the story seem to recede into the realm of myth, a myth interesting and significant but quaint and alien to the modern temper. Even now the story of creation, of Paradise, and the Fall can only be regarded as a piece of primitive folklore which the theologians made the basis of the dominant Western cult with Christ, the Mediator and Saviour, at the heart of its potent mystery. The ethical principles which Christ taught surely contain a permanent core of truth. Some now speak bluntly of the "demise" of Milton's ideas. "Milton's ideas and some of the feelings which go with them cannot be inter-

---

[30] William Ralph Inge, "An Old Man Looks at the World," *The Hibbert Journal*, L (July, 1952), 388–89. This essay was first published in January, 1948.
[31] *Christian Faith and Life* (London, 1954), p. 131.

preted into modernity; they are dead," declares one critic with the greatest confidence.[32] With equal assurance others have insisted upon the permanence of the religious and ethical values of Milton's poetry. Milton is occupied, we are told, with the problem not of reforming society but of making individuals better; and he makes us better not merely through his imaginative and poetical beauties but through the total effect of his religious and ethical theme, through his profound concern with "man, the heart of man, and human life." Bush boldly proclaims the prime reason for reading Milton: "We need the shock of encountering a poet to whom good and evil are distinct realities, a poet who has a much-tried but invincible belief in a divine order and in man's heritage and responsibility, who sees in human life an eternal contest between irreligious pride and religious humility."[33] This seems to mean that Bush, like the cultured fundamentalist Lewis, demands that the reader accept the theology of the epic as well as the ethics: the "distinct realities" of good and evil, the "divine order," and man's divine heritage and responsibility as well as the "rational and philosophic conscience" which "links man with man and God." This is indeed a formidable assignment. The critical reader may reject the theology and the story of the Fall as what Santayana calls a "fanciful dramatic mythology" having no basis in the universe that we know. To demand the acceptance of the theology may be to erect a barrier between the intelligent reader and the poem. Some, trusting, perhaps too much, in their own reason and resenting the claim of God's sovereignty, may rebel against the Protestant theology of the epic, perhaps instinctively admiring the dynamic character of Satan though totally misconceiving his diabolic purpose and role. In fact the rationalists and the romantics here meet and join hands. Renaissance humanism, from which modern rationalism descends, abounds in jealous resentment of God's sovereignty, "a tendency which . . . finds expression in Milton's Satan, even in the midst of what is sincerely intended to be a Christian epic."[34] Of the attitude of the romantics Shelley is perhaps the best known example. This meeting of minds, the rationalist and the romantic, is passing strange.

We thus reach an impasse: the religious and the rationalistic minds cannot possibly agree in their views of *Paradise Lost.* Regarding the course of history, the epic, for example, presents the view of the

[32] Robert M. Adams, *Ikon: John Milton and the Modern Critics* (Ithaca, 1955), pp. 214 ff.

[33] Bush, *Paradise Lost in our Time*, pp. 27 ff.

[34] Casserley, *The Retreat from Christianity*, p. 31.

church, which has never held or encouraged the belief that this world is steadily improving. It was "only in the eighteenth century that Western Europe began to dream of an approaching millenium without miracle, to be gradually ushered in under the auspices of a faculty which was called Reason."[35] Rationalists apparently accept this view. They would reject Milton's interpretation of history. The Greeks, who prided themselves on being the degenerate descendants of the gods, put their Golden Age in the past. We, who take pride in being "the very creditable descendants of monkeys," put ours in the future or, in our more optimistic moments, in the present. "The law which we cannot escape," Dean Inge ironically says, "is the blessed law of progress—'that kind of improvement that can be measured by statistics.' We had only to thank our stars for placing us in such an environment, and to carry out energetically the course of development which Nature has prescribed for us, and to resist which would be at once impious and futile." Despite wars and taxes this is the faith of a smug America, enjoying a phenomenal prosperity, rich beyond the dreams of wealth, and at least nominally grateful to God for all its blessings. How can we doubt the bounty of God? How can we possibly accept the orthodox religious view of history? Thus, I think, runs the argument. Milton's view of history is wrong. The millenium is assured and may even now be dawning; for, as Herbert Spencer avowed, "Progress is not an accident but a necessity. What we call evil and immorality must disappear. It is certain that man must become perfect. . . . Always towards perfection is the mighty movement—towards a complete development and a more unmixed good."

The most cursory survey of events of the last four decades would discredit this absurd optimism, this gospel of inevitable movement toward perfection, this superstition of progress which has "invaded and vitiated our history, our political science, our philosophy, and our religion." The scientist's report of the nature and destiny of our species is quite different from that of these ostensibly democratic and rationalistic rhapsodists. We now know that the alleged law of progress has no scientific basis whatever. "Ancient civilisations were destroyed by imported barbarians; we breed our own." Realistic study should convince the most resolute and confirmed optimists that moral wrongs, human vices, and what used to be called sins can scarcely be corrected or cured by secular methods of reform, though modern

[35] William Ralph Inge, "The Idea of Progress," *Diary of a Dean* (New York, 1950), p. 192.

drugs and medical skill may often alleviate physical ills. Perhaps the world will at last realize that in the realm of the spirit true and undefiled religion is essential; that the Gospel contains universally valid truths; that, as Tyndale said more than four centuries ago, the Christian faith is "the mother of all truth" and the solid "rock" against which "no sin, no hell, no devil, no lies, no error can prevail"; that, in Niebuhr's words, Christ "is the savior, not of a selected band of saints, but of the world."

Thus even though the story of the Fall and the somewhat rigid or limited theology of *Paradise Lost* may be questioned or perhaps merely tolerated, something of lasting value may indeed survive. It may be inadequately and vaguely defined as a spirit of devotion to God and to the best ethical standard, a sort of code of spiritual values set in but not strictly limited by the frame of conventional orthodoxy, and essentially a moving appeal that man with God's grace should work out his own spiritual salvation. As God's advocate against man but for man's eternal welfare Milton presents in a noble poem a lofty ideal of obedience and righteousness which seems to be the essence of Protestant Christianity. Without this spiritual code, this standard of righteousness and obedience, this doctrine of faith in Christ as the Redeemer of sinful man, life would surely have been much more selfish, vicious, and cruel than it was, though there is much reason to doubt that we are now actually "more humane and more sympathetic or juster or less brutal than the ancients." For the Christianization of Western society—in so far as it has been Christianized—the Bible, the church, the faithful ministry, and unnumbered devout communicants should of course receive the largest share of credit. Upon life and conduct the impact of *Paradise Lost* was probably unappreciable. However, the poem was widely read, as the numerous editions show. Important now mainly as literature, the poem was the product of a flourishing Christian culture and more especially the work, almost the lifework, of a poet inspired by the Protestant Reformation and, to some extent, by the apparent failure of the Reformation. Its main appeal was to devout Christian readers, who doubtless missed some of its distinctive literary merits and some of the evidences of Milton's store of ripened learning but were nevertheless instructed and edified. We should, I am now convinced, not uncritically accept the statements and assumptions regarding the learning of Milton's audience: that, for example, many of his readers knew the work of Natale Conti, the greatest of Renaissance mythographers; that his audience was "familiar with the sophisticated notion of hell in pagan and Christian tradition"; that his readers were acquainted not only with the tradition of Christian thought but also with contemporary Christian mysticism, Stoic philosophy, and the demonology of Florentine Neo-Platonists.[36] There can be no doubt that some of Milton's readers were well-read; but the blithe assumption that they were as universally learned as are some of his modern critics, who are the professional voices of a kind of cumulative and composite erudition, seems simply preposterous. This assumption is based, I believe, upon a total misunderstanding of the nature and the qualifications of Milton's average audience and perhaps upon an equally serious misconception of the real character and purpose of Milton's poem, which is now sometimes the occasion for the scholar or critic to display his extensive learning. In fact erudition may be a definite encumbrance, and it may interfere with the genuine appreciation of the poem, which needs either devout readers or, at the very least, those who will consider with sympathy and understanding the Christian faith, the Christian doctrine, and the incalculable contributions of Christianity to civilization.

We live in a time of change, of chaos, and, as some think, a time of catastrophe. But there is reason to believe that the climate of Christian reality, as of Christ, is "a climate of catastrophe," in which the rhythm of eternity strikes athwart the mortal with an immortal music. Milton might have said:[37]

To sigh for the naive simplicities and harmony of Eden or Athens is an infantilism of the spirit; to foresee through storm the co-ordination of our contraries in Christ, that dawn beyond death, is the essential of Christian faith.

It is the law of the spirit and of life that only after suffering comes salvation, only after adversity joy, only after death life. We look forward to the ultimate day and the inexorable hour: "Venit summa dies et ineluctabile tempus." In art as in life we should look at things *sub specie aeternitatis*, living soberly, righteously, and humanely in this present world and awaiting in hope the fulfillment and the vindication of truth in eternity, which, as Dr. F. H. Brabant in his Bampton Lectures said, may in the truest sense be described as completeness and perfection.

Meanwhile, though we may at times be discouraged when we see the gate of Paradise "With dreadful Faces throng'd and fierie Armes,"

[36] Hughes, "Myself Am Hell," *Modern Philology*, LIV (November, 1956).
[37] M. Chaning-Pearce, *The Terrible Crystal: Studies in Kierkegaard and Modern Christianity* (London, 1940), p. 221.

we should be much more cheered with "meditation on the happie end." Our poet, bearing the relics and the proofs of his life and culture and that faith which survived all trial and tragedy, moves toward the heights, guided by a star, "the bright and morning star," which shines over the church of the Spirit and over all those who worship Him in Spirit and in Truth. No matter how the intellectual climate may change, no matter how violently the winds of literary criticism may blow in this age of "Tumult and Confusion all imbroild,/And Discord with a thousand various mouths," no matter how indifferent or apathetic or skeptical the public may be today,—it is reassuring to know that *Paradise Lost* survives, towering o'er the wrecks of time: a monument to the character and ideals of Protestantism; a memorable synthesis of religious and ethical truth; a poem to be read and cherished as one of the most inspired and perfect creations of Christian culture; a guide to that inner paradise which is no mythical land of dreams but a spiritual state more to be desired than all the riches and power of the world and all the knowledge of nature's works—a spiritual kingdom prophetic of that ideal kingdom founded upon righteousness and peace and love "To bring forth fruits Joy and eternal Bliss."

VI

The Pattern of Time and Eternity

O fleeting joys of paradise, dear bought with lasting woes!

It is futile to ignore or deny the fact that one who would understand and appreciate Milton's poetry must be prepared to overcome uncommon obstacles, which are partly due to the poet's learning but are more essentially related to the Biblical myth, the theological fabric, and in some degree the poet's religious philosophy—all of which are in some measure outmoded or obsolescent. These difficulties are not negligible. But they have been misrepresented or exaggerated by a group or crew of sophisticated and dogmatic critics who apparently have never made an honest effort to understand the poet or his thought. These condemn Milton as a bad artist if not a bad man, whose style is mere rhetoric, conventional and artificial, and whose principal work is just a monument to dead ideas. They even deny that Milton is a genuine religious poet and declare that as an exponent of the Christian spirit he cannot be ranked with Herbert or with Donne, who is their idol. For these smart modern critics Milton's poetry does not possess even that pathetic and melancholy charm evoked by architectural ruins, as, for example, the sandstone columns of the Temple of Juno in Agrigento, with their echoes of a vanished civilization.[1]

[1] Irwin Edman, *Philosopher's Holiday* (New York, 1938), p. 90.

And after all what is there here to thrill
The senses, what live beauty here that sings
Deep to the heart? Ruined temples on a hill,
Passion and pathos of dead perfect things,
Golden brown columns, rhythmic spaces, blue
That throbs intensely in the sky and sea;
Soft rolling mountains and the reddening hue
Of sun on sandstone. What else can there be?
Or do there loiter in this falling light,
White slender forms that once made music here?
Do we catch echoes on the wind tonight
Of unstilled voices rising cool and clear?
    Or do the young gods once more as we gaze
    Stand bright and breathing in the twilight haze?

Time has made these ruins beautiful and impressive: "a facade of symmetry, an image of order, built by perishing men two thousand years ago against a changing but eternal sea, a moment of time made into a monument of eternity." To the sophisticated modern critic, who does not admire or understand the civilization of Puritan England, the art of Milton is neither beautiful nor impressive. Supremely confident—perhaps less so since the recent recantation of Eliot—that their judgment and taste are superior to those of two centuries of critics who ranked Milton as the greatest of English nondramatic poets or simply as the greatest English poet, these critics have dethroned and buried Milton. They have a rather large body of disciples, sophisticated and unsophisticated, who privately or publicly dismiss Milton as dull and old-fashioned and who then incontinently embrace the latest critical fad.

It is not my purpose to expose the prejudices and whims of the anti-Miltonists. The fallacies of the modern reaction against Milton, the lack of perception, the arrogant prejudice, the unfailing habit of erecting personal impressions into laws, the "curious mixture of ultra-sophistication and naïveté,"—all this and more has been convincingly demonstrated by Douglas Bush, who then points out one of Milton's great merits. Noting the current zeal for making a better world, Bush shrewdly observes: "to judge from the millions of words poured into print and into the air, much of that zeal is directed toward making other people better, or making more and better gadgets. In all his major poems Milton is occupied with the far more real and fundamental problem of making one's self better. And he makes us better not merely through his imagination and 'poetical' beauties but

170

through the total effect of his religious and ethical theme, through his profound concern with 'man, the heart of man, and human life.' "[2] This is a compelling motive for the thoughtful reading of Milton, whose religious and ethical thought, in spite of the decay of orthodox religion and the triumph of science, may still have great vitality and significance for us. It is, of course, useless to pretend that Milton is really very modern, that he is, in fact, a harbinger of the modern world, though his contemporary John Locke has been described as "a Victorian in essence" two hundred years before Queen Victoria.[3] In Milton's thought there are marked traditional and medieval elements which cannot be ignored, which must be accepted and understood as part of the framework of his religious and ethical thought. These elements from the past are, in a sense, the form or shape of his thought, but they do not constitute the essence or soul of his doctrine.

The general problem or dilemma of the reader has been clearly presented by Charles E. Raven, Regius Professor Emeritus of Divinity of the University of Cambridge, in the Gifford Lectures for 1952. If a Christian is to live in the world[4]

he must come to terms with it, must form some opinion of its significance for him and of his place in it; he must, as a child of the twentieth century, face the problems that have made his traditional religion so often appear an anachronism; the scale and character of a universe measured in terms of astronomical space and geological time; the worth of a world in which struggle and suffering have played so large a part; the purpose of existence when progress is so precarious, sin so manifest and devilry at times so triumphant.

Raven contrasts the size and age of this world with that of the earth of the New Testament:

We realize that in the days of the New Testament when the earth was pictured as a flat and relatively tiny ring of land around the Mediterranean, covered at no great distance by the vaulted heavens, it was easy to feel a direct and intimate relationship between God and the human individual: everything was small and cosy, a realm not much larger than the Roman empire. In such a world the Babe of Bethlehem, His birth heralded by star and angels, was a lovely proof of the Father's nearness and care. Throughout the Middle Ages and even when Copernicus and his successors

[2] Douglas Bush, *Paradise Lost in Our Time* (New York, 1948), pp. 27–28.
[3] George Santayana, *Some Turns of Thought in Modern Philosophy. Five Essays* (Cambridge, 1933), p. 4.
[4] Raven, *Natural Religion and Christian Theology.* The Gifford Lectures 1951. Second Series: *Experience and Interpretation* (Cambridge, 1953), p. 107.

had displaced the earth from its central position, the Manger and the Cross stood out with dramatic fitness as the twin reminders of the divine condescension.

Now the antiquity of the earth, the scale of the solar system, the unimaginable size of the universe have made the span of human life insignificant, the immensity of creation overwhelming.

In this regard let us consider the pattern of time in *Paradise Lost* to determine what the pattern is and then, if possible, its effect on the structure and meaning of the poem. First a word about the structure and the meaning, which are intimately related, and in which time is an important factor. Matthew Arnold deplored the fact that the English, unlike the Greeks, care only for the parts, that they lack architectonic power, the ability to impose unity upon a mass of material. This flaw is notoriously apparent in some of the Romantic poets, whose imagination or inspiration, like the wind, bloweth where it listeth. Milton, on the other hand, has in a supreme degree this architectonic power. If the reading of *Paradise Lost* is, in Lamb's words, "a celestial recreation," part of the pleasure must be ascribed to Milton's mastery of form. In Milton's treatment of his universal theme, in which the characters are God and His creatures, which extends over unimaginable spaces and distances, and which embraces the histories of heaven, earth, and hell—in all this there is, as Sir Walter Raleigh remarked, not an incident and hardly a line but leads backward or forward to those central lines in Book IX, 780–84:

> So saying, her rash hand in evil hour
> Forth reaching to the Fruit, she pluck'd, she eat:
> Earth felt the wound, and Nature from her seat
> Sighing through all her Works, gave signs of woe,
> That all was lost.

"From this point," Raleigh observes, "radiates a plot so immense in scope, that the history of the world from the first preaching of the gospel to the Millenium occupies only some fifty lines of Milton's epilogue." Even the personal passages, in the preludes to Books I, III, VII, and IX, which were once considered as digressions, are now regarded as valuable guides to the construction or form of the poem.

In the development of the vast plan with its single theme there appear to be, Tillyard said, three movements, which are closely linked or integrated. The first movement is hell with its tortures and terrors, the punishment of the rebel angels, and their plans for revenge. This movement ends, for the time, with Satan's journey to this pendant world, suspended from heaven by a golden chain. The second movement is heaven with its purity and peace and God's plan for the redemption of man, whose fall is foreseen. This movement is interrupted by the return to Satan, whom we follow as he makes his way through the universe and finally alights on Mt. Niphates, on the borders of Eden. The third movement is Paradise with man as the center of the action, which involves both heaven and hell. This movement is introduced in Book IV and thereafter remains the principal one. We hear the story of the war in heaven and of the fall of the rebel angels; we hear the story of creation. But throughout Raphael's extended narrative one is or should be aware that Adam and Eve are the ones chiefly concerned, that over the bliss of Paradise and over them hangs the inevitable doom. Finally, having fully executed his divine mission and having explicitly warned Adam, Raphael withdraws, leaving man to his own resources and his fate. Heaven has done all it could. Fully instructed and armed with knowledge man is free to stand or fall. Deceived by Satan's casuistry Eve sins. Led astray by his love of Eve, that is, overcome by passion, Adam sins, knowing that he sins. The natural, the rational, the divine order of the world is broken. Sin and Death in person invade the universe. In a sort of epilogue Milton reveals not only the tragic consequences of this mortal sin but also the ultimately successful working out of God's plan for the salvation of man and the restoration of the divine order.

Having surveyed the general movement of the epic, we must return to a closer scrutiny. After the immediate effects of the mortal sin are traced in the unrestrained passion of Adam and Eve, in their mutual recriminations, in God's denunciation of punishment—after all this, Milton turns in Books XI and XII to the future. By God's command Michael surveys for Adam, first in vision and then in story, the history of the world, a history which illustrates the fatal effects of Adam's sin. Some such thing, Bush reminds us, was prescribed in the story of the Fall, which culminates in Christ's mediation and sacrifice and in man's salvation. It is in this survey of history that Milton makes use of a conventional pattern of time, to control a vast mass of material and to achieve a sort of structure or outline that is necessary.

Apparently this pattern of time has not been detected. Readers have been misled by the introduction of the classical divisions of time. Verity, for example, finds in Book XII a picture of the Silver Age, when, after the Flood, men, diligent and prosperous,

> Shal spend thir dayes in joy unblam'd, and dwell
> Long time in peace by Families and Tribes
> Under paternal rule.

which is not very much like Hesiod's Silver Age, when men could not keep from sinning and wronging one another and would not serve the immortals.[5] This age is followed, Verity says, by the Age of Iron, of political tyranny under Nimrod. Verity may assume that the period in Paradise corresponds to the classical Age of Gold, when men lived like gods without sorrow, remote and free from toil and grief, and the fruitful earth bore all things needful abundantly and without stint. Verity does not find any classical label for the period of violence and wickedness which preceded and occasioned the Flood. Although there may be some echoes of the classical ages, the events of *Paradise Lost* do not follow or correspond to the classical divisions of time. The classical scheme is entirely inapplicable to the periods of scriptural history. One must look to scriptural or Christian authorities for a scheme or pattern which will explain Milton's structure and his emphasis on events and persons. Much, of course, must be attributed to Milton's inspiration, to his prayerful solicitation of "that eternal Spirit, who can enrich with all utterance and knowledge, and sends out his seraphim, with the hallowed fire of his altar, to touch and purify the lips of whom he pleases." But inspiration alone does not explain *Paradise Lost*. Milton relied upon the implements of poetic and philosophic thought. One sees him before 1652 seated in his study with the Holy Bible "open majestically before him, and beside it that other revelation—the terrestial globe," not to mention much besides. One sees him later, "In darkness, and with dangers compast round,/ And solitude; yet not alone," drawing upon the reservoirs of his select and comprehensive reading. A minor but important phase or item of this knowledge included, I am sure, the Biblical divisions of time, from creation to the present.

We begin with creation, which Milton in *The Christian Doctrine* defines as "that act whereby *God the Father produced everything that exists by his Word and Spirit . . . for the manifestation of the Glory of his power and goodness.*" It seems to have been agreed that as there was no matter before creation so there was no time or measure of time. Ussher in *The Summe and Substance of Christian Religion* (1649) says that before the creation "there was no measure of time by

[5] *Paradise Lost*, ed. Verity (Cambridge, 1929), II, 641; *Hesiod, The Homeric Hymns and Homerica*, with an English Translation by Hugh G. Evelyn-White (London, 1914), p. 13.

men or Angels." Milton, of course, held that all things were made "not out of nothing, but out of matter," and he believed also that motion and time, which is the measure of motion, could have existed before this world was made. The time of creation was not undetermined, though there was not complete agreement on the date. Calvin believed that the world was not quite six thousand years old. John Lightfoot, Vice-Chancellor of the University of Cambridge, declared, as the result of his exhaustive study of the Scriptures, that heaven and earth were created all together, in the same instant, and that this "work took place and man was created by the Trinity on October 23, 4004 B.C. at nine o'clock in the morning."[6] Raven recently stated:[7]

Three hundred years ago in Western Europe every educated man from Thomas Hobbes to Robert Boyle and from John Milton to Isaac Newton would have agreed that creation was an event taking place at a fixed and calculable date some 4000 years before Christ; that at that date and, as most supposed, in the autumn of the year the earth gave birth to its plants and trees, its fishes and birds, its reptiles and mammals, each as we still know it, and that when all was complete man was made and supplied with a mate.

Raven says that this view persisted well on into the nineteenth century. The point of departure for our pattern is creation, from which Biblical time was reckoned. As creation was often a process or series of acts covering six days, with a final day of rest, so the history of the world was divided into ages, with notable scriptural events marking off the limits.

One of the first to indicate this division of time was St. Augustine, whose *De Civitate Dei* is thought to have influenced Milton's interpretation of the Fall and his account of the creation of man as well as his conception of Christ. Hanford thinks that the Protestant poet was influenced even when he was in fundamental disagreement with "this mighty elaborator of Catholic Christianity." The statement of chronology, which, of course, would not excite theological rancor, being apparently mere statement of fact, occurs in Book XXII, chapter 30, which is entitled "Of the eternall felicity of the City of God, and the perpetuall Sabbath." It runs as follows:[8]

[6] Andrew D. White, *A History of the Warfare of Science with Theology in Christendom* (1910), I, 8–9. Hereafter cited as *A History of the Warfare of Science.*

[7] Raven, *Natural Religion and Christian Theology,* II, p. 129.

[8] St. Augustine, *The Citie of God . . . Englished* first by J. H. (London, 1620), p. 859.

If therefore that number of ages, as of daies be accompted according to the distinctions of times, which seeme to be expressed in the sacred Scriptures, that Sabbath day shall appeare more euidently, because it is found to be the seauenth, that the first age, as it were the first day, be from *Adam* to the floud; then the second from thence unto *Abraham*, not by equality of times, but by the number of generations. . . . From hence now, as *Mathew* the Euangelist doth conclude, three ages doe follow euen unto the comming of Christ; euery one of which is expressed by fourteene generations. From *Abraham* unto *Dauid* is one, from thence euen untill the Transmigration into Babilon, is another; the third from thence unto the incarnate Natiuity of Christ. So all of them are made fiue. Now this age is the sixt, to bee measured by no number.

After the sixth age, God shall rest as on the seventh day; and at the end of the seventh there shall be not the evening but the Lord's day, as the eighth eternal day, when "we shall rest, and see, we shall see and love, we shall love, and we shall praise: Behold what shall be in the end without end! . . . in that Kingdome of which there is no end." With minor variations St. Augustine's division of time is accepted. Having the sanction of a distinguished Father of the Roman Catholic Church and the authority of Holy Writ, it becomes the orthodox and official pattern of time.

This division of time was adopted by Isidore of Seville, in whom "Biblical tradition dominated all historical thinking." As a Christian writer he substituted the Scripture for pagan authority and, like Augustine and Orosius, he reshaped knowledge so that it would have a subordinate place in the religious scheme. Anything in Graeco-Roman intellectual culture that could not be amalgamated with or made to support the religious idea was ignored or discarded. Isidore's chief distinction, according to Henry Osborn Taylor, is that he "gathered and arranged in his treatises a conglomerate of knowledge, secular and sacred, exactly suited to the coming centuries." Others have condemned Isidore's vast encyclopaedic compilation, the *Etymologies,* as a pretentious and feeble performance tending to encourage intellectual laziness and stagnation and providing for learned and unlearned alike "the fruits of a very much decayed tree of ancient knowledge."[9]

One of the bits of knowledge of the "vastly influential" Bishop of

[9] Taylor, *The Medieval Mind* (4th ed.; Cambridge [Mass.], 1951), I, 103; Floyd S. Lear, "St. Isidore and Mediaeval Science," *The Rice Institute Pamphlet,* XXIII (1936), 77. Lear exonerates Isidore in the light of his milieu—an era of "epitomes of epitomes, . . . the text-book habit of mind."

Seville was the scriptural division of time. This appears in his *Ety-mologies*.[10] The first age includes the creation: "Prima aetas continet in exordio sui creationem mundi." This age extends to Noah and the Flood: "Noe autem, an. DC, factum est diluvium." The second age extends from Noah to Abraham. It includes the building of the tower of Babel, the founding of the kingdom of the Scythians, and the discovery of witchcraft by Zoroaster. The third age extends from Abraham to David. In this age the Hebrews endured servitude in Egypt and received letters and laws; Troy was captured; Homer lived; Apollo invented the art of medicine. The fourth age runs from David to the captivity of the Jews. In this age the Temple in Jerusalem was built, and Carthage and Rome were founded. The fifth age runs from the captivity of the Jews to the birth of Christ. In this age Sophocles, Euripedes, Plato, and Demosthenes flourished; Alexander captured Jerusalem; the Romans subdued Syria. In the sixth age, from the birth of Christ to the end of the world, the Gospels were written, the Lombards invaded Italy, and heresies arose. The sixth age began in the year 5155 from creation or by another reckoning in the year 5211. After observing under the date 5808 that the Jews in Spain are being made Christian, Isidore says, "The remainder of the sixth age is known to God alone." Isidore's ages correspond with those of St. Augustine, but Isidore adds dates and includes a meager list of events in each age. Probably, St. Augustine and St. Isidore had much to do with establishing and making current this scriptural division of time.

The same chronology appears in the following works: *Chronica Hungaorum* (1472), the first of the printed chronicles; *Fasiculus Temporum*, which enjoyed more than a score of reprints before 1492, having been translated into French, Spanish, German, and Dutch; and *Supplementum Chronicarum* (1483), which was artistically the best of the chronicles before the *Nuremberg Chronicle*, which appeared in 1493. In this, which is also called *The Book of Chronicles*, the first age is before the Flood; the next includes the building of the Ark and extends to the destruction of Sodom and Gomorrah; the third age is Abrahamic; the fourth is Davidic; the fifth extends to the birth of Christ; the sixth is the Christian era. The material of the Chronicle is arranged under these divisions. The first two are mainly scriptural. In the third, Schedel, the compiler, brings Europe prematurely into the world scene with pictures of Corinth, Paris, Naples, Venice, Pisa, and London. At the end of the third age he inserts an account of the

10 I have used the edition printed at Augsburg in 1472 and that in the *Pat. Lat.*, LXXXII, cols. 223–28.

province of England. The illustration of the destruction of Jerusalem is interesting mainly on account of its anachronisms. In an illustration of the events of the year 587 B.C. the mountains in the background show Satan pointing out to Christ the kingdoms of the world. Like Isidore, Schedel mixes the true and the legendary at his pleasure. The sixth age extends to the coronation of Maximilian I, which occurred in 1493, within a few months of the completion of the Chronicle. On folio 245 there is the earliest known picture or illustration of Siamese twins, male and female. Prodigies and portents are noted: for example, a human being with the head of a wolf, a lion with a woman's head. In the year 1493 several comets and eclipses foretell disaster. The return of Columbus to Palos in 1493 is not recorded.

The *Nuremberg Chronicle* is regarded as a great monument of the Middle Ages, presenting "medieval ideas more elaborately in text and picture than any other book of that age." The first pages paraphrase the first chapters of Genesis and illustrate the life of Adam and Eve. One cut shows them standing by the Tree of Knowledge, each modestly holding a branch in front; another shows an angel with a sword driving them from Paradise; another, Cain slaying Abel; another, the building of the Ark. Near the end a few pages are left blank, "For none of us can do everything." Following the third blank page there is the heading "Septima etas mundi," and this considers the reign of Antichrist and the near approach of the end of the world. After the final battle between the heavenly hosts and the minions of Satan, vividly depicted, and the defeat of Antichrist, the dead, illustrated by a spirited engraving of the Dance of Death, arise. Then three pages are devoted to the last age of the world, with a full-page picture of the last judgment. It might be convincingly argued that something of the structure and the spirit of the *Nuremberg Chronicle* is reflected in *Paradise Lost*.

Other examples of this scriptural chronology are not hard to come by. There is the *Cursor Mundi*, a Northumbrian poem of the fourteenth century—but here the fifth age begins with the parentage of the Virgin Mary and extends to John the Baptist, and the sixth runs from the baptism of Jesus to the finding of the Cross. The Day of Doom and the state of the world after doomsday constitute the seventh age. The *Cursor Mundi* is said to have been very popular. In Richard Grafton's *Chronicle at Large and Meere History of the Affayres of Englande* . . . (1569) we find the usual division. In the first age God made heaven and earth and all creatures, including man; in

178

the second He sent the universal Flood; in the third He made the covenant with Abraham, and so forth. But in Grafton the seventh age is from the birth of Christ to the end of the world. He also gives the number of years in each age. The first age, as always, is the longest, numbering 1656 years. He finds that from creation to the birth of Christ there were 3963 years, according to the computation of Scripture, which "must of force be true." The first volume of Grafton's *Chronicle* is arranged in seven parts, corresponding to the seven ages, and carries us to the victory of William the Conqueror, with a mixture of sacred and secular history.

In Lambertus Danaeus' *Wonderfull Woorkmanship of the World* . . . (1578), "made English by Thomas Twyne," the familiar classification appears: from creation to Noah; from the Deluge to the promise of Abraham; from this event to the departure of the children of Israel from Egypt; and so on. But here the present age, from the birth of Christ to "our" time, 1578, is the seventh age, not the sixth. This division and computation are said to be based on the Scriptures and the "best learned auctours that have written most truly in this behalf." The number of years since creation is estimated to be exactly 5298. As a matter of course, the same divisions appear in *A Fruitfull Commentarie upon the Twelve Small Prophets,* written in Latin by Danaeus and turned into English by John Stockwood in 1594, with precise figures for each period.

The preface to the chronography of *The Ancient Ecclesiastical Histories of . . . Eusebius, Socrates, and Evagrius*[11] surveys the events preceding the birth of Christ and recommends the chronography: "the English tongue hath not at this day extant any Ecclesiasticall Chronographie continued for so long a time." Since Milton is known to have been acquainted with this work, I reproduce the leading statements:

"The first age of the world from *Adam* to *Noah* hath 1650 yeares." [The deluge] "drowned the whole world in the six hundredth yeare of *Noah*" [in the year 1656, as Augustine writes in his *De Civitate Dei*].
"The second age of the world from *Noah* to *Abraham* hath 292 yeares." [The time from Adam and the creation of the world to Abraham was 1948 years. The patriarchs went into Egypt in the year 2238; they left Egypt in the year 2453.]
"The 3. age of the world from *Abraham* to *David* hath 942 yeares."

[11] I have examined the editions published in 1577, 1607, and 1636.

179

"The 4. age of the world from *David* unto the captivity in Babylon hath 473 yeares."

[Hanmer supplies a full list of the kings of Israel and Judah. In the margin we learn that Bath, Leicester, and Rome were built in this age. London had been founded in the third age.]

"The fift age of the world from the captivity of Babylon, unto Christ hath 596 yeares." [Our Saviour was born in the forty second year of the reign of Augustus. But the year of His birth has not been exactly determined. Eusebius gives the year 5199; Jerome, 3965; the old Rabbis, 3759; Luther, 3960; and so on. Without prejudice to the rest, Hanmer prefers the date 3965 or 4000. He remarks that according to the received opinion of Augustine, Justin Martyr, Irenaeus, Munster, and others, the world shall last six thousand years: two thousand before the Law; two thousand under the Law; two thousand under Messias.]

The sixth age was the Christian era, for six hundred years of which Hanmer gives a detailed chronography. It is clear that Hanmer followed St. Augustine and other authorities of the church in his division or pattern of time, as was to be expected in an ecclesiastical history.

One of the most popular poems of the sixteenth and seventeenth centuries—in fifty years it went through approximately two hundred and thirty editions—and one that may have influenced Milton in *Paradise Lost* is Du Bartas' *Deuine Weekes and Workes,* to use the title of Joshua Sylvester's famous translation. This divides the subject into two weeks: seven days of creation in the first, seven days in the second, whereof three were not finished. In the second week the four days are labeled Adam, Noah, Abraham, and David, corresponding to the traditional division of time. In the last division of the first day of the second week Adam tells his son how many ages the world shall endure:[12]

> The *First* begins with me: the *Seconds* morn
> Is the first Ship-wright, who doth first adorn
> The hils with Vines: that Shepherd is the *Third*
> That after God through strange Lands leads his Heard,
> And (past mans reason) crediting Gods word,
> His onely Son slayes with a willing sword:
> The *Fourth's* another valiant Shepheardling,
> That for a Cannon takes his silly sling,
> And to a Scepter turns his Shepheards staff,
> Great Prince, great Prophet, Poet, Psalmograph:

[12] *Du Bartas His Deuine Weekes and Workes.* Translated by Josuah Sylvester. (London, 1611), pp. 293–94.

> The *Fift* begins from that sad Princes night
> That sees his children murdred in his sight,
> And on the banks of fruitfull *Euphrates,*
> Poor *Iuda* led in Captiue heauiness:
> Hoped *Messias* shineth in the *Sixt*:
> Who, mockt, beat, banisht, buried, cruci-fixt,
> For our soul sins (stil-selfly-innocent)
> Hath fully born the hatefull punishment:
> The *Last,* shall be the very *Resting-Day,*
> Th' Ayr shall be mute, the Waters work shall stay:
> The Earth her store, the stars shall leaue their measures,
> The Sun his shine: and in eternall pleasures
> We plung'd, in Heav'n shall ay solemnize, all,
> Th' eternall *Sabboths* end-less *Festiuall.*

The Treasurie of Ancient and Moderne Times . . . of Pedro Mexio and others (1613), a compilation of learned readings, memorable observations, divine, moral, and philosophical, along with much other miscellaneous information, includes a long chapter (here summarized and paraphrased) on the division of time, which "the greater part of Authors" divide into six ages, though divers others number them seven. The author is guided by Eusebius and the common judgment of all historians that have set down their rest in the number six. The first age is from creation to the universal Deluge. This age, which was the world's infancy or childhood, lasted a long time, and there were probably notable accidents, of which there is no record. Cain builded in the east the first city, Henoch; Lamech was the first twice-married man "that durst adventure upon two wives"; Tubal invented the art of music. In this age there were giants. Finally, after 1656 years, or 2272 according to the seventy-two interpreters, came the universal Flood for the sins of men. Of the second age, from Noah's coming forth from the Ark to the birth of Abraham, we know very little. Noah begat children and so did his sons, with the natural result that the world began "to be greatly peopled." At this time the tower of Babel was built, Tubal went into Spain, the kingdom of the Scythians began, the art of magic was discovered; and at the end the potent reign of the Assyrians began, with Belus the first king; and Ninus built Nineveh, three day's journey in circuit. The third age, from Abraham to David, contains "without all contrarietie" 942 years, to which Isidore adds two more. It may be called the world's adolescence, for now all things increased greatly. Semiramis rebuilt Babylon; the Pharaohs ruled; the kingdom of the Amazons was founded; Joseph was sold into Egypt; Hercules traveled into Spain, and the city of Seville was founded; Troy flourished; Jason made his conquest of the Golden Fleece; the Trojan war followed, Troy was destroyed, and Aeneas came to Italy. The fourth age, from David's reign to the transmigration of the Jews, is the lusty or sprightly age, in which infinite events occurred "wherewith all Histories are plentifully enriched." David conquered the Philistines; Solomon built the Temple; the empire of the Assyrians fell to the Medes; Rome and Carthage were founded. Finally Nabuchadonosor destroyed Jerusalem and carried away captive the children of Israel. The fifth age lasts to the nativity of Christ and includes much alteration of states, with wonderful levying and mustering of armies. The Jews were set free at the death of Cyrus; learning and chivalry flourished in Greece; Alexander became the monarch of the world. Finally, "the full accompaniment of all things beeing come," the fifth age ended with the birth of Christ. The sixth age, the last of the world, is the Christian; but the empire of Christendom has been much reduced by Mahomet and the inroads of the Goths. Discords increase and faith waxes cold. Plainly the end of the world is drawing near.

The authorities cited for these several ages are Augustus, Isidore, Bede, Eusebius, Philo Judaeus, Orosius, "all singuler Historians," with Vincentius, Petrus de Alicus, and especially Johannes Driodonus, surely an impressive array. Relying upon these authorities, the *Treasurie* hands on the traditional division or pattern of time, one which, it is clear, no historian might lightly reject.[13]

For good measure, I add a chronological table, entitled "A perfect Supputation of the yeeres and times from the creation of the world, unto this present yeere of our Lord God 1580, proued by Scriptures, after the collection of diuers Authours," which was published in the Geneva Bible. Here the main divisions are:

From the creation of the worlde unto the flood are 1656 yeeres and 6

[13] Raleigh rejects it, dividing his *History of the World* into five books: (1) from the creation to Abraham; (2) from Abraham to the destruction of Solomon's Temple; (3) from the destruction of Jerusalem to Philip of Macedon; (4) from Philip to the kingdom of Antigonus; (5) from the rule of Alexander's successors to the Roman conquest of Asia and Macedonia. Raleigh's first two periods cover the first four of scriptural time; to his third, fourth, and fifth he assigns his own secular limits. In Book I, chapter 5, section 5, Raleigh seems to be aware of the old division, observing that men "of the first age" lived much longer than those "after the Flood." Andrew D. White says that Raleigh followed the chronology of the Septuagint version (*op. cit.*, I, 254), pointing out the danger of adhering to the old system.

Creation of the Stars, Birds, and Fishes
(Perugia, Augusta Library, MS. L. 59, Fol. 2)

dayes. . . . From the said flood of Noah unto Abrahams departing from Chalde, were 423 yeeres and ten dayes. . . . From Abrahams departing from Ur in Chalde unto the departing of the children of Israel from Egypt, are 430 yeeres. . . . From the going of the Israelites from Egypt unto the first building of the Temple, are 480 yeeres. . . . From the first building of the Temple unto the captiuitie of Babylon, are 441 yeeres & a half. . . . Jerusalem was reedified and builded againe after the captiuitie 143 yeares. The children of Israel were delivered out of captivitie and restored to their freedome, in the first yeare of Cyrus, & in the second yeare the foundation of the Temple was laide. . . . From the reedifying of the Citie, unto the death of Christ our Saviour, are 478 yeares. . . .

According to this table the time from creation "unto this present yere of our Lord God. 1580 . . . amounteth unto 5597 yeres, six monethes, and 16. dayes."

This is exactly the same number of years as would be ascertained by consulting Ussher's *Annals of the Ancient and New Testaments* (1650), which became "the greatest authority for all English-speaking peoples." Ussher's dates were "inserted in the margins of the authorised version of the English Bible, and were soon practically regarded as equally inspired with the sacred text itself."[14] There were a few who dared to question the accepted chronology, but they were almost without influence; and throughout the seventeenth century the orthodox view prevailed. It was expected that all Christians would rely upon "the infallible annals of the Spirit of God." For our purpose the exact date of the creation of the world and the number of years in each period are not important. Milton was not interested in such detail. But the division or pattern of time is important, as I hope to show by applying this traditional pattern to the poem, in which time is a factor and, I believe, a sort of structural principle. This will perhaps be made clear by analyzing the poem from this point of view.

In surveying sacred history Milton, it seems, should be influenced by the conventional time pattern. This pattern might lighten its task by simplifying the choice and arrangement of the material. Milton was, of course, thoroughly familiar with Scripture; but his undertaking was not an easy one. He must traverse speedily, clearly, and with proper emphasis a vast scope of Biblical history. Here the orthodox division of time would come to his aid. He would disguise its rigid outlines to achieve a free flow or continuity of narrative, and he would inevitably impart to his treatment the force and individuality of his genius, as far as this is possible in dealing with such material.

---

[14] White, *A History of the Warfare of Science*, I, 253.

These seem to be reasonable assumptions in the light of the subject and the tradition. It is possible to contrast time before creation with time afterward.

Time before the creation of the world was naturally or rather supernaturally indefinite. It is known that God and light existed eternally with His Son and Holy Spirit. We know that Milton's Muse conversed with eternal Wisdom "Before the Hills appeered, or Fountain flow'd." We know that God had exalted His Son to be His vice-regent, before whom all knees in heaven should bow. We are told that there was war in heaven, "so neer the Peace of God in bliss," a war which on the third day resulted in the overwhelming defeat of Satan and his rebellious hosts, who for nine days fell through chaos, pursued by eternal wrath "to the bottomless pit." We know that for another nine days Satan

> with his horrid crew
> Lay vanquisht, rowling in the fiery Gulfe
> Confounded though immortal.

We know that for an indefinite time the rebel angels debated at length about their future course of action: whether by open war or secret fraud they should prosecute their war against God. We learn finally that, in the meantime, at some unspecified time between their fall and Satan's journey through chaos, God had created a new universe, to repair His "damage fondly deem'd." As he draws near, Satan sees this universe, near the empyreal Heaven:

> fast by hanging in a golden Chain
> This pendant world, in bigness as a Starr
> Of smallest Magnitude close by the Moon.

All this had taken place in eternity, in that time before which at God's command the universe at last emerged out of the boundless deep, this universe in all its beauty and perfection, with all its creatures and with man made in the image of God to crown His work, a work divine celebrated

> with acclamation and the sound
> Symphonious of ten thousand Harpes that tun'd
> Angelic harmonies.

This work of creation, related in detail in Book VII, was accomplished in six days, as in Genesis 1. It was followed by a seventh day of rest and jubilation when the Creator returned

> Up to the Heav'n of Heav'ns his high abode,
> Thence to behold this new created World
> Th' addition of his Empire, how it shew'd
> In prospect from his Throne, how good, how faire,
> Answering his great Idea.

This full-dress recital of creation is not, however, our subject. We are interested in the vision and the survey of the future after the Fall; for it is there, I think, that Milton used the conventional and authoritative scriptural pattern of time.

God's messenger here is Michael the archangel, who, accompanied by a select band of warriors, must without remorse expel the disobedient human pair from the holy ground of Paradise, first, however, revealing "To *Adam* what shall come in future dayes," and disclosing also God's covenant of grace to the penitent and regenerate, so sending them forth "though sorrowing, yet in peace." Michael, the "gentle Angel," circumspectly and faithfully performs his task. He conveys Adam to the highest hill in Paradise,

> from whose top
> The Hemisphere of Earth in cleerest Ken
> Strecht out to amplest reach in prospect lay.

Having purged Adam's sight with three drops from the well of life, the archangel speaks:

> *Adam*, now ope thine eyes, and first behold
> Th' effects which thy original crime hath wrought
> In some to spring from thee, who never touch'd
> Th' excepted Tree, nor with the Snake conspir'd,
> Nor sinn'd thy sin, yet from that sin derive
> Corruption to bring forth more violent deeds.
> (XI, 423–28)

Milton devotes the remainder of Book XI, that is more than half (some 468 lines out of a total of 901), to the events of the first age, including the Deluge. This is the longest part of the survey, as the first age was the longest, 1656 years at least. He emphasizes the wickedness of the sons of Adam, who are guilty of murder, luxury, war, riot, rape, adultery, and finally universal corruption, which brings on the universal Flood. This vision, a pageant of evil in the world, begins with the murder of Abel. Adam is dismayed and exclaims,

> O sight
> Of terrour, foul and ugly to behold,
> Horrid to think, how horrible to feel!

185

Michael then explains that this is death and adds that there are

> many shapes
> Of Death, and many are the wayes that lead
> To his grim Cave, all dismal.

Immediately there appears a lazar-house, sad, noisome, and dark, crowded with those who suffer from all maladies and over whom

> triumphant Death his Dart
> Shook, but delaid to strike, though oft invok't
> With vows, as thir chief good, and final hope.

In the same age there follows a scene of society at peace, having arts that polish life and indulging in mixed marriages, all of which pleases Adam much; but he is sternly informed that these are the tents of wickedness, that these good men have been corrupted by a "Beavie of fair Women, richly gay/In Gems and wanton dress," who seemed goddesses but were empty of all good,

> Bred onely and completed to the taste
> Of lustful appetence, to sing, to dance,
> To dress, and troule the Tongue, and roule the Eye.

The inevitable result of all this immorality will be a world of sorrow—which follows immediately. In a wide territory of country and cities with lofty gates and towers Adam sees "Concours in Arms, fierce Faces threatning Warr," pillaging of flocks, deserted fields strewn with carcasses and arms, and oppression and violence throughout the land. Thereupon follows a time of jollity and feasting, dancing, luxury, and riot, which is succeeded at once by the building of the Ark and then the Flood and at last the rainbow, "Betok'ning peace from God, and Cov'nant new." So ends the first age of history. The age is not numbered, of course; but it is clearly the first.

When in the edition of 1674 Milton divided Book X into Books XI and XII, he added at the opening of Book XII the following lines:

> As one who in his journey bates at Noone,
> Though bent on speed, so heer the Archangel paus'd
> Betwixt the world destroy'd and world restor'd,
> If *Adam* aught perhaps might interpose;
> Then with transition sweet new Speech resumes.

The survey of history, measuring "this transient World," continues. It is completed in some 370 lines of Book XII or in 550 lines if we include the dissolution of this world, beyond which lies "Eternitie, whose end no eye can reach."

In what corresponds to the second age in our chronology (Milton, of course, does not use numbers), the poet describes first a God-fearing, pastoral society living at peace under paternal rule. Then appears the first tyrant, Nimrod, who arrogates to himself dominion over his brethren and quite dispossesses "Concord and law of Nature from the Earth." Nimrod builds or casts to build "A Citie & Towre, whose top may reach to Heav'n." Tyranny is denounced, but Adam is reminded that since his original sin true liberty

> Is lost, which alwayes with right Reason dwells
> Twinn'd, and from her hath no dividual being:
> Reason in man obscur'd, or not obey'd,
> Imediately inordinate desires
> And upstart Passions catch the Government
> From Reason, and to servitude reduce
> Man till then free.   (XII, 84–90)

The latter world will thus tend from bad to worse till God "Wearied with their iniquities, withdraw/His presence from among them," leaving them to their own polluted ways and selecting one peculiar nation for his own.

The next period, the third age, begins with one "faithful man" of this nation. Called by vision from his father's house, "He leaves his Gods, his Friends, and native Soile/Ur of Chaldaea," and with a cumbrous train of herds, flocks, and servants passes to Haran, "Not wandring poor, but trusting all his wealth/With God, who call'd him, in a land unknown." This patriarch is, of course, "faithful *Abraham*," whose departure from Ur inaugurates the third age of our chronology. Michael then relates the sojourn of the Israelites in the land hereafter to be called Egypt, the tyranny of Pharaoh and the plagues which finally tame the River-Dragon, the miraculous escape from Egypt, the wanderings in the desert, the delivery of the Law to Moses, the building of the Ark of the Covenant, and at last under Joshua (the type of Christ) the return of the Israelites to Canaan. This return, "With glory and spoile back to thir promis'd Land," marks the close of a distinct period. The entire passage (there are 155 lines, from 114 to 269) depicting these events is extremely interesting and extraordinarily vivid and picturesque, and it is certainly not open to the charge of dullness sometimes brought against the historical survey in the last two books. Adam's interposition at the end of

Michael's graphic narrative of these events shows clearly that Milton wished to mark the close of a distinct period:

> Here *Adam* interpos'd. O sent from Heav'n,
> Enlightner of my darkness, gracious things
> Thou hast reveald, those chiefly which concerne
> Just *Abraham* and his Seed: now first I finde
> Mine eyes true op'ning, and my heart much eas'd,
> Erwhile perplext with thoughts what would becom
> Of mee and all Mankind; but now I see
> His day, in whom all Nations shall be blest, . . .
>
> (XII, 270–77)

These events, from Abraham's departure from Ur to the return of the Israelites to Canaan, with their theme of the wanderings of "Just *Abraham* and his Seed," form a separate and unified part of sacred history, which the reader who is acquainted with the traditional divisions of sacred story will immediately recognize as a familiar unit constituting the third age. Even without a number to mark it off, it stands out conspicuously, as also do other periods of the survey, which, nevertheless, form a continuous story.

Michael then imparts to Adam suitable information regarding the sin resulting from man's natural depravity, sin that can be removed not by the Law and ceremonies but only by a "better Cov'nant" of grace, not by works of the Law but by works of faith, not by Moses but by

> *Joshua* whom the Gentiles *Jesus* call,
>
> . . . .
>
> who shall quell
> The adversarie Serpent, and bring back
> Through the worlds wilderness long wanderd man
> Safe to eternal Paradise of rest. (XII, 310–14)

Meanwhile in Canaan the Israelites shall dwell for a long time and prosper until their sins provoke their enemies, from whom God saves them by judges and kings. Among the latter the most important is "The second, both for pietie renownd/And puissant deeds," who shall receive a promise irrevocable that "his Regal Throne For ever shall endure," and from him shal spring a son. In Him all nations shall trust and of his reign there shall be no end.

This king, who marks the beginning of the fourth age, was, of course, David. Now the building by Solomon of the glorious Temple, which shall enshrine the Ark of God, is followed by foul idolatries

188

and other sins, which so incense God that He abandons His people, leaving "Thir Citie, his Temple, and his holy Ark/With all his sacred things, a scorn and prey" to that proud city Babylon. The destruction of Jerusalem marks the close of the fourth age.

The captivity of the Jews, briefly mentioned, marks the beginning of the fifth age. Remembering mercy and His covenant sworn to David, God brings the Israelites back after seventy years to a rebuilt Temple and city. Here for a while they live in mean estate; but later, increased in wealth and multitude, they grow factious. The contention of their priests pollutes the Temple and leads to the dethroning of David's sons. This prepares the way for the anointed Messiah, whose birth, marking the end of the fifth age, is beautifully related:

> at his Birth a Starr
> Unseen before in Heav'n proclaims him com,
> And guides the Eastern Sages, who enquire
> His place, to offer Incense, Myrrh, and Gold;
> His place of birth a solemn Angel tells
> To simple Shepherds, keeping watch by night;
> They gladly thither haste, and by a Quire
> Of squadrond Angels hear his Carol sung.
> A Virgin is his Mother, but his Sire
> The Power of the most High; he shall ascend
> The Throne hereditarie, and bound his Reign
> With earths wide bounds, his glory with the Heav'ns.
>   (XII, 360–71)

With the birth of Christ, who is the fulfillment of the prophecy that Eve's seed shall bruise "our Foe" and whose ministry and reign are so exquisitely described in the preceding narrative, we enter the sixth or Christian era, the last age of the world. The theme now is the ministry of Christ in a world of sin. Adam, whose heart has been filled with joy at the tidings of Christ's birth, "O Prophet of glad tidings, finisher/Of utmost hope!" and who confidently looks forward to the final defeat of Satan in mortal combat with the Saviour, is saddened to learn that for his and man's transgressions Christ must suffer death, "shameful and accurst, naild to the Cross," but he learns also that in this shameful death Christ really conquers, nailing to the Cross man's enemies, unjust law and the sins of all mankind, which will "Never . . . hurt them more who rightly trust/In this his satisfaction." On the third morn Christ shall rise from the grave, "fresh as the dawning light,/Thy ransom paid, which Man from death redeems," and after appearing to His disciples, to whom is committed the charge

189

"To teach all nations what of him they learn'd/And his Salvation,"
Christ shall ascend to glory at the right hand of God. Then at the last
day, at the dissolution of the world, He shall return "To judge th' unfaithful dead, but to reward/His faithful, and receave them into
bliss," in heaven or a new earth,

> for then the Earth
> Shall all be Paradise, far happier place
> Then this of *Eden*, and far happier daies.   (XII, 463–65)

In this very reassuring survey of Christ's ministry and man's potential salvation, the time is most indefinite. The life and the death of
the Saviour, the preaching of the Gospel, and Christ's victory and
exaltation—all this takes place in a future quite dateless, with no
secular events to indicate the passing of time, with, it may be said,
no marking of time except the phrase "the third dawning light" referring, of course, to Christ's resurrection. All that may be said is that
in Adam's unrealistic expectation of Satan's almost instantaneous defeat the word "now" in the lines "Needs must the Serpent now his
capital bruise/Expect with mortal paine" is obviously to be contrasted
with an indefinite future when through Christ's mediation, death, and
resurrection there shall ultimately spring "To God more glory, more
good will to Men/From God, and over wrauth grace shall abound."
But, though it may be implied, the word "ultimately" or any similar
word does not occur. Milton's habitual indefiniteness in such matters
is here, as elsewhere, obviously a very great advantage, for the apparently unlimited future is both impressive and, in effect, true.

The story does not end here: there are the unfaithful, the unre-
generate. Santayana, in *The Idea of Christ in the Gospels*, says, "The
idea of Christ crucified has had many worshippers, and has inspired
many saints. But it has not converted the world or saved it. The world
does not wish to be saved." Michael tells Adam that in the room of
the Apostles of Truth will come wolves, "grievous Wolves,"

> Who all the sacred mysteries of Heav'n
> To thir own vile advantages shall turne
> Of lucre and ambition, and the truth
> With superstitions and traditions taint,
> Left onely in those written records pure,
> Though not but by the Spirit understood.
>   (XII, 509–14)

These shall appropriate to themselves the spirit of God, whence heavy
persecutions shall arise, and most "Will deem in outward Rites and

specious formes/Religion satisfi'd." Truth shall retire, and works of faith shall rarely be found: "So shall the World goe on,/To good malignant, to bad men benigne," until at length the Saviour shall return

> In glory of the Father, to dissolve
> *Satan* with his perverted World, then raise
> From the conflagrant mass, purg'd and refin'd,
> New Heåv'ns, new Earth, Ages of endless date
> Founded in righteousness and peace and love,
> To bring forth fruits Joy and eternal Bliss.   (XII, 546–51)

In this prophetic vision time is as indefinite as before; but it is still time, which is to be succeeded by eternity, as Adam perceives:

> How soon hath thy prediction, Seer blest,
> Measur'd this transient World, the Race of time,
> Till time stand fixt: beyond is all abyss,
> Eternitie, whose end no eye can reach.   (XII, 553–56)

As Adam says, Michael has measured the race of time in this transient and pendant world. The measure is undoubtedly that of the universally accepted pattern. For the sake of the free flow of the narrative and its unbroken continuity the ages are not numbered. The scale of the survey is very extensive, more so than that of the story of creation with its precise account of the work of each day; but the structure, as was prescribed by tradition, is similar. Days there correspond to ages here: six days of creation and six ages of history, each followed by a sabbath of rest, "One sabbath deep and wide." The symmetry, a heritage of the Middle Ages, is perfect. The scriptural division of time was adopted. The orthodox chronological divisions of scriptural history provided the basis for Milton's selection and organization of the material. This was the basis of his structure. It should be emphasized that the pattern of time in the traditional chronology served as a guide for the kind and the proportion of material to be chosen from the vast and varied storehouse of Scripture. There was, in fact, no other pattern than this, which had indeed almost the authority and prestige of Holy Writ.

The theme and the character of the survey, with its emphasis on the corruption and violent deeds resulting from Adam's "original crime," must be defined as scriptural and doctrinal. Indeed this digest of history illustrates the fact that man "is very far gone from original righteousness, and is of his own nature inclined to evil, so that the flesh lusteth always contrary to the spirit," to use the words

191

of the *Book of Common Prayer*. For this corruption every person born into the world "deserveth God's wrath and damnation." And this "infection of nature" remains even in them that are regenerate. History then is inevitably an illustration of the corruption and depravity of human nature. In the conviction that the history of mankind is a continued and endless story of human lust, cruelty, oppression, and wickedness and in the persistently dark view of human fate in this world, some may find a quality which they like to call uniquely Miltonic. But this view is unjust. Milton's survey of history is scriptural and orthodox—and, as indicated in the epilogue, much nearer the truth than the rosy visions of man's inevitable progress, much more credible than the eighteenth-century dream of an approaching millenium to be ushered in "under the auspices of a faculty which was called Reason." Milton was no optimist who worshiped the Goddess of Reason. He did not believe in following implicitly the course of development which Nature has prescribed. He had never heard of the doctrine that progress is "not an accident but a necessity," that what we call "evil and immorality must disappear," and that man must become perfect. Milton believed in sin. He says that "all are born servants of sin," which to a great extent obscures "that right reason" which enabled men to discern the chief good and which was the life of the understanding. He believed that the natural consequence of sin was "the death of the spiritual life." In this way the sinner becomes "more miserable, more vile, more destitute of the divine assistance and grace, and farther removed from his primitive glory."

On the other hand, Milton declared that "some remnants of the divine image still exist in us, not wholly extinguished by this spiritual death." He believed that these "vestiges of original excellence" are visible in the understanding and in the liberty of the will, which is not entirely destroyed. The real basis of Milton's hope was of course his belief in regeneration through Christ. He was deeply moved by the conception of the "incarnation of God in man, and the divinisation of man in God," by the spiritual aspiration and the striving for ideal perfection which Santayana describes as "something perfectly Greek."[15] By the deepest springs of his nature and his culture Milton was impelled to embrace not the monotonous and servile worship of the God of Hebraism but that universal and ideal "infusion of Greek thought"

[15] George Santayana, "The Christian Epic," *The Life of Reason or the Phases of Human Progress* (New York, 1954), p. 219. Hereafter cited as *The Life of Reason*.

which distinguishes mature Christianity. His poetry as a whole and *The Christian Doctrine* show that Milton was profoundly moved by the conception of regeneration through Christ, "by the Word and the Spirit, whereby the old man being destroyed, the inward man is regenerated by God after his own image, in *all the faculties of his mind*, insomuch that he becomes as it were a new creature, and the whole man is sanctified both in body and soul, for the service of God, and the performance of good works." Through repentance, which is the gift of God, the regenerate man perceives with sorrow that he has offended God by sin, and he "detests and avoids it, humbly turning to God through a sense of the divine mercy, and heartily striving to follow righteousness." Through faith he believes that whatsoever things God has promised "in Christ, are ours, and especially the grace of eternal life." From faith arises hope, "a most assured expectation ... of those things which are already ours in Christ." By regeneration, repentance, and faith, natural ignorance is removed and the understanding is enlightened "for the perception of heavenly things"; and love or charity, "arising from a sense of the divine love shed abroad in the hearts of the regenerate by the Spirit," brings forth good works "spontaneously and freely."

Perfection is of course not to be expected in this present life; but *"it is our duty to strive after it with earnestness, as the ultimate object of our existence."* There is a victory to be gained over the world, over death, and over Satan. Those who are strenuous in this conflict and who "earnestly and unceasingly labor to attain perfection in Christ" are, though imperfect, by imputation and by divine mercy "called in Scripture perfect, blameless, and without sin." The true Christian patiently cultivates and cherishes virtue, humility, temperance, obedience, and love, the soul of all the rest, and he earnestly strives for perfection as the ultimate goal of life.

It should not be at all surprising that along with this vital system of morality and true religion Milton accepted and employed the traditional pattern of time, on which he depicted the "sad pageant of life," a sacred history "interpreted as a temporal execution of divine decrees," and in conclusion the plan of salvation "as an ideal necessity."

Milton's acceptance and use of material sanctioned by Scripture and religious tradition—God's power and providence, the rebellion of the angels, a paradise of beauty and bliss, the Fall of man through Satan's temptation, man's depraved nature, his redemption through grace, the pattern of time as a framework for all—this and much besides in the epic poses the issue previously stated: the dilemma of the Christian reader who has inherited this ancient religious system and who is ineluctably confronted by the modern universe. If thoughtful, he realizes that in "the scale of a universe measured in terms of astronomical space and geological time" his religion embodying a much smaller and more intimate universe presided over by a loving Father is an anachronism. To appreciate this fact one has only to try the simple experiment suggested by Raven: stand at night under the stars and repeat, "God reigns and Christ died for the salvation of man." This experiment may inculcate humility in the presence of the infinite universe, but it is hardly one to confirm religious faith in a personal Father and His Son as the Redeemer. The dilemma must be faced now when, to quote Santayana, "every emancipated prig creates his theology."[16] Here we cannot rely upon the sophisticated aesthete who, "armed with his supercilious sensibility and transcendental freedom, intrudes into the workshop of the arts with his nose in the air." Through lack of training and knowledge such critics are quite unprepared to understand the art and culture of the past. We dare not trust as guides or interpreters the modern critic who is "contemptuous of the stupid public and the traditional styles" and especially contemptuous of traditional religion and its spiritual values.

The problem, however, remains, now that the story of *Paradise Lost* is relegated to the area of myth, the theology is becoming antiquated, and even the very idea of obligation or duty as "an original and permanent endowment of the human race" is dismissed as old-fashioned.[17] How can the modern student, who investigates all things, tolerate Adam's conception of knowledge within bounds, his apparent willingness to shun intellectual curiosity, his submission to authority? Is the modern reader not rightly repelled or diverted by the fantastic myth, the old-fashioned theology, the fancied absence of intellectual stimulus—in short, by what Santayana calls "the brief time and narrow argument into which Christian imagination squeezes the world"?[18] It is no satisfactory solution of the problem to praise, on the one hand, the sustained grandeur of conception, the mastery of design, and the distinction of style and, on the other, to condemn Milton's thought and theology as merely "a superior branch of po-

---

[16] George Santayana, *The Philosophy of Santayana*, ed. by Irwin Edman, (New York, 1953), p. 771.

[17] Sir William David Ross, *Foundations of Ethics* (Oxford, 1939), p. 15.

[18] Santayana, *The Life of Reason*, p. 222.

litical science" and his imagination as that of a philosopher, lucid and concrete but "unlit by heavenly gleams."

It is perhaps not very difficult to dispose of some of these objections or strictures, which are posed because of changes in concepts in the course or pattern of time. It may be said that the fable as myth is a delightful one with an extremely valuable moral. It may plausibly be argued that the essential and universal meaning of this ancient story can be grasped only when "the story is set free from any connection with an actual occurrence in time and space."[19] Though not literally true in the sense that man fell, that by sin he forfeited his right to live in Paradise in innocence and bliss, "the story of the fall is true . . . if man is *in fact* alienated from God and thus *actually* falling short of the glory of his own true nature and destiny." The scriptural story or myth which is the basis of *Paradise Lost* attempts to express "an understanding of the relation in which God *actually* stands to human life." And the story is true only if that understanding is true. As for the story of redemption, that is true only if in fact Christ is our redeemer from sin and death. The truth, as Christians believe, is the truth which was actually discovered in the event itself. It is important that Christians should realize that it is a story that they believe. Once this view is accepted, the critical reader may be reassured and may with equanimity and profit meditate on the story for its essential spiritual truth. If hard pressed, one may be unable to explain his belief in philosophical or historical terms; but one may still believe the spiritual truth, which is as true as "the faith which it was created to express."

The downright skeptic who dismisses Christianity as mere superstition will be deaf to such an interpretation. As we know, the scientific mind or method is now triumphant. What Joseph Butler said in *The Analogy of Religion* is even truer today: "It is come, I know not how, to be taken for granted, by many persons, that Christianity is not so much as a subject of enquiry; but that it is now at length discovered to be fictitious." From the point of view of science God has been found to be "an unnecessary hypothesis in one field after another of study and experience," until He seems to have become a silent actor in the play or the ghost of a dead faith. For many, science is the "cohesive force" in modern society, the ground on which may be built "a secure way of life for man and for communities." One

19 John Knox, *On the Meaning of Christ.* The William Belden Noble Lectures delivered at Harvard University, 1947 (New York, 1947), p. 90.

cannot disregard the scientist and the skeptic who believe that when the scientific truth is known, religious notions will disappear like phantoms of the night when the day dawns.[20] I am not much concerned with such confirmed and hardened infidels, who in any case are unlikely to take a real interest in *Paradise Lost* or to appreciate its spiritual truth.

So much for the "narrow argument." As for the charge that time as conceived by the Christian imagination is brief, it is clear that in *Paradise Lost* time is indefinite and the space unlimited. In fact both time and space have a sweep and scope that stimulate thought and imagination. The spaces of the poem, even within the world, are infinite. In spite of the pattern, which is partly concealed, time seems to be unlimited, not being tied to years or dates. The vastness and indefiniteness of space and time add much to the sublimity and grandeur of the poem, giving the impression of universality and immensity. At crucial moments, however, attention is focused upon the human pair and the fruit "Of that Forbidden Tree, whose mortal tast/Brought Death into the World, and all our woe." The theme is both personal and universal, the trial of Adam and Eve being "a universal example of the trials and weaknesses of every man and every woman." The scale, in space, time, and action, is indescribably immense.

Bush has declared that Milton is great because of his moral and ethical teaching. He is not a great artist in the sense that he prayerfully devoted "his life and faculties to the manipulation of vowels and consonants"; and his greatness does not consist primarily in the noble design and the epic machinery. These are all means to an end, not the end themselves. The end of Milton's religious and ethical teaching is the making of one's self better, the inculcation of an inner morality, the conduct of life by enlightened reason directed by the spirit of grace. Bush emphasizes the moral doctrine and its application in conduct. He adds that Milton is "thoroughly orthodox in making Christ the incarnation of divine love and the atonement the great manifes-

---

[20] The opposed views of religion and science are well illustrated by the following excerpt: "When we build our University physics laboratories today, we no longer adorn their main gateways as the gateway of the Cavendish Laboratory at Cambridge is adorned: 'The works of the Lord are great: sought out of all those that have pleasure therein.' In fact, when the Royal Society Mond Laboratory for low temperature research was opened at Cambridge in the 1930's it was the carving of a stone crocodile that decorated its entrance" (C. A. Coulson, *Science and Christian Belief* [Chapel Hill, 1955], p. 13).

tation of that love."[21] In addition, Bush insists that for Milton as for other Christian humanists Christ is also, in the words of Whichcote, "the principle of divine life within us, as well as a Saviour without us" and is virtually "identified with right reason."

It is certainly true that in Milton's thought the moral and ethical doctrine and the principle of right reason must be supplemented or implemented by the doctrine of regeneration. As already explained, this is a spiritual experience by which, through *faith, not reason,* the natural ignorance of man is removed and the understanding is enlightened "for the *perception of heavenly things.*" As explained in *The Christian Doctrine,* regeneration by the "Word and the Spirit" destroys the "old man" and renews or regenerates the 'inward man" in "all the faculties" of the mind, so that the regenerate is *"sanctified both in body and soul for the service of God."* The language and thought here are wholly religious, and the experience is not natural but rationalistic in the theological sense. The primary functions of the new man in the new life are *"comprehension of spiritual things, and love of holiness."* Thus believers are *"ingrafted in Christ"* and are made *"partakers of Christ,"* meet for becoming one with Him. By the "teaching of God" the regenerate *"know all that is necessary for eternal salvation and the true happiness of life."* They are blessed with love or charity, which arises *"from a sense of the divine love shed abroad in the hearts of the regenerate by the Spirit,"* whereby they *"become dead to sin, and alive again unto God, and bring forth good works spontaneously and freely."* It is our duty, as explained before, to strive earnestly for perfection as "the ultimate object of our existence," and perfection is defined as *"perfection in Christ."* This spiritually regenerated life is the consequence of repentence and faith; *"it is a habit or condition of mind produced by God."* It is the effect of divine enlightenment—not of right reason, a term which Milton does not use. The purpose and ultimate goal of life is union and fellowship with the Father through Christ. By striving earnestly and unceasingly to be perfect in this life the faithful Christian is assured of salvation, and he will "most certainly attain to everlasting life and the consummation of Glory."

This is the orthodox doctrine of regeneration, which Bush identifies with right reason. It may not completely explain the character and rôle of Christ in *Paradise Lost,* where He represents not only divine

[21] Bush, *Paradise Lost in Our Time,* p. 45.

love but also the irresistible power of order, truth, and right. But the doctrine of regeneration is fundamentally Christian, and it is fundamental in the last books of the epic, where Christ is depicted as the Redeemer of sinful mankind. Christ proclaims "Life to all who shall believe in his redemption," and he pays man's ransom,

> which Man from death redeems,
> His death for Man, as many as offerd Life
> Neglect not, and the benefit imbrace
> By Faith not void of workes: this God-like act
> Annuls thy doom, the death thou shouldst have dy'd,
> In sin for ever lost from life.

This conception is certainly in marked contrast with the best kind of secular and civic morality today, which is usually an effort "to be as Christian as possible" within the much narrower context in which the secular and civic kind of man supposes himself to live. As Casserley says, "His is a kind of semi-Christian, although very sincere, morality, narrowed, truncated and modified precisely because he has accepted a much narrower conception of what the universe is and what human life means and involves."[22] With the dimension of eternity cut out, life and reality become for us "very little things" with the range of interests narrowed and the philosophy of life and morals "inevitably bourgeois and provincial." For the secularist the horizon is the boundary and "he neither dreams nor looks beyond it." Casserley exclaims, "Poor little blinded child of God, his is indeed a case that calls for profound prayer and infinite compassion."

Though this kind of smug secularism was probably not unknown in Milton's day, it at least was uncommon; and Milton himself was not afflicted by spiritual blindness. But his ideal of perfection was, as he knew, not to be attained in this world. Here, as he himself sadly declares—though the words are the Archangel's—the enemies of Truth will always persecute the faithful few. Here the elect are always menaced by worldly power, by "Wolves . . . grievous Wolves,"

> Who all the sacred mysteries of Heav'n
> To thir own vile advantages shall turne
> Of lucre and ambition, and the truth
> With superstitions and traditions taint.

Here truth is forever on the scaffold, wrong forever on the throne.

[22] J. V. Langmead Casserley, *The Retreat from Christianity in the Modern World* (London, 1952), p. 160.

198

"To go against Reason," said Benjamin Whichcote, "is to go against God." With this idea Milton agrees. Whichcote also said, "Reason is the Divine Governor of Man's life; it is the very Voice of God." Unfortunately, this is not true; for after the Fall there is, to quote *The Christian Doctrine,* a "general depravity of the human mind"; and man is unable by nature to obey the voice of Reason. All men sinned in Adam, and all men are guilty of personal sin; they are "enthrall'd/ By sin to foul exorbitant desires." However, it is true that the freedom and efficiency of the will are not wholly lost and that there are "some remnants of the divine image" still in us, "not wholly extinguished by this spiritual death." Almost all mankind "profess" some desire of virtue and turn with abhorrence from the more atrocious crimes. But these "vestiges of original excellence" are not in themselves sufficient for man's salvation. Actually man is saved only by the grace and mercy of God:

> Man shall not quite be lost, but sav'd who will,
> Yet not of will in him, but grace in me
> Freely voutsaft; once more I will renew
> His lapsed powers, though forfeit and enthrall'd
> By sin to foul exorbitant desires.

Man must know "how frail" his fallen condition is, and he must recognize the truth that he owes to God all his deliverance. Through Christ man is redeemed, and the will is restored so that we have it "in our power" to obtain salvation. Through faith, which springs from the will, not the understanding, the mind is enlightened for the perception of heavenly things and the free and spontaneous performance of good works. Cultivating all the virtues, the good Christian strives earnestly and unremittingly to attain *"perfection in Christ."*

This is of course the orthodox plan of salvation for the individual. As for society at large or in the mass, the greater part is irreclaimable. It is clearly implied that many will neglect and scorn God's mercy, His sufferance, and His day of grace. By their own perverse natures hardened and blinded, they will stumble on and deeper fall. Only these are excluded from divine mercy. It is obvious that in this world evil generally triumphs. Here the regenerate exist or persist only precariously in the midst of universal wickedness and injustice; for the world is "to good malignant, to bad men benign." Nevertheless there is hope, for there is also "a victory to be gained over the world, over death and over Satan." This struggle will end only when Christ shall defeat all His foes, "Death last, and with his Carcass glut the Grave." Then only will justice and truth finally prevail in

> New Heav'ns, new Earth, Ages of endless date
> Founded in righteousness and peace and love,
> To bring forth fruits Joy and eternal Bliss.

This story with its devotions and aspirations, its successes and its failures, its sacrifices and its tragedies, its mysteries and its martyrdoms, which made real the meaning and the truth of the Christian vision of righteousness, was, Santayana said, to fill the ages, "Till time stand fixt: beyond is all abyss,/Eternitie, whose end no eye can reach." The student who would understand our society and its civilization cannot afford to ignore this history or the epic which enshrines much of the doctrine and the spirit of Christianity.

VII

Samson Agonistes and the Geneva Bible

A little onward lend thy guiding hand

If *Samson Agonistes* has often been admired, it has also and not infrequently been disparaged. It has been praised as the most simple, direct, powerful, and finished of Milton's poems; but strictures on the structure, the subject matter, and the style are not unheard; and the spirit has been variously interpreted. Some critics object to the harshness of the story; some regard Milton's choice of the subject as a fundamental mistake. Tillyard, who prefers the two epics, finds in the drama complete adequacy of expression, a complete story, and no evidence of the relaxing of Milton's grip; but he is distressed by the unamiable qualities of the poem. Bowra thinks that in *Samson* Milton rediscovered his taste for action and that in Samson's triumph over his enemies Milton's own feelings are mirrored.[1] In the cool, ironical gloating over the destruction of the Philistines, Tillyard, who works out a rather close analogy between Samson and the poet, discovers proof of the "settled ferocity" of Milton's mind and character. He declares that the poem is too austere: there is nothing to mitigate the starkness of the story, which makes no mention of Christ or the vicarious atonement.

[1] E. M. W. Tillyard, *Milton* (New York, 1930), pp. 332 ff.; C. W. Bowra, *Inspiration and Poetry* (London, 1955), p. 113.

201

Such criticism ignores the fact that *Samson Agonistes* is essentially a dramatic version of the Biblical story of Samson, in which there is no gentleness or amiability. It must be remembered that Samson, a hero of the Old Testament, was subject to the Mosaic Law, which was written "by Gods own fingers in the two Tables of the Law" and administered by judges and rulers appointed by God or when these failed by God Himself. William Chillingworth noted that the rigorous Mosaic Law imputed "a sudden violent untimely death, together with all kind of misfortune, that could make this life miserable" if one swerved in any point from the Law. This Law enjoined hatred "without all pity and consideration" of enemies. It imposed a strict outward discipline, with the threat of punishment unto death "without mercy upon the transgressours."[2] Until the coming of Christ there was no law of mercy, no promise of salvation and everlasting life. The harsh Mosaic Law allowed no redemption, no satisfaction, no commutation, but only a "certain fearful looking for of judgment and fiery indignation to consume Gods Adversary." This accounts for the Hebraic spirit of *Samson Agonistes*, which repels some critics, who apparently would have had Samson remodeled—a thing quite impossible, for only Christ is able through the Covenant of Grace to purge our consciences from dead works to serve the living God. The Jews of the Old Testament were, however, not quite excluded from the promise of the Gospel, for through Abraham they were by faith heirs of the promise made to him and his seed. Thus despite the primitive legend and the Mosaic Law Samson's reconciliation with God is possible, though God remains severe and inexorable. The God of Israel, as Milton knew, was a jealous God who ruthlessly destroyed His enemies. The austerity and the harshness of the poem is in complete harmony with the character of Hebrew religion. As Chillingworth says, there is no need fruitlessly to "trifle away the time in insisting upon the nature and quality of the Mosaical Law" and emphasizing the "incomparable excellency of the Covenant of Grace." Critics should realize the truth of Chillingworth's observation: that "*Moses* his Liturgy and Ceremonies" were only civil and legal and that the "eyes of the Israelites were too weak to serve them to pierce through those dark clouds and shadows" without a special revelation from God. The application to *Samson Agonistes* is obvious: Samson and his compeers lacked this special revelation, "the inward sanctify-

[2] "The Eighth Sermon," *The Religion of Protestants* . . . (4th ed.; London, 1674), pp. 418 ff.

ing spiritual Grace" of the Gospel, "the New Covenant, the Covenant of Grace."

This leads us to the consideration of a matter that is essential, difficult, and controversial: the definition of the tone of *Samson Agonistes*. In a famous essay, read before the British Academy (Dec. 10, 1908), the classical scholar Sir Richard C. Jebb asserted that in language and structure the poem is classical but that in idea and spirit it is Hebraic.[3] Milton's mind, Jebb declared, was in the literal and proper sense Hebraic. Milton believed, as did the Hebrews, that God is the personal king and leader of His people, that the Hebrews were His servants, and that from time to time God selects and inspires those who reveal His will. Sometimes Milton substitutes the English for the Hebrews as God's chosen people; and he almost habitually regards himself as God's prophet and interpreter. It is essentially in this character—not in the implied and in some respects fanciful analogy between the personal fortunes of Samson and Milton—that Milton is revealed in *Samson Agonistes*. In the poem the treatment of the subject, Jebb maintained, is genuinely Hebraic:

It would be needless to point out how, or how thoroughly, the spirit of the *Samson Agonistes* is the spirit of Hebraism. Samson is the champion of the Israelites against the Philistines. Jehovah is the God of the Israelites; Dagon is the protecting deity of the Philistines. Samson, through disloyalty to himself, has been permitted to fall into the hands of the idolaters; and Israel shares in his humiliation. Yet, even in this abasement, Samson is confident that the Lord of Hosts will finally assert His own majesty against the idol. This confidence is justified: the honour of the true God and of His chosen people are [sic] vindicated by the catastrophe which punishes the weakness, as it closes the penance, of His individual minister. This is the issue of the drama—Jehovah has prevailed over Dagon; Israel is avenged on Philistia.

Jebb also insisted that the conflict between man and fate, the theme of all Greek tragedy, is not present in *Samson Agonistes*. In Milton's poem there is no conflict between free will and destiny, between "an absolute inward liberty and an inexorable external necessity." Samson is not the victim of fate but, on the contrary, the heroic though fallible champion of the Hebrews and of Jehovah. He is "first victorious, then abased, then finally triumphant in a national cause," which is also the cause of Jehovah. The famous classical scholar there-

---

[3] "*Samson Agonistes* and the Hellenic Drama," *Proceedings of the British Academy 1907–1908* (London, 1908), pp. 341–48.

fore concluded that *Samson Agonistes* is in spirit and idea essentially and genuinely Hebraic.

For many years this sound interpretation stood unchallenged. Finally, W. R. Parker, our eminent iconoclast, entered the lists. He intrepidly, not to say recklessly, attacked Jebb's evidence and conclusions and confidently offered his own interpretations.[4] Parker admitted that there are Hebraic elements in *Samson Agonistes* but he insisted that there are also Hebraic elements in Greek tragedy. He declared that spirit or tone is not at all a matter of ideas. He maintained that we cannot pin spirit down to a specific belief in fate or indeed to any specific belief whatever. In fact most of our standards are, he asserts, completely inadequate to measure Milton's artistic sympathies. Our standards are more than inadequate; they are an insult to Milton's genius. Having thus discarded the normal or rational standard of value and judgment, based upon ideas, Parker then proceeds to consider "in a larger sense" the real meaning of spirit. Spirit is, first, the tone or temper resulting from controlling artistic principles; second, spirit is the tone resulting from dominant ideas "other than artistic"; and, third, spirit is a combination of these two. For Parker, tone is expressed or designated by such words as serious, reflective, earnest, didactic, religious, sublime. These qualities he finds in Greek tragedy; he finds them also in *Samson Agonistes*. Therefore he concludes that *Samson Agonistes*, though admittedly Puritan or Hebraic in origin, is truly Hellenic in spirit, "truly Hellenic" in the combination of all the five qualities of tone.[5]

Parker also insists that there is very little difference between the conception of fate in Greek tragedy and the idea of fate in the poem, though he admits that the word does not occur in the drama. He declares that we must not be misled by words. He turns to *The Christian Doctrine* for a definition of fate: it is "a divine decree emanating from some almighty power." In Greek drama and in *Samson* the universal law of justice is fate; fate is a mysterious divine decree. He concludes that God and fate are similar or indeed practically identical. Parker also declares that Samson is a "Hebrew only by accident."

We see now the result of abandoning the idea in the definition of the spirit or tone of the poem. In this kind of special pleading words

[4] "The Greek Spirit in Milton's *Samson Agonistes*," *Essays and Studies by Members of the English Association*, XX, 21–44; W. R. Parker, *Milton's Debt to Greek Tragedy in Samson Agonistes* (Baltimore, 1937), pp. 189–211.
[5] This is the conclusion of an argument that is extended, ingenious, but, I think, fundamentally sophistical.

seem to have no precise meaning: Aeschylus is Hebraic; God is just another name for fate; Samson is a Hebrew only by accident; *Samson Agonistes* is Hebraic only in origin; and so on. The informed reader will not be convinced by such assertions. Consider briefly the statement that Samson is a Hebrew only by accident. The obvious truth is, of course, that the legend of Samson is nationalistic, that Samson is the hero, the champion of the Israelites, "The glory late of *Israel,* now the grief," as the Chorus, made up of Samson's friends, sings. The reader knows that Samson's birth was "from Heaven foretold." He knows that Samson "Should *Israel* from. *Philistian* yoke deliver." He knows that Samson's impotence and shame are Israel's disgrace. He knows too that Samson's final deed brings honor and freedom to Israel. The reader does not for a moment believe that Samson is a Hebrew only by accident. The critical reader, unmoved by sophistry, is sure of one fact: that in his zealous efforts to prove the poem truly Hellenic, Parker has misrepresented and distorted its true spirit and meaning—the spirit and meaning which Jebb, in his short study, understood and clearly stated with sure insight and true wisdom.

Incidentally, it has recently been argued that Milton's relationship to Greek tragedy can be precisely determined only by study of the Greek plays in the form or the editions in which Milton and his age knew them. Parker obviously read Greek tragedy in modern versions; Milton did not. Only when we know how Greek drama was interpreted in the commentaries of Renaissance editions can we be prepared to understand how Milton may have understood these tragedies,[6] assuming, of course, that Milton was influenced by these commentaries. Parker's rejection of Jebb's interpretation of the spirit of *Samson Agonistes* is to be understood as a phase of the much wider conflict of two schools of Miltonic criticism: an older school which emphasizes the Christian and the Puritan spirit of a stern and austere poet; a younger school which, zealously reinterpreting and revaluating, stresses almost exclusively the poet's broad humanism and genuine Hellenism. The reaction against the traditional view was inevitable and is in some respects desirable. It has undoubtedly discovered and emphasized very significant values. But in the case of *Samson Agonistes* the ardent revaluation has perhaps gone too far, for it denies or minimizes the fundamental religious and Hebraic spirit which pervades the drama as it does the scriptural story of Samson which is its

[6] F. Michael Krouse, *Milton's Samson and the Christian Tradition* (Princeton, 1949), pp. 8 ff.

immediate source. If Milton's debt to the Renaissance and to Hellen-ism is exclusively emphasized, there is grave danger that the student will lose sight of his true character, which, of course, is that of a sin-cere Protestant and religious poet.

Returning, then, to the religious ideas of the poem, without losing sight of the fact that *Samson Agonistes* is in form an imitation of tragedy "as it was antiently compos'd," we are obliged to conclude that Parker's attempt to isolate spirit from idea results in a vague something, unrelated to the obvious sense of the drama. Realistically or rationally defined, as we understand it in the poem, the spirit of *Samson Agonistes* is, as Jebb explained, undeniably Hebraic. The poem is also, as I hope to show, definitely Protestant and even Puritan in character.

Some evidence to prove this assertion may be found by comparing *Samson Agonistes* with the annotations on the story of Samson in the Geneva Bible. This Bible, sound in scholarship and copiously an-notated, was essentially a Protestant version, which for many years enjoyed great popularity. "It became the people's Bible, was Shake-speare's Bible, and is usually known as the Breeches Bible, from the rendering of Gen. iii.7 'and they sewed figge tree leaves together, and made themselves breeches (margin: Ebr. things to gird about them to hide their privities)'."[7] After its first publication in 1560 there were numerous reprints. The following statement is most important for our purpose:

> The popularity of the Geneva Bible, and above all its controversial notes from the extreme Protestant point of view, was distasteful to the Bishops. Moreover, the marked excellence of the Geneva renderings had drawn attention to the notorious defects of the Great Bible, which was almost completely ousted in popular esteem.

The Geneva Bible was, of course, never approved for use in the An-glican Church, but it was widely read and revered, and it exercised a profound influence. The marginal commentary is of the greatest im-portance in this study. It is my belief that some of the ideas in this commentary on the story of Samson emerge and may be identified in *Samson Agonistes*.

Admittedly, there is no external proof that Milton owned a copy

[7] Sir William Craigie, *The Bible in Its Ancient and English Versions*, ed. by H. Wheeler Robinson (Oxford, 1940), p. 182; Brooke F. Westcott, *A General View of the History of the English Bible*, rev. by W. A. Wright (3d ed.; London, 1905), pp. 93 ff.

of the Geneva Bible. In fact it is known that the Bible of the Milton family was the Authorized Version.[8] There is, however, an inherent probability that Milton would know the Geneva Bible and its commentary which expressed opinions which he as a Protestant and a Puritan would approve. At the very least the commentary must be accepted as presenting a terse and authoritative statement of Protestant scriptural exegesis which in this form had the widest currency and a quite incalculable influence. It is almost inconceivable that Milton would not be influenced by the ideas expressed in this famous Protestant Bible and its controversial notes, which were distasteful to the bishops. At any rate the evidence deserves serious consideration as an indispensable segment of the vital intellectual background of the poem, which is a superb synthesis of complex elements.

As understood in this inquiry, the words *Protestant* and *Puritan* are taken in their most essential and inclusive meaning. They do not here refer to liturgical reforms or to church discipline, though it is, of course, recognized that Protestants and Puritans wished to "eradicate all in church services which seemed to them to inculcate false ideas" and to purify and simplify the service so that it would conform with the Gospel. In this study the words imply a religious and theological belief or principle "that brought every man to a direct experience of the spirit and removed intermediaries between himself and the Deity," between the individual and the Word of God. This belief is an affirmation that "man's salvation is God's free gift, not man's purchase by any kind of meritorious works, whether moral or ritual." This Protestant principle, "first stated by Luther," is known as "justification by faith." It affirms that "God has graciously provided a way by which the broken harmony between rebellious and sinful man and a righteous and loving God can be restored" by man's acceptance of the "overture" that God has made. This acceptance is faith, and the result is man's justification. Puritanism has recently been described as an "enterprise which began in the sixteenth century by exhorting men to prepare themselves for a miracle of grace and ended by asserting the presence of the Holy Spirit in every individual."[9] The essence of Puritanism is "an experience of conversion which separates the Puritan

---

[8] J. Milton French, "Milton's Family Bible," *PMLA*, LIII (June, 1938), 363–66; Harris F. Fletcher, *The Use of the Bible in Milton's Prose*, The University of Illinois Studies in Language and Literature, XIV (August, 1929), 20 ff.

[9] Alan Simpson, *Puritanism in Old and New England* (Chicago, 1955), pp. 1–2 *passim*. Ralph B. Perry, *Puritanism and Democracy* (New York, 1944), pp. 90 ff.; Godfrey Davies, *The Early Stuarts 1603–1660* (Oxford, 1937), p. 301; W. E. Garrison, *A Protestant Manifesto* (New York, 1952), p. 29.

from the mass of mankind and endows him with the privileges and the duties of the elect." Puritans believed in the direct revelation of the divine will and purpose to the individual and in man's individual responsibility to God. Having this abiding sense of individual responsibility the Puritan was supported by his faith that nothing in the world is due to chance or blind fate. With fear and trembling each individual must achieve his salvation by obedience to the divine will. The root of Puritanism, as distinguished from Protestantism, of which Puritanism was a special English development, was always "a new birth, which brings with it a conviction of salvation and a dedication to warfare against sin."

In this sense *Samson Agonistes* is essentially Protestant and Puritan, though in the conception of God as stern and inexorable and in the virtual exclusion of love and mercy there is obviously also an Hebraic quality. The spirit of the drama may be defined as a synthesis of Hebraism and Puritanism, both of which are present in Milton's character. In the Geneva Bible the annotations on the story of Samson emphasize God's purpose and indicate that between Samson and God there is a spiritual relationship that does not appear in the Biblical text. In the commentary Samson is the conscious and voluntary agent of the Deity. In the commentary and in *Samson Agonistes* Samson is presented as an individual consciously acting within a scheme or a pattern of religious values that are definitely and recognizably Protestant and Puritan. In origin a "lusty folkhero," Samson is in the commentary and the poem a Protestant and a Puritan, one of the elect. He is not perfect, of course; in his shame and despair he is overwhelmed by a conviction of sin; but he is reborn and becomes a knight of God, a saint, distinguished by his faith and obedience. It may even be said that Samson experiences a "new birth" and it is certainly true that he was reconciled to God.

Let us now examine the evidence.

The tone of the commentary in the Geneva Bible is indicated by the note that accompanies the following text: "Then there was a man in Zorah of the familie of the Danites, named Manoah, whose wife was baren, and bare not."[10] The note reads: "Signifying that their deliuerance came onely of God and not by mans power." This clear statement of divine interest and direct intervention prepares us to understand the leading role that God played in the life of Samson. In the commentary of the Geneva Bible the Lord takes a direct and

---

[10] Judg. 13:2. All quotations are from the 1580 edition.

continuing interest in Samson from his birth until his death. In turn Samson recognizes the divine purpose and his obligation. This idea is reinforced by the note on the text: "For loe, thou shalt conceiue and beare a sonne, and no rasor shall come on his head: for the childe shalbe a Nazarite unto God from his birth." The note on "Nazarite" is: "Meaning, he should be separate from the world and dedicate to God." This seems to express the ideal of the sincere and devout Puritan. In *Samson Agonistes* Samson asks, perhaps somewhat querulously,

> Why was my breeding order'd and prescrib'd
> As of a person separate to God,
> Design'd for great exploits; . . . ?   (30–32)

Both the commentary and the poem emphasize Samson's separation from the world and his dedication to God. Both stress the divine calling and mission of Samson. By God's will Samson was set apart from the world and dedicated to the service of his country and God. The notes explicitly state this idea. Surely the devout and sincere Puritan would have recognized in Samson a kindred spirit.

The willingness of man to obey God's will is asserted in the note on the text: "Then Manoah prayed to the Lorde." The note reads:"He sheweth him selfe ready to obey Gods will, and therefore desireth to knowe farther." Characteristically Protestant and Puritan, Manoah is ready to obey God's will. In the text "Then Manoah took a kid with a meat offring, & offred it upon a stone unto the Lord: and the Angel did wonderously," the phrase "did wonderously" carries this note: "God sent fire from heauen to consume their sacrifice, to confirme their faith in his promise." The statement of God's purpose, the confirming of their faith, is important. Note also the comment on the Lord's accepting the burnt offering: "These graces that we haue receiued of God, & his accepting of our obedience, are sure tokens of his loue toward us, so that nothing can hurt us." Perhaps no statement could reveal more forcefully the unique relationship between man and God, as previously explained.

In the Geneva Bible the commentary on the first part of the story states explicitly the active interest and participation of the Lord. This assurance of God's grace and favor seems to envelop the story. The notes present a religious or theological idea for which the text supplies only a slender basis. This tone is, I believe, reflected in *Samson Agonistes*.

At this point there is one discrepancy that should be mentioned.

Where the text reads "And Manoah arose & went after his wife, & came to the man, and said unto him . . . ," the note explains: "He calleth him man, because he so seemed, but he was Christ the eternall word, which at his time appointed became man." Milton does not say that the angel or man of God was Christ. If he had read this note, he ignored it or decided not to use it.

When Samson asked his parents to obtain for him as wife the woman of Timnath, they replied: "Is there neuer a wife among the daughters of thy brethren, & among all thy people that thou must goe take a wife of the uncircumcised Philistins?" The Geneva version presents this note: "Though his parents did iustly reproue him, yet it appeareth that this was the secret worke of the Lord." In *Samson Agonistes* Samson's parents did not know but he knew that what he "motion'd was of God." Samson somehow understood God's purpose:

> From intimate impulse, and therefore urg'd
> The Marriage on; that by occasion hence
> I might begin *Israel's* Deliverance
> The work to which I was divinely call'd.   (223–26)

Opposite the text "that hee should seeke an occasion agaynst the Philistims" stands in the margin of the Geneva Bible this note: "To fight against them for the deliuerance of Israel." The idea and even the phrasing of this note are repeated in Milton's line "I might begin *Israel's* Deliverance."

At this point there is in the commentary no support for Milton's idea that from intimate impulse Samson knew God's purpose, but this thought is stated in a later note. After Samson had slaughtered the Philistines, he was thirsty and he called upon the Lord. Here the commentary runs thus: "Whereby appeareth, that he did these things *in faith,* and so *with a true zeal to glorifie God and deliuer his country.*" This is, of course, a very important point and fundamental in our argument. Faith and zeal for his divinely appointed work characterize the young and invincible Samson.[11] It is important to recall this glorious Samson, the zealous and obedient servant of the Lord. In reading the poem our attention is at first fixed upon the blinded and wretched slave who has fallen into shame and misery. The reader must remember that Samson was once the Lord's faithful servant. The text of Scripture affords little basis for this interpretation. The commentary in the Geneva Bible may acount for this remodeling or

[11] On Samson as an exemplar of faith see Krouse, *Milton's Samson and the Christian Tradition,* pp. 31 ff. Italics added.

shaping of Samson's character. The commentary and the poem agree in this fundamental and most significant matter. The idea that Samson was the conscious and faithful servant of God is traced to Protestant and even Roman Catholic tradition. As Krouse has said, many writers "in the patristic period called attention to the fact that Samson was impelled and strengthened throughout his career by the Holy Spirit."[12] Indeed Samson was regarded as a saint who "believed and was resplendent in faith." This idea, which is essential, appears in the Geneva commentary.

The marriage to the woman of Timnath affords no further evidence. But in the following episode there seems to be positive evidence that the poem is related to the commentary. After Samson had smitten the Philistines with a great slaughter, he withdrew to the rock Etam, in Judah; and the Philistines pursued him for revenge. Then the men of Judah came to bind Samson and deliver him to his foes, asking, "Knowest thou not that the Philistims are rulers over us?" This abject surrender of their champion is emphatically condemned in the Geneva version. A note in the commentary reads thus: "Such was their grosse ignorance, that they iudged Gods great benefite to be a plague unto them." Surely the reader of this Bible would condemn the men of Judah. Another note is equally outspoken in its condemnation: "Thus they had rather betray their brother, then use the means that God had given for their deliverance." Almost the same opinion is expressed in Samson's reply to the Chorus's reminder that "Yet *Israel* still serves with all his Sons." Samson indignantly replies:

> That fault I take not on me, but transfer
> On *Israel's* Governours, and Heads of Tribes,
> Who seeing those great acts which God had done
> Singly by me against their Conquerours
> Acknowledg'd not, or not at all consider'd
> Deliverance offered.   (241–46)

Declaring that his own people had basely betrayed him to the Philistines and thus had forfeited their chance and hope of freedom, Samson goes on to say that political bondage is the inevitable result of vice and that nations grown corrupt often despise, envy, or suspect him "Whom God hath of his special favous rais'd/As thir Deliverer." Doubtless these lines might be applied to Milton and the other men of the Commonwealth, who, as they thought, were champions of liberty and who were repudiated at the Restoration. But the idea seems

[12] *Ibid.*, pp. 38 ff.

to be a restatement and elaboration of two notes in the Genevan commentary; the men of Judah, grossly ignorant and ungrateful, failed to recognize in Samson the champion of God; and they betrayed their brother, who was the means that God had given for their deliverance. If he read them, it is difficult to believe that Milton was not influenced by these notes.

We come now to Samson's greatest folly and his most grievous sin, his infatuation for Delilah and his revelation of the secret of his strength. Since it profaned the mystery of God, this action brought about his ruin and it deserved the most severe punishment. Milton was scarcely more vigorous in condemning Samson's infatuation than were the authors of the annotations in the Geneva Bible. After the failure of her first attempts to learn the secret of Samson's strength, Delilah persists, saying, "See, thou hast mocked me and told me lies. I pray thee nowe, tell me wherewith thou mightest be bound." Here is the commentary: "Though her falshode tended to make him lose his life, yet his affection so blinded him, that he could not beware." In the poem Samson perceives the design of Delilah, but he is so bewitched that he cannot resist her importunity. With a grain of manhood he might have shaken off her snares,

> But foul effeminacy held me yok't
> Her Bond-slave; O indignity, O blot
> To Honour and Religion! servil mind
> Rewarded well with servil punishment!   (410–13)

Even his present humiliating servitude, Samson exclaims, is not so base or so ignominious as was his former enslavement; and that blindness was worse than this, "That saw not how degenerately I serv'd." As the commentary explains, Samson was so blinded by his affections that he could not beware.[13]

When Samson does not rebuke or chide Delilah for her continued solicitations, the Geneva version utters this clear warning: "It is impossible, if we giue place to our wicked affections, but at length we shalbe destroyed." Finally, when Samson tells Delilah the secret of his strength, a note offers this pertinent comment: "Thus his immoderate affections toward a wicked woman, caused him to lose Gods excellent giftes, and become slaue unto them, whom he should haue ruled." Incidentally, this, it may be noted, is another phase of the fundamental theme of *Paradise Lost:* the surrender to passion, the failure to obey reason and God. Samson's sin is punished by the loss of his

[13] See Krouse, *Milton's Samson and the Christian Tradition*, pp. 38 ff.

strength, which was the gift of God. When his locks are cut off and his strength departs from him, the commentary informs us that he lost his strength "Not for the losse of his heare but for the contempt of the ordinance of God, which was the cause that God departed from him." In the poem Samson exclaims, "O impotence of mind, in body strong!" His physical suffering, though severe, is light as compared with his mental anguish, which springs from his realization that he has been the fool of a deceitful woman and that he has brought dishonor upon Israel and God, whose peculiar servant he was. Although the Chorus may presume to question God's providence and to suggest that He sometimes abandons the elect, "With gifts and graces eminently adorn'd," Samson blames only himself for the loss of God's gifts and favor. He concludes that only death can release him from his miseries, "So many, and so huge, that each apart/Would ask a life to wail." But almost insupportable as are his miseries, they are not in fact out of proportion to his sin, which, as both Milton and the commentary in the Geneva Bible explain, was his surrender to passion and his contempt for the ordinance of God. To say, as Parker does, that Samson suffered far more than he deserved[14] is quite misleading. Such a statement indicates a complete misconception of the God of the Hebrews and of Protestant and Puritan theology, which required severe punishment of those who sinned and disobeyed the Lord. By this standard Samson was not unjustly punished. And he was not, as Parker says, the victim of fate. He was the victim of his own lust and moral blindness, which inevitably brought about his fall, his misery and remorse, and the sharpest grief of all, the desolating consciousness of his having forfeited God's favor. This is the plain truth, not to be concealed by facile essays on the Greek spirit or smart assertions to the effect that Milton "caught the Greek spirit and the Greek spirit caught him." As interpreted in the commentary of the Geneva Bible and in *Samson Agonistes,* Samson's life illustrates the providence of God and the varying fortunes of God's chosen, valiant, but fallible servant. One fact is unmistakable: Samson is responsible for his own sufferings. He laments his condition but he "blames no one but himself." Like a foolish pilot he has shipwrecked his own vessel. As has recently been said, "He is so conscious of his fault, and so contrite for it, that he confesses it even to Harapha and claims that he deserves all, and more than all, his sorrows."[15] Samson's sufferings are not due to fate but to "his own wrong actions." Invincible

---

[14] W. R. Parker, *Milton's Debt to Greek Tragedy in Samson Agonistes,* p. 226.
[15] C. W. Bowra, *Inspiration and Poetry,* p. 117.

while virtue was his mate, Samson has fallen to the "lowest pitch of abject fortune" solely through his own fault; and for all the miseries of his life, "Life in captivity/Among inhuman foes," he blames no one but himself. As Havens said, his misery is deserved, and his punishment though severe is just.

In the light of Samson's calamity, the following note in the Geneva Bible, referring to the angel's wondrous action in response to Manoah's sacrifice, may seem irrelevant: "Those graces that we have receiued of God, & his accepting of our obedience, are sure tokens of his loue toward us, so that nothing can hurt us." From this comment the devout doubtless derived consolation, though Samson's state for a time at least seemed quite hopeless. The note, however, provides some basis for Manoa's assurance, after his son's "noble" death, that God had been with him:

> And which is best and happiest, all this
> With God not parted from him, as was feard,
> But favouring and assisting to the end.   (1718–20)

Samson's prime sin was that he had broken his solemn word or obligation to serve God. This, as Samson says, was due to his pride:

> Fearless of danger, like a petty God
> I walk'd about admir'd of all and dreaded
> On hostile ground, none daring my affront.
> Then swoll'n with pride into the snare I fell
> Of fair fallacious looks, venereal trains,
> Softn'd with pleasure and voluptuous life.   (529–34)

He was, Josephus said, "more elate . . . then he ought to have been." Condemning his own folly, Milton's Samson declares that he was strong in body but weak in mind: immeasurable his strength but his wisdom "nothing more than mean." The Chorus tries to console him with the reflection that wisest men have by "bad Women been deceiv'd," but Samson, insisting that he himself was the prime cause of all sufferings, is inconsolable.

In the Argument of Judges, in the Geneva Bible, it is said that there are two principal points in this book: first, "the battel that the church of God hath for the maintenance of true religion against idolatrie and superstition"; second, "what great danger that common welth is in, when as God giueth not a magistrate to reteine his people in the pureness of religion and his true service." Both of these points, the first religious, the second semipolitical, are significant ideas in *Samson*

214

Agonistes. They stamp the poem as fundamentally Protestant and Puritan.

Samson's indictment of the rulers of Israel for their base surrender of him, their deliverer, to the Philistines has already been considered. The cause of even more poignant grief and remorse is Samson's realization that his folly and sin have brought honor and fame to Dagon but dishonor and obloquy to God. Manoa says that Dagon is magnified, but God

> Besides whom is no God, compar'd with Idols,
> Disglorifi'd, blasphem'd and had in scorn
> By th' Idolatrous rout amidst thir wine.   (441–43)

The realization of this ignominy is his chief affliction. It has brought shame and sorrow and anguish to his soul. But whatever may happen to Samson, he is sure that Dagon must stoop and that the Lord will destroy His enemies. This affirmation of Samson's faith occurs early in the poem. Samson says,

> This only hope relieves me, that the strife
> With me hath end; all the contest is now
> 'Twixt God and *Dagon; Dagon* hath presum'd,
> Me overthrown, to enter lists with God,
> His Deity comparing and preferring
> Before the God of *Abraham*. He, be sure,
> Will not connive, or linger, thus provok'd,
> But will arise and his great name assert:
> *Dagon* must stoop, and shall e're long receive
> Such a discomfit, as shall quite despoil him
> Of all those boasted Trophies won on me,
> And with confusion blank his Worshippers.   (460–71)

Accepting Samson's assurance as a prophecy, Manoa is confident that God will not long defer "To vindicate the glory of his name."

There is no doubt of the ultimate outcome. Samson's lot is in his own opinion hopeless and his woes are incurable, but the close of his life is characteristically and inevitably triumphant. We should consider the reason for this triumph. Jebb declared that Samson's will is the agent of the catastrophe, and in a sense this is true. We must not, however, make the mistake of ignoring God's part in Samson's triumph. It is clear that as God's servant Samson should not act blindly and that his last act should be a vindication of his life. To triumph and to die fittingly Samson must regain the favor if not the grace of God. He must be reconciled to God. The key to the last hours of Samson's life is to be found in the commentary of the Geneva Bible. On the text "And the heare of his head beganne to grow againe after that it was shauen" there is the following marginal comment: "Yet had he not his strength againe, til he had called upon God, and reconciled himselfe." This is the necessary explanation of Samson's spiritual regeneration. In *Samson Agonistes* it is, I think, implied that Samson was spiritually reborn and reconciled to God. When he is on the point of leaving to obey the command of the lords of the Philistines, Samson has regained some degree of confidence and self-respect. He declares that he will do nothing dishonorable, nothing to discredit himself and God. He will not abuse his "Consecrated gift"; he will not prostitute himself before idols or vaunt his strength in honor of Dagon. He will not stain his vow of Nazarite. This assured state of mind, this resolution could not have been achieved without Samson's consciousness that God is with him. With a will reborn and restored to harmony with God's will, Samson is prepared to vindicate himself and the honor of God. On any other basis his final heroic act is impossible and indeed inconceivable.

In the Geneva Bible the text "Call Samson, that he may make us pastime. So they called Samson out of the prison house, & he was a laughing stock unto them" has the following comment: "Thus by gods iust iudgements they are made slaues to infidels which neglect their vocation in defending the faythfull." We are reminded of the point in the Argument: the battle of the church to maintain true religion against idolatry and superstition, which is also the implied theme of *Samson Agonistes*. In the poem we know that Samson will not make pastime for the lords of the Philistines. By his rejection of the Officer's first imperative message, by his indignant refusing to perform feats before Dagon, the "worst of indignities," we are assured that Samson has regained his right mind. Thus we are prepared for his last deed as the servant of God. The commentary explains that Samson's strength had gone from him "Not for the losse of his heare but for the contempt of the ordinance of God, which was the cause that *God departed from him.*" It should be remarked that in Manoa's last speech Milton apparently echoes the last clause. Samson died heroically,[16] "With *God not parted from him,* as was feared,/But favouring and assisting to the end." Actually, of course, God had departed from Samson or had withdrawn his favor; but at the last He returned, and Samson with God's favor "quit himself like Samson."

---

[16] In both quotations the similar clauses are italicized.

216

It is dramatically fitting that Samson's full reconciliation with God apparently occurs just before the catastrophe, which presents Israel's champion in his true character as God's avenger. Here all themes merge; here is the culmination of *Samson Agonistes* as a Protestant and Puritan drama. The reconciliation and the principal theme are stated in the Geneva Bible. Here is the text: "Then Samson called upon the Lord, and said, O Lord God, I pray thee, thinke upon me: O God, I beseeche thee, strengthen me at this time onely, that I may be at once avenged of the Philistims for my two eyes." Here is the marginal commentary: "According to my vocation, which is to execute Gods iudgements upon the wicked." The comment, of course, characteristically interprets Samson's act as more than a deed of personal revenge. The note indicates that throughout his life (except, of course, in his infatuation with Delilah) Samson was conscious of his vocation. This is also true of Milton's Samson, of whom the Chorus chants,

> Living or dying thou hast fulfill'd
> The work for which thou wast foretold
> To *Israel.*

He executes God's judgment upon the wicked idolaters, enemies of Israel and God. He did so not in pride but in humility, "humbling himself for neglecting his office & the offence thereby giuen," as the commentary explains.

Manoa emphasizes this point. He takes pride in the heroic death of his son, in his crushing revenge upon his enemies, in the opportunity of freedom thus offered Israel. But most of all Manoa rejoices because God was not parted from Samson, "But favouring and assisting to the end." This is why Manoa is not inconsolable for his son's death. He knows that Samson's final deed was not a mere display of physical strength. He knows that Samson's spiritual regeneration preceded and made possible his astounding demonstration of physical prowess. He knows that Samson was enabled to revenge himself upon his enemies and to execute God's purpose only because his faith had been renewed and he had found favor with God. In the words of the Chorus, God, who had seemed to hide his face, unexpectedly returned and bore witness to His glorious champion. In his heroic death Samson was obedient to his heavenly duty. His is a spiritual victory. It is the most illustrious proof of his divine vocation, which like that of all loyal Protestants and Puritans was to defend true religion against idolatry and superstition.

217

Averting our gaze from the blind, wretched, despondent prisoner at the opening of the poem and recalling the entire career of Samson, a career consciously devoted to God, we should recognize in Samson a character, a pattern, a religious attitude unmistakably Hebraic but also Protestant and Puritan in spirit. The specifically Protestant and Puritan character is identified by the two themes of Judges: the battle to maintain true religion against idolatry and superstition, and the danger to the commonwealth when the magistrate does not retain the people in true religion and God's service. The Samson of the Geneva Bible and of *Samson Agonistes*, quite unlike the crafty strong man of Hebrew legend,[17] is, on the whole, the chosen and dedicated servant of God, definitely conscious of his vocation, animated by faith and zeal, invincible against the idolatrous enemies of Israel, undone by his folly which forfeits God's favor, and in the end signally triumphant by repentance and reconciliation with God. Obviously, then, it is not primarily Samson's will but his faith and his obedience to God that are the keynotes of his character and the proof that, in spite of his faults, he is one of the elect.[18]

It strengthens the conception of Samson as God's champion to survey the tradition to which the poem is probably indebted. Through patristic and medieval commentaries Samson, purified by allegory, emerges as a type of Christ as well as, somewhat incongruously, a moral example of the dedicated man who falls through lust; Israel had been blamed for failing to back him; and his repentance had been made explicit. To this traditional view of Samson Milton adds, as Krouse observes, the intelligence, the noble speeches, and the traditional temptations which provide the vital thought, the dramatic action, the spiritual tension of this psychological drama, this "theatre of the soul."[19]

The commentary in the Geneva Bible, which is, of course, only one

[17] Kenneth Fell, "From Myth to Martyrdom," *English Studies*, XXXIV (August, 1953), 145–53. Fell argues that *Samson Agonistes*, although rich in spiritual insight, is limited by the story, "which lacks a mature teaching of the true way of dealing with one's enemies." By the "true way" he means, I suppose, the Christian way of forgiving. But he must be reminded that in the seventeenth century it was no part of Protestant policy to tolerate what was regarded as idolatry and superstition.

[18] See M. E. Grenander, "*Samson's* Middle: Aristotle and Dr. Johnson," *University of Toronto Quarterly*, XXIV (July, 1955), 377–89. In this article, which appeared long after my study was completed, Grenander observes, I am glad to see, that the relation between Samson and God is the most important one in the play. He also regards as crucial Samson's loss of and restoration to God's favor (p. 381).

[19] Cf. Una Ellis-Fermor, *The Frontiers of Drama* (New York, 1946), pp. 24 ff.

in a long series, is important because of its well-known Protestant stamp: its emphasis upon Samson's separation from the world and upon his divine vocation to serve God and destroy idolatry. It is, I think, inconceivable that Milton was not influenced by Protestant interpretations of Scripture, which, concisely stated, were readily accessible in the famous commentary of the popular Geneva Bible. Under this influence, I assume, Milton in his characteristically individual way, with allusions to his own personal misfortunes and even to recent or contemporary political conditions, wrote the drama of Samson's life, which therefore takes on a specific meaning and value which has no conceivable relation to the ideas and the spirit of Greek tragedy.

In form, except in the choruses, which are a blending of the Greek and Italian styles, *Samson Agonistes* is, of course, Greek. It was written after the ancient manner, avoids comic matter, strictly observes the unities, and illustrates Aristotle's definition of the purpose of tragedy. But all this, excepting the purpose or the catharsis, does not greatly affect the essential thought or meaning. The theory that *Samson* is Greek in spirit is untenable. The theory ignores the thought, the intellectual content and spirit of the poem, which is a unique and imaginative synthesis of the Hebrew legend, the Christian tradition, and the Protestant character by a poet who was both a true humanist and a sincere though independent and cultured Puritan.

It need hardly be said that this study deliberately ignores certain aspects of Puritanism: the gloomy view of life, the contempt for beauty, the occasional hypocrisy, the stereotyped other-worldliness, and other features and limitations which are sometimes taken as proof that medieval orthodoxy and the Puritanism of the Reformation were fundamentally related.[20] Doubtless English Puritanism of the sixteenth and seventeenth centuries had a high ancestry—but such comparative views, however enlightening, are not pertinent here. Nearer home strikes the following truth: "The hand of God rested upon the Puritan, and he observed a world of sin and ignorance which could be saved only by the imposition of the order of society, civil and religious, which God had revealed to him."[21] In their unremitting struggle against Satan and the powers of darkness in the world and in particular against the papists, commonly scorned and feared as

[20] G. G. Coulton, "The High Ancestry of Puritanism," *Ten Medieval Studies* (Cambridge, 1945), pp. 46–51.
[21] W. K. Jordan, *The Development of Religious Toleration in England* . . . (London, 1932), pp. 240 ff.

idolatrous and superstitious, militant Puritans would have hailed Samson as a worthy prototype. "The eyes of the Puritans were fixed entirely upon the purging of the Church so as to concentrate its energy more effectively on the struggle with Rome." For Puritans the Word of God was a divine law, the absolute rule of faith and discipline, whereas the Church of England may be regarded as "an attempt to nationalize the religious organization with loyalty to the Queen as its fundamental article." In theory at least Puritans were loyal subjects, but they owed their deepest allegiance to God. Although some of these meanings are not excluded as overtones, it seems best here to take Puritanism in its most absolute sense. The Puritan was one who by God's grace was set apart from the world, who had a conviction of his divine vocation, and who dedicated himself to unceasing warfare against sin.

In this sense *Samson Agonistes,* the last work of the devout and disillusioned poet, is Protestant and Puritan. Beyond the betrayed, imprisoned, degraded slave of the Philistines, "Eyeless in *Gaza* at the mill with slaves," we behold the outlines of a noble and loyal servant of God, the holy Nazarite, the judge and invincible champion of Israel, not perfect but dedicated and except for one fatal lapse obedient. After a heroic life of service to Israel and God he is undone by his own folly: he is "Blind among enemies, O worse then chains,/ Dungeon, or beggery, or decrepit age!" But although he despairs he does not rashly doubt "Divine Prediction." He neither sues for life nor seeks an easy way out of his calamity. In spite of all he is still the "Image" of God's strength as he is God's "mighty minister." At last, repentant and with faith renewed, he goes resolutely as God's servant to a triumphant death. In the ending of this "life Heroic" there is, Manoa says, nothing for tears,

> no weakness, no contempt,
> Dispraise, or blame, nothing but well and fair,
> And what may quiet us in a death so noble.

As the champion of Israel and the servant of God, Samson has earned his reward, a monument planted round with shade

> Of Laurel ever green, and branching Palm,
> With all his Trophies hung, and Acts enroll'd
> In copious Legend, and sweet Lyric Song.

Here shall resort Israel's valiant youth to be inspired "To matchless valour, and adventures high." And virgins too shall

> Visit his Tomb with flowers, only bewailing
> His lot unfortunate in nuptial choice,
> From whence captivity and loss of eyes.

With this prudent reflection and the final assurance of God's inscrutable wisdom the drama closes, a drama which in thought and spirit is deeply indebted to Scripture and to Protestantism.

Samson exemplifies that side of Protestantism which emphasized dynamic individual action. Herschel Baker says that the influence of Protestantism can hardly be said to have been toward "causing man to retire from the world and resign himself to his well-merited damnation."[22] Damnation suggests Calvinism, in which there were two basic facts: "a God of power and righteous anger rather than love and bland rationality, and a man of impotence and sin rather than virtue and rational self-sufficiency." Pausing only to remark that a man of rational self-sufficiency would be an alien in any church and would probably have no need of religion, one may say that the God of *Samson Agonistes* is mainly Hebraic, with perhaps something of the Calvinist Deity added—the stern God of our fathers, to whom are due both reverence and fear. But Samson is not passive and he is far from impotent. Though he has a proper conviction of sin, he rather conforms to Milton's conception of active and purposeful virtue within a society or a tribe owing allegiance to God. At his best Samson is loyal to his country, to God, and to himself as God's servant. Essentially a Hebrew, he is in his vocation or calling and in his sense of duty to God a symbol of the Protestant character and, it might be argued, a hero of "Geneva print," literally one of the elect, a "person separate to God." But he also has a deep conviction of sin and weakness, for he has shipwrecked the vessel trusted to him from above. The cause of his greatest shame and sorrow is the realization that he has brought scandal to Israel and to feeble hearts distrust and doubt of God; hence his anguish of soul that suffers not his eyes to sleep or his thoughts to rest. He does not, however, blame God for his humiliation and affliction, which, as he admits, is due only to his own folly. And as the end draws near his faith is renewed, and he goes resolutely to face the enemy and vindicate the glory of his name.

It is not improbable that Milton intended to suggest in Samson the prototype of the militant Protestant and Puritan, the servant of God, whose prime obligation was to live righteously and—to use a phrase sanctioned by more than a century of belief and practice—to

---

[22] Baker, *The Dignity of Man* (Cambridge [Mass.], 1947), p. 313.

defend true religion against idolatry.[23] This idea, implicit throughout the poem, is explicitly stated by the Chorus just as Samson departs on his fateful mission:

> Go, and the Holy One
> Of *Israel* be thy guide
> To what may serve his glory best, & spread his name
> Great among the heathen round.

With the assurance that the heathen had sunk down into the pit that they had made and with the knowledge that Samson had died not ingloriously as God's servant, the reader is dismissed with poignant realization of the overwhelming tragedy of Samson's life but also "With peace and consolation . . . /And calm of mind all passion spent."

[23] This subject is treated incidentally in Ann Gossman's doctoral dissertation entitled "The Synthesis of Hebraism and Hellenism in Milton's *Samson Agonistes*" (The Rice Institute, 1957), a distinguished contribution to Milton scholarship.

VIII

The Paradise Within

And speak the truth

To think and speak intelligently about religion and poetry one must have from within
an experience and an understanding of the
real meaning and value of religion and poetry. If the study of Milton's poetry is to be
significant and moving, the student must
have or must cultivate a genuine interest in religion and some understanding of the rich religious background of Milton's life. It is essential to have or to acquire an informed imagination, "the utmost
sympathetic imagination," and a keen appreciation of the value of
religion. With initial sympathy and with diligence and intelligence
one may understand and appreciate the poetry of religion. The truth
is that religion and poetry have much in common. In the words of
Santayana, there was in Christianity "a new poetry, a new ideal, a
new God. . . . The moving power was a fable" which "carried the
imagination into a new sphere."[1]

It was a whole world of poetry descended among men . . . so that they
might move through supernatural realms in the spirit while they walked
the earth in the flesh . . . . The idea of Christ himself had to be constructed
by the imagination in response to moral demands, tradition giving only
the barest external points of attachment. The facts were nothing until they

[1] George Santayana, *Interpretations of Poetry and Religion* (New York, 1900),
pp. 86–94.

223

became symbols; and nothing could turn them into symbols except an eager imagination on the watch for all that might embody its dream . . . . The whole religious doctrine is thus religious and efficacious only when it becomes poetry, because only then is it the felt counterpart of personal experience and a genuine expansion of human life.

The language of religion is often sheer if conventional poetry, the imaginative expression of aspiration and reverence, of love and faith, of grief and hope. Faith is nourished by poetry. Poetry of language and ritual is essential to the expression of religious ideas, which appeal to the profoundest thoughts and emotions of human nature, emotions and thoughts hallowed by experience and time. Poetry endows with a more vivid and intense life, beauty, and meaning the conventional conceptions of religion, so that we may in imagination see, for example, the "Star-led Wisards" hastening to the manger of Jesus, the Attendant Spirit in his pure ambrosial weeds descending to succor the innocent children benighted in the wild wood, and Satan "In shape and gesture proudly eminent" standing like a tower or on swift wings exploring in solitary flight the wild abyss of chaos. The rhythm and the imagery of poetry should carry spiritual truth to the receptive heart directly and convincingly. The hymn, which provides for many people their principal experience of poetry, is the best example of the power of rhythmic language to stir the imagination and the emotions. The heartfelt supplication of one of the most simple and sincere hymns must have touched the souls of millions:

> Swift to its close ebbs out life's little day;
> Earth's joys grow dim, its glories pass away;
> Change and decay in all around I see;
> O thou who changest not, abide with me.

There is, however, a problem. There is a barrier between the modern reader and the understanding and genuine appreciation of Milton's poetry. It is the secularism, the rationalism of our time, which is nominally but in fact not sincerely and consistently religious. The contrast between the temper of the present and the past may be indicated by two statements: first, the development of the conquest of nature makes the modern American and European "look exclusively to the control of material objects for the way of happiness"; second, "ancient wisdom sought self-control by spiritual exercise." These extremes can hardly be reconciled. Between them a great gulf is fixed; between them yawns a great abyss; between them flows the unplumbed salt estranging sea. Only by rejecting material standards of goodness and happiness, only by cultivating genuine spiritual values, humility, sincerity, seriousness, love, faith, and charity—only thus may the reader approach Milton intelligently and in the proper spirit. Self-sufficiency, superficiality, pride are fatal handicaps.

More than this is required. One needs to understand the religious character and spirit, its rituals and symbols, its traditions and even its doctrine which helped to shape individual lives and the history of many centuries. Unless the rationalistic faculty is held in check and the sympathetic understanding of the reader is engaged, the reading of Milton's poetry may become a mere literary exercise, limited to the study and appreciation of style and metrical matters, as has too frequently been the case. In fact some modern criticism of Milton has been completely divorced from serious consideration or real understanding of his thought. Of this latter fault Mark Van Doren may serve as an illustration. In *The Noble Voice* he presents an endless catalogue of Milton's alleged faults: his imagination in *Paradise Lost* was unregulated by a right conception of his task; before Book X the story fails "as the impossible must always fail"; a bungling and prolix writer, Milton merely assembled property from a miscellany of sources; he gives us no definite images, the pagan deities, for example, thronging "the dark avenues of *Paradise Lost*" and "glittering illicitly"; his Christ is "an abysmal failure" in the role of Redeemer; Milton misconceived the Fall, for our loss of Paradise really came "not through our weakness but through our strength." In *The Art of Poetry* William P. Ker averred that the scenery of the epic is merely childish or quaint and that Milton realized too late his great failure: he had not brought God and Satan face to face, and so Satan had "all the heroism to himself." How could Milton have overlooked this scene, a great duel between God and Satan! For modern sophisticates Yvor Winters may be allowed to speak. It is significant that "many years ago" he found Milton's method in *Paradise Lost* "more nearly defensible" than he does now. Obviously the years have brought wisdom. He now grows extremely tired of the poem's "meaningless inflation," its "tedious falsification of the materials by way of excessive emotion." He condemns especially the use "of cannon in the angelic war," the "preposterous, cloudy, and tedious" but "extremely circumstantial details of the highway from Hell," and "above all" the "disquisitions" addressed by God to the Son in Book III. He concludes: "It requires more than a willing suspension of disbelief to read most of Milton; it requires a willing suspension of intelligence."[2] Obviously *Paradise Lost* is a colossal failure. Ignoring the thought or misrepresenting it, these critics concentrate their fire upon Milton's alleged faults as an artist and a man—and even in their recantations they damn him with the faintest praise.[3]

It should be obvious that these are extreme and generally indefensible personal opinions or prejudices, depending in part on the reigning literary taste, the style or thought of the moment, and quite detached from or unrelated to the great and vital religious tradition which his poetry reflects and which I have attempted to indicate. The traditional, humanistic, Christian conception of truth is not highly valued in our modern scientific utopia, where[4]

We are setting out to "conquer space" (as, absurdly, we call it)—and tremble that the force that should convey us to the moon may convey us to—the other place instead; we have delved into the silent depths of our souls—and return shaken; we have unearthed the secrets of the past and, burdened by them, know no longer whither we are going. Rich as never mankind was, surrounded by all the wonders of the world, of the Now and the Past, we live among them (if "live" be the word) as the worm lives among corpses. "And yet quite comfortably": so the cynic retorts. Yes; comfort we have achieved. Not indeed that comfort for which anxious souls once longed; which they found in the surrender of self to the mystery of divine grace, but the comfort of the oyster that dozes in its shell.

In our utopia there is no dearth of information. It is wafted at us unceasingly, overwhelmingly, day-in, day-out: a fund of irrelevancies; and the inevitable effect is that "the riches of the world—spiritual, artistic, historic of every kind—all are ground to dust in the same mill." What is modern society, for all its boasted efficiency and its smug conceit? The monotony of the office and the factory, the dreariness of the slum, the feverish quest for thrills, the escape into rootless fancy or bloodless artistry! There is only one slender thread[5]

by which our age seems to reach, or at least to grope after, reality—the emotions of sex; and these have been talked about, analyzed, represented

[2] Yvor Winters, "Problems for the Modern Critic of Literature," *The Hudson Review*, IX (Autumn, 1956), 256. This antipathy, it may be added, is evident in Norman Douglas' biased article "Another Source of *Paradise Lost*," *Atlantic Monthly*, CII (1908), 696–703—an article which was not published in England.

[3] T. S. Eliot, "Milton," *Proceedings of the British Academy* (London, 1947).

[4] G. Zuntz, "Knowing—Learning—Living," *The Hibbert Journal*, LIV (July, 1956), 350.

[5] *Ibid.*

and misrepresented so endlessly, so devastatingly, that only the most abstruse perversion may still draw a passing attention. Who would dare, in our disillusioned days, to praise the simple, unfathomable might of world-creating Love?

There is another way, another spirit, another purpose in life, as Christians know: God is love and as such He is revealed in Christ, "and *love is not a metaphysical essence but personal moral will and action.*"[6] The basis of this life is the Spirit, which "authenticates itself both as a divine Spirit—it comes from God—and also as the Spirit of Christ. No argument can establish the fact that the Spirit is from God or that it is the Spirit of Christ." But one who belongs to the community knows the Spirit and knows whence the Spirit comes and knows also who the Spirit is. The Spirit comes from God and is the abiding presence of Christ. The one remembered is still known. The one known as the divine center of the church's life is the very one who is also remembered. The Spirit is the Lord; the Lord is the Spirit. The Christian life is life not only in Christ but also with Christ. The one who lived and died lives still; and it is possible still to walk with Him and to know Him in the breaking of the bread. This is the real meaning of the resurrection.[7] Upon this revelation the meaning of human history depends. It is not easy to believe in the meaning of history. Knox says we have come "to a realization of the depth and recalcitrance of moral evil in ourselves and in all men, to a recognition of the limitations implicit in our finitude, to an understanding of the realities of man's political, economic, and social life, which makes any easy optmism impossible." Reading history we note the rise and fall of nations and cultures "in cycles which in perspective seem as short and are apparently as final and futile as the lifespan of man"; we see "evil manifesting itself continually in the same hideous forms, good winning its victories but also suffering its defeats, as century follows century and our tiny planet is hurled on its precarious way among the stars." We may well ask, "What does it all come to?" If, as Christian faith affirms, God revealed Himself in history, that act is[8]

the sign and guarantee of a purpose of God in history, a purpose to which all of nature is subordinate. History ceases to be formless and void; it takes on character and order. It is seen to have a center, and by the same token we know it will have an end—not merely a fortuitous end, as by an accident

[6] John Knox, *On the Meaning of Christ*. The William Belden Noble Lectures delivered at Harvard University, 1947 (New York, 1947), p. 57. Italics mine.
[7] *Ibid.*, pp. 39–40.   [8] *Ibid.*, pp. 112–13.

to our planet or a burning out of the sun, but a true end, a decisive end, because God's purpose in and through it will have been fulfilled.

As Christians believe, that purpose is "the bringing of many sons to glory"; it is "the creation of the family of God, from whom every family in heaven and earth is named; the coming to pass, whether in heaven or on earth or in some new heaven and earth, of the Kingdom of His Love."

The actual application of Christian principles to social, economic, and political life is not the subject here. For that we must turn to genuine Christian statesmen, such as Sir Stafford Cripps, who declared that the accomplishment of economic and social justice should be our present objective. He said:[9]

This is not to press for an ideal other-worldly society, but for our society as it actually exists. We are not primarily concerned with individual preparation, in a hopeless world of evil, for an ideal world to come hereafter. We are concerned with the creation, out of the present drab unhappiness, of a new and joyous life for the people in "our green and pleasant land."

The scriptural saying "By their fruits ye shall know them" does not mean "by their hopes or imaginings of something better or different hereafter." It means, he says, "by what you see them actually do." We must not, he insists, "seek to save our souls by our religious exercises, for then assuredly we shall lose them." We must by our "selfless devotion in a great cause" and by our "continuing and continual" acts, each one small and insignificant, actually "build the Kingdom of God on earth in the most real and tangible form."

Milton certainly had no expectation that the kingdom of God would be established in his "green and pleasant land," though Adam is assured that God will be present in valley and plain, as He was in Paradise, and that there will be

> of his presence many a signe
> Still following thee, still compassing thee round
> With goodness and paternal Love.

Milton's vision was rather of "New Heav'ns, new Earth,"

> Founded in righteousness and peace and love,
> To bring forth fruits Joy and eternal Bliss.

Nor was Milton's religion quite that of John Knox, for whom divine love is central. As a Protestant and a Puritan Milton emphasized

[9] Cripps, *Towards Christian Democracy* (New York, 1946), p. 6.

228

man's sin and guilt, which made the world a place of evil; but he also made man under God and with God's grace responsible for his own salvation. Admittedly his religion was austere and singularly individualistic. There is in it little or no thought of social service, for obviously Christ expressed Milton's thought when He said that the people are "a herd confus'd, A miscellaneous rabble." Apparently there is no conception of the *community* of saints on earth, though a spiritual community is doubtless implicit in his vision of heaven. Milton's religion or theology is inadequately characterized as merely Hebraic or Puritan, with reference no doubt to his sense of God's absolute sovereignty and man's obligation to obey implicitly. This is only part of his faith. In Christianity there are, it has been said, two distinct elements or principles: "world renunciation" and "world penetration." Although Milton had no faith in the reformation or amelioration of society and was no believer in progress,[10] he renounced only the evil of the world and did not withdraw from it, except, of course, as he was isolated by his blindness and the restoration of the Stuart monarchy. Milton's religion may be partly described as somewhat restrictive but not negative, as morally constructive but not fanatical or evangelistic, as realistic but not optimistic, as individualistic and intelligently and independently Protestant. Milton said that in "matters of religion, he is learnedest who is simplest." Such phrases as these have little meaning, however, unless they are illustrated and embodied in his ideas, which as previously sketched I may informally recaptitulate.

In reading Milton's poetry one must reflect on the nature and the origin of good and evil. One may speculate that Paradise represents the "wholeness of nature, the realm of instinct" and that the myth of the lost Paradise symbolizes "the genesis of consciousness in the development of the spirit," consciousness born of pain and suffering, through which one ascends to regeneration and bliss in God. The truth, then, is a paradox: the myth of the Fall does not humiliate man but in fact exalts him. If man is a fallen creature and if he fell by virtue of the freedom inherent in him from the first, his is a lofty and

[10] In this matter Milton's view is in accord with the best modern thought, which on the soundest evidence has wholly rejected the eighteenth-century dogma of progress. We now know that social development is slow, uncertain, and precarious; that man swiftly reverts to savagery, more terrible because technified, a savagery which has made "our century and our lifetime perhaps the bloodiest and cruellest in human history"; that "progress as a secular faith is plainly doomed." (J. V. L. Casserley, *The Retreat from Christianity in the Modern World* [London, 1952], pp. 99–100.)

a free spirit. Thus the myth of the Fall is a myth of man's greatness, and the possibility of evil is the condition of real virtue. This is not precisely the orthodox Christian dogma, which is rather that man's fall is proof of his frailty and his failure to obey God and that man's "First Disobedience . . . /Brought Death into the World, and all our woe."

But Christian doctrine also holds that the Fall was fortunate in that it made possible and necessary man's redemption through Christ. As Milton states in *The Christian Doctrine*, the restoration of man is "the act whereby man, being delivered from sin and death by God the Father through Jesus Christ, is raised to a far more excellent state of grace and glory than that from which he had fallen." In the words of St. Ambrose, Adam's sin "has brought more benefit to us than harm." This story attempts to express an understanding of "the relation in which God *actually* stands to human life": God is "*in fact* our Redeemer from Sin and Death." The truth of this story is the "meaning which was actually discovered" in the event through man's experience. Believing the story, Milton emphasizes man's freedom before and by grace after the Fall, embraces the doctrine that toleration of evil is an essential part of God's providence, and proclaims the truth that through faith, suffering, obedience, and grace a spiritual paradise may be attained. It is one of the unique values of Milton's poetry that it stimulates thoughtful and serious reflections upon man's character and destiny, for which man alone under God's providence is responsible.

In an age of extreme political and religious agitation, conflict, and change, Milton's thought was essentially that of an independent Protestant. It is one of those half-truths described by a Victorian poet as "the blackest of lies" that the Reformation was "the recovery in the Church of Scriptural Christianity." The real truth in this statement is "that the Reformation was in part the cause and in part the consequence of an unprecedented spread in the popular knowlege of the Scriptures."[11] From this knowledge there followed a new critical alertness and a new emphasis on "the literal sense of Scripture at the expense of the other traditional modes of interpretation." The Reformers decided that nothing could be required to be believed and practiced "than what was plainly to be read in the title-deeds of the faith," that is, in Scripture. Reform was justified by an appeal from existing customs or doctrine "to the witness of Scripture." For Milton

[11] The Rt. Rev. F. J. Taylor, "Scripture and Tradition in the Anglican Reformation," *Scripture and Tradition* (London, 1955), p. 59.

the Bible was, of course, the basis of Christian doctrine, which he defined as "Faith, or the knowledge of God,—and Love, or the worship of God." The Holy Scriptures were written not for occasional purposes only but "for the use of the church throughout all ages"; they are, partly by their own simplicity and partly by divine illumination, "plain and perspicuous in all things necessary to salvation, and adapted to the instruction even of the most unlearned, through the medium of diligent and constant reading." The Scriptures in themselves are sufficient "to make men wise unto salvation through faith, that the man of God may be perfect, thoroughly furnished unto all good works."

Protestantism may be defined as the assertion of the right of the individual to private judgment in matters of conscience. Among the Reformers there was not, of course, complete freedom. In practice the Bible was the principal, if not the sole, source of Christian belief; but the Bible was interpreted in accordance with the creeds and the opinions of the holy doctors of the Church and the leaders of the Reformation. Milton's position was that of an extreme Protestant. In *The Christian Doctrine* he said: "Every believer has a right to interpret the Scriptures for himself, inasmuch as he has the Spirit for his guide, and the mind of Christ is in him." In *Paradise Lost* he declares that the truth is "Left onely in those written Records pure,/Though not but by the Spirit understood."

The foundation of Milton's faith and doctrine was the same as that of other Protestants: the Scriptures, which Archbishop Sandys said God caused to be written for our learning and which he extolled thus:[12]

This most precious jewel is to be preferred before all treasure. If thou be hungry, it is meat to satisfy thee; if thou be sick, it is a present remedy; if thou be weak, it is a staff to lean unto; if thine enemy assault thee, it is a sword to fight withal; if thou be in darkness, it is a lanthorn to guide thy feet; if thou be doubtful of the way, it is a bright shining star to direct thee; if thou be in displeasure with God, it is the message of reconciliation; if thou study to save thy soul, receive the word ingrafted, for that is able to do it: it is the word of life.

The meaning is clear: in "the spiritual tabernacle, in matters of religion, pertaining to the service and worship of God, all things should be done according to the rule of his own will, which is set down in his

---

[12] Edwin Sandys, *The Sermons of Edwin Sandys . . . Archbishop of York,* ed. for the Parker Society by the Rev. John Ayre (Cambridge, 1842), p. 113.

written word." God is well pleased when men "are so religiously affected, that they dare not swerve a hair's breadth from his word."

Based upon the Holy Scriptures as interpreted by the Spirit, this
Protestant doctrine emphasized what has been called the basic ethical
concern of Christianity: "the inviolable dignity and importance of the
individual person." Milton insisted upon the right and the obligation
of the individual to drink directly from the fountain of truth. He denounced those who turned the sacred mysteries of religion to their
own selfish advantage. He protested that the Spirit of God and of
Truth was promised and given to "all Beleevers," and he declared
that spiritual laws are engraven on the heart. The faith of each individual is sacred. Milton was the consistent champion of freedom of
thought and conscience.

His religious thought and imagination were, as I have tried to show,
sustained and stimulated, as well as circumscribed, by Scripture and
the Christian tradition. In his major poems he was inspired by the
Christian Muse, whose sacred oracles Milton interpreted as directed
by the Holy Spirit. The material is scriptural, elaborated and em-
bellished by his vigorous but discreet imagination; the pattern is influenced or determined by his sound classical culture; the tone
throughout is serious and frequently somber. Although Milton is preoccupied with religion and specifically with scriptural themes, it is a
grave error to think of him as a dogmatist, as one interested in or
limited by a narrow and arid theology. "Platonic thinking is," it has
been said, "at the root of all Milton's theology, deeper than his Evan-
gelicalism, deeper than his Puritanism,"[13] though, as we have seen,
Milton's Platonism may, in Bush's words, be "a little altered by the
selective instinct of a cultivated puritan of the Renaissance." From
Comus onward, virtue, enlightened by reason and guarded by Providence, is of cardinal importance. Knowledge must serve virtue, the
highest good, which can teach mortals how to climb "Higher then
the Spheary chime."

The ladder of perfection, the *scala coeli*, is thus a true and appropriate symbol of Milton's Christian-Platonic idealism:

> Yet some there be that by due steps aspire
> To lay their just hands on the Golden Key
> That ope's the Palace of Eternity.

Milton has been called a Christian humanist. He might also be called

[13] A. E. Dyson, "The Interpretation of *Comus*," *Essays and Studies*, N.S.,
VIII (London, 1955), p. 99.

a Christian Platonist or a Protestant-Puritan idealist. In any case, in his thought and poetry Christian-Platonic idealism is the path, the ladder to salvation. His message and his doctrine are for the elect, those who conscientiously, earnestly, intelligently, and devoutly, "by due steps," aspire to godliness, virtue, and truth. With the Attendant Spirit he might have said:

> To such my errand is, and but for such,
> I would not soil these pure Ambrosial weeds,
> With the rank vapours of this Sin-worn mould.

Striving always to be true to himself, to be obedient to his heavenly vision, and never divorced from the vital spiritual influences of his time, he exemplified to the rest of us, as Adams has recently said, "what the armed soul impelled by its own conscious destiny can endure and accomplish." As the years passed, the way if anything became straiter, the world more sin-worn, the prospect of reform more dim, the ideal of perfection more unattainable except in the realm of religious poetry. Fallen on evil days and evil tongues, "In darkness and with dangers compast round,/And solitude," the blind poet found consolation in his visions, invoking his sacred Muse to find fit audience but to drive far off the profane,

> the barbarous dissonance
> Of *Bacchus* and his Revellers, the Race
> Of that wilde Rout that tore the *Thracian* Bard
> In *Rhodope*, where Woods and Rocks had Eares
> To rapture, till the savage clamour dround
> Both Harp and Voice.

Here, in this dim spot called earth, there could be, he realized, no abiding city. Here true religion and works of faith will rarely be found. So shall the world go on, "To good malignant, to bad men benigne," until the day of judgment, when the Lord will destroy "Satan with his perverted World" and finally establish His kingdom of righteousness and peace and love.

In the epic the day of judgment is not described at length though it was the inevitable result of men's obdurate wickedness and, of course, the keystone of orthodox faith, as Lewis R. Farnell has emphasized. Grandiose and awe-inspiring, this cosmic catastrophe was to be the "perfect consummation of God's justice." Farnell says, "No other dogma has exercised so momentous an influence on life and conduct, or has coloured so deeply the minds and the moods of men and their theory of life. At times it has worked with such morbid influence upon

233

certain imaginations as to darken wholly the earthly life and to belittle its value, with uncivilizing and anti-social effects."[14] As contained in a vast body of literature sacred and profane, in Jewish apocalyptic books and the writings of the Christian fathers, in the works of theologians of the Middle Ages and the Reformation, down to the most recent times, the ideas of divine justice have, we discern, "been infected with human passion, human vindictiveness and intolerance," and the award of salvation and happy immortality has been made to depend "not on pure righteousness, but on dogmatic belief, ceremonial sacraments, or . . . the knowledge of certain formulae. . . ." It is indeed, as Farnell asserts, repugnant to our thoughts and our highest conception of divine justice that a man's life should be judged by his dogmatic creed. Still more repugnant is the doctrine of eternal damnation, a doctrine that is losing its hold on the popular mind and is "no longer clamant in our pulpits." Some religious thinkers now declare that hopeless souls are not punished after death but extinguished. This is a dispensation "which Milton's Belial eloquently declares is worse than Hell." Farnell quotes the lines expressing Belial's aversion to the idea of being swallowed up and lost "in the wide womb of uncreated night"; and then he remarks, "But the Archangel, like his poet, was a highly intellectual spirit. Painless extinction has probably no terrors for the multitude."

Although Milton mentions the day of judgment and the punishment of the wicked, it is significant that he does not dwell or brood upon its horrors; he does not gloat, as Dante does, over the eternal torments of the damned. It must of course be remembered that Milton's hell is inhabited only by the fallen angels, though Satan, who carries his own hell with him, generously extends to Adam and Eve and thus to all mankind his hospitality:

> League with you I seek,
> And mutual amitie so streight, so close,
> That I with you must dwell, or you with me
> Henceforth; my dwelling haply may not please
> Like this fair Paradise, your sense, yet such
> Accept your Makers work; he gave it me,
> Which I as freely give; Hell shall unfould,
> To entertain you two, her widest Gates,
> And send forth all her Kings; there will be room,
> Not like these narrow limits, to receive

[14] *The Attributes of God.* The Gifford Lectures delivered at the University of St. Andrews, 1925 (Oxford, 1925), p. 171.

> Your numerous ofspring; if no better place,
> Thank him who puts me loath to this revenge
> On you who wrong me not for him who wrongd.
>
> (IV, 375–87)

There will be ample room. Meanwhile let there be no despair. With faith, humility, patience, temperance, virtue, and love the true Christian strives to overcome evil here, creates a spiritual paradise within, and hopes for eternal bliss hereafter.

There is clear insight and truth in Coleridge's tribute:

My mind is not capable of forming a more august conception, than arises from the contemplation of this great man in his latter days: poor, sick, old, blind, slandered, persecuted,

> Darkness before, and danger's voice behind,

in an age in which he was as little understood by the party, *for* whom, as by that, *against* whom he had contended; and among men before whom he strode so far as to *dwarf* himself by the distance; yet still listening to the music of his own thoughts, or if additionally cheered, yet cheered only by the prophetic faith of two or three solitary individuals, he did nevertheless

> Argue not
> Against Heaven's hand or will, nor bate a jot
> Of heart or hope; but still bore up and steer'd
> Right onward.

Still he strides on ahead while we listen to the music of his thoughts.

At the end of his pilgrimage Mr. Valiant-for-Truth left his sword to him that should follow him; his skill and courage he left to "him that could get it"; but he carried with him his marks and scars to be a witness that he had fought for his Redeemer. Milton's legacy was all this and something more. It was a supreme poetic achievement won by his artistic synthesis of many elements: a thorough knowledge of Scripture and the Christian tradition; an unrivaled command of classical culture; unshaken faith, which is the knowledge of God; courage never to submit or yield and not to be overcome; a profound conviction that enlightened reason with freedom of the will and conscience is the foundation of mortality and true religion; unswerving fidelity to a liberal Protestant doctrine, enlightened and inspired by the Spirit of Truth; incomparable verse embodying his conviction that truth and virtue guided by reason and illuminated by faith are invincible, but that

> evil on it self shall back recoyl,
> And mix no more with goodness, when at last

Gather'd like scum, and setl'd to it self
It shall be in eternal restless change
Self-fed, and self-consum'd.

Nightly or when "Morn Purples the East" Milton's Muse brought him visions of truth and tidings of hope, "hopes unrealisable" in this world but divinely inspired and leading upward "to fuller knowledge and higher, purer aspirations." It has been written that all things are taken from us and "become portions and parcels of the dreadful past." But though much is taken much abides. One thing is certain: to each will come the time when the whole of life will lie behind and before only eternity, only the entrance into that undiscovered country from whose bourne no traveler returns. Meanwhile, here on the darkling plain, it is our privilege to strive to achieve the spiritual life: to overcome vices, to cherish virtue, to attain the Pauline triad of faith, hope, and charity, or life, light, and love—"the divisions of the *Scala Perfectionis*," a *scala* suggested by the magnificent structure ascending in lone splendor from the sea of jasper to the ramparts of heaven, a spiritual ladder, made up of the cardinal and religious virtues, "Life, Light, and Love . . . essential attributes of the Divine nature and essential conditions of human salvation."[15]

Bernard, Abbot of Clairvaux, says in *De Gradibus Humilitatis*,

Sic arcta via cautius strictim inceditur, sic ardus scala tutius pedetemptim ascenditur; sic miro modo ad veritatem licet pigrius tamen firmius claudicando acceditur. . . . Est ergo via descensionis, sicut et ascensionis. Et via est ad bonum, et via est ad malum. Cave malam, elige bonam.

Thus straitly and cautiously we advance along the narrow way; thus securely, step by step, we climb the steep ladder; thus haltingly, slow but sure, we miraculously draw near the truth. . . . There is then a way down and a way up, a way to the good and a way to the evil. Shun the evil one, choose the good one.

Milton was eminent among those "That labour up the Hill of heav'nly Truth." Let us join, he urges, in the quest of truth, in the unremitting search for the scattered parts of the dismembered body of divine truth—a search that will end only with "her Master's second coming; he shall bring together every joint and member, and shall mould them into an immortal feature of loveliness and perfection."

While analyzing Milton's thought and celebrating his virtues, I would not forget that his poetry presents some difficulties. There is, for example, the old problem: did Milton inadvertently make Satan

---

[15] William Ralph Inge, *Faith and Knowledge* (Edinburgh, 1905), p. 231.

a hero? The problem has recently been restated and answered by a doctor of divinity and fellow of Trinity College, Oxford. Milton's intention was twofold: first, to show how Satan, the proud and rebellious will, thinks about God; second, to show how what Satan thinks compares with the truth of his relation to God. Milton tried to do both things. He succeeded with the first. Satan, the rebel, is a tragic hero; and, further, he is a "symbol of the quality of the human will at all times." Milton did not succeed in the second. The true relation of Satan to God is not felt; it does not "live with the same poetic life."[16] Obviously this opinion is based upon a superficial reading of the poem. In the epic as a whole, Satan does not have the "titantic quality" and the heroic character which are attributed to him by some critics, who must be thinking mainly of the first books. Mr. C. S. Lewis' brilliant analysis of Satan's character and "progress" from archangel to snake should have settled this matter.[17]

A more difficult problem is the attitude of the modern reader to religious poetry expressing ideas and doctrines once universally believed but now challenged. The old attitude is represented by what F. D. Maurice said of the Apostles' Creed:[18]

There is actually found at this present day, in every Christian country, a certain document called a creed. . . . It has lasted through a great many storms and revolutions. . . . It is substantially what it was, to say the very least, sixteen hundred years ago. During that time it has not been lying hid in the closet of some antiquarian. It has been repeated by the peasants and children of the different lands into which it has come. It has been given them as a record of facts with which they had as much to do as any noble. In most parts of Europe it has been repeated publicly every day in the year; and though it has been hawked about, and, as men would say, vulgarised, the most earnest and thoughtful men in different countries, different periods, different stages of civilization, have felt that it connected itself with the most permanent part of their being, that it had to do with each of them personally, and that it was the symbol of that humanity which they shared with their brethren. . . .

For earnest and thoughtful readers of such a pious public as this in England *Paradise Lost* was written. Such simple faith as this, based on Scripture, is perhaps now rarely found, and certainly not in aca-

[16] Austin Farrer, *The Glass of Vision*. The Bampton Lectures (Westminster, 1948), p. 123.
[17] Lewis, "Satan," *A Preface to Paradise Lost* (London, 1946), pp. 92–100.
[18] John Baillie, *The Idea of Revelation in Recent Thought* (New York, 1956), p. 103.

demic circles.[19] It cannot be restored; and literary appreciation, which often tends to be a matter of "outward Rites and specious formes," cannot take its place. But, as I have tried to show, it is not impossible to cultivate in respect to the Christian faith—its spiritual truth, its doctrines and traditions, its inestimable contribution to civilization— both a true insight and a genuine sympathy which may, after all, be some compensation for the loss of simple faith. So qualified and prepared the student may more truly understand and appreciate Milton's unique achievement: his consistent reconciliation of poetry with morality and religion; his admirable synthesis of Platonic thought and Christian theology; his sure command of noble verse and clear structure not unworthy of his great themes;—and the actual composition of his "heroic Song." He had long been delayed; he had suffered frustration and grievous disappointment; the calamity of his blindness had cut him off from the cheerful ways of men, from

> sight of vernal bloom, or Summers Rose,
> Or flocks, or herds, or human face divine;
> . . . .
> And wisdome at one entrance quite shut out.

But he still bore up and steered right onward. "Smit with the love of sacred song" he did not cease

> to wander where the Muses haunt
> Cleer Spring, or shadie Grove, or Sunnie Hill,
> . . . but chief
> Thee *Sion* and the flowrie Brooks beneath
> That wash thy hallowd feet, and warbling flow.

His firm faith and his resolute will saved him from despair and did not permit him merely to stand and wait. In his affliction, blinded by no fatuous optimism and deluded by no false philosophy, he appealed not to the world of nature or science but to a moral and spiritual order under God, who was for him the embodiment of justice, truth, and love. He invoked a divine understanding, a supernal illumination. He aspired to prepare the hearts and minds of men to understand and to receive the Holy Spirit, whose office is to lead men to the Truth.

In our modern Babylon, so preoccupied with secular interests and worldly goods, so prone to forget "all the sacred mysteries of Heav'n"

---

[19] In *Poetry, Religion, and the Spiritual Life* (1951), the Rockwell Lectures at The Rice Institute, George F. Thomas attributes the "wide-spread" neglect of Milton, Wordsworth, and Browning to our "secularism and disillusionment" (p. 62), one form of our "moral and spiritual disintegration."

238

in the inexorable pursuit of "lucre and ambition," so prompt to force "the Spirit of Grace it self" and bind "His Consort Liberties"—in this predicament we are discovering that practical reforms, economic, social, political, are merely palliatives, demonstrably inadequate. To save civilization from destruction at the hands of its friends—secularists, specialists, militarists, and politicians—we must have a real renaissance of the spirit, a cultural synthesis in which a revitalized religion, enriched by philosophy and science, renews the challenge of the ideal life. It is true that all ages have fallen short of the ideal of Christianity. That was inevitable. No ideal worth pursuing will ever be achieved fully. But it has been truly said that the better, the more exacting, and the more valid the ideal which we pursue, the further we shall advance. Devotion to a true not a sham ideal will expose the deplorable self-righteousness and hypocrisy of our day. It should rescue us from the blind materialism, the frantic indulgence in sensual pleasures, the narrow intellectualism, the complacent moralism, the arrogant egotism of technical and military leaders and their political henchmen, the domestic fury and the international strife which fill our days with anxiety and threaten ultimate extinction. A genuine spiritual renaissance might even transform man the vegetative animal into a living, self-critical, and self-sacrificing citizen of the commonwealth whose leader gave His life for the salvation of man.

In the meantime we shall not wait for this spiritual renaissance. We shall depend upon native intelligence, instinctive sympathy, and diligent study to acquire the insight, the information, and the understanding which are essential if we would hear the song that Apollo sings and truly comprehend our poet's purpose, which is old but ever new, simple but manifold. His purpose is to show the path of moral and spiritual virtue and truth, conceived generously as purity, obedience, patience, temperance, and love. It is to justify the ways of God to man and to teach man to know God aright, to show that God is omnipotent but merciful. It is to explain that man is free, free to choose the way of life or of death, and that thus man is responsible for his own sin and by God's grace for his salvation. It is to show Christ as the merciful Redeemer and the perfect pattern for overcoming temptation. It is to show that God's ways are just and "ever best found in the close." In the words of Holy Scripture, which contains all things necessary for salvation, his purpose is to declare that God is light and that in Him there is no darkness at all; to reprove the world of sin, and of righteousness, and of judgment; to reveal that Christ hath redeemed forever them that are sanctified and that

239

the Lord will remember their sins and iniquities no more. In no narrow sense was it his purpose to voice "the aspirations of English Puritans in the seventeenth century."[20] In fact part of Milton's essential thought might be expressed in the language of the *Book of Common Prayer* of the Church whose hierarchy he repudiated but whose Christian doctrine he espoused. He declares that man "is very far gone from original righteousness, and is of his own nature inclined to evil, so that the flesh lusteth always contrary to the spirit"; that "every person born into the world deserveth God's wrath and damnation"; and that we have "no power to do good works without the grace of God by Christ preventing us, that we may have a good will, and working with us, when we have that good will." He would implant in us reverence for Him who alone can order the unruly wills and affections of sinful men, so that our hearts and all our members "being mortified from all worldly and carnal lusts" may in all things obey God's holy will. He would show us how by the light of the Spirit we may have "a right judgement in all things" and thus live godly, righteous, and sober lives, that so, among the sundry and manifold changes of the world," our hearts may surely there be fixed, where true joys are to be found." His prayer is for grace that "we may cast away the works of darkness, and put upon us the armour of light, now in the time of this mortal life" and that we may "so pass through things temporal, that we finally lose not things eternal."

In his poetry Milton looked beyond the temporal, alluring surfaces of life to the abiding sources of value in conduct and worship, to the Word of God, the life of the spirit, and the things which were deemed necessary for salvation. Though not unmoved by sensuous pleasures, by the delights of music, the sight of vernal bloom, of summer's rose, and human face divine, by all this world so fair—he was not tempted to devote his genius to the gratification of the affections and the passions, the lusts of the flesh and the world, or mere physical pleasure however innocent and unreproved. His poetry reveals his lifelong preoccupation with spiritual and religious values, his devotion to things not ephemeral but eternal. In effect this was his prayer: "O God, who hast prepared for them that love thee such good things as pass man's understanding; Pour into our hearts such love toward thee, that we, loving thee above all things, may obtain thy promises, which exceed all that we can desire; through Jesus Christ our Lord." For Milton this was not a mere form of words, to be recited and for-

[20] *Ibid.*, p. 79.

240

gotten. It was the statement of the most important truth in life. In his youth he undertook an "assiduous" course of study of the Old and the New Testaments in their original languages. By this study and by constant diligence he had acquired, as he said, a precious aid for his faith and an inestimable treasure for his future life. Milton maintained the right and the liberty of the individual to sift and winnow every doctrine by the authority of Scripture. He believed that only the Christian religion could "rescue the lives and the minds of men from those two detestable curses, slavery and superstition." For the Word of God, so studied and interpreted, was for the intelligent Christian both a shield against ecclesiastical and political tyranny and in fact the way of liberty and divine truth. In this spirit and with this conviction and faith Milton lived. With darkened eyes but with mind and spirit illuminated by celestial light, he aspired to tell of the spiritual world, invisible but real, of hell and heaven, of damnation and redemption, of the Christian ideal, the paradise within, and the

> New Heav'n and Earth wherein the just shall dwell
> And after all thir tribulations long
> See golden days, fruitful of golden deeds,
> With joy and Love triumphing and fair Truth.

Bibliography

Adams, Robert M. *Ikon: John Milton and the Modern Critics*. Ithaca: Cornell University Press, 1955.

Adams, Thomas. *A Spirituall Navigator Bound for the Holy Land*. London, 1615.

Alcuin, Saint. "Commentariorum in Apocalypsin libre quinque," *Patrologiae Latinae*, C.

Allen, Don C. *The Harmonious Vision: Studies in Milton's Poetry*. Baltimore: Johns Hopkins Press, 1954.

Ambrose, Saint. "Hexaemeron libri sex . . . De Jacob et vita beata libri duo," *Patrologiae Latinae*, XIV.

———. "Expositio septem visiones libri Apocalypsis," *Patrologiae Latinae*, XVII.

Anselm, Saint. "Expositio in Apocalypsim," *Patrologiae Latinae*, CLXII.

Aquinas, Saint Thomas. *Opera omnia*. . . . XVIII, XXX, XXXI. Paris, 1876.

Auerbach, Erich. *Mimesis The Representation of Reality in Western Literature*. Translated from the German by Willard R. Trask. Princeton: Princeton University Press, 1953.

Augustine, Saint. "Expositio in Apocalypsim," *Patrologiae Latinae*, XXXIV.

———. *The Citie of God*, with the Learned Comments of Io. Lodovicus. Englished first by J. H. . . . London, 1620.

———. *Confessions and Enchiridion*. Translated and edited by Albert C. Outler. *Library of Christian Classics*, VII. London: S. C. M. Press, 1955.

Baillie, John. *The Idea of Revelation in Recent Thought*. New York: Columbia University Press, 1956.

Baker, Herschel. *The Dignity of Man*. Cambridge [Mass.]: Harvard University Press, 1947.

———. *The Wars of Truth: Studies in the Decay of Christian Humanism in the Earlier Seventeenth Century*. Cambridge [Mass.]: Harvard University Press, 1952.

———. "Where Liberty Lies: Freedom of Conscience in Milton's Day and in Ours," *Southwest Review*, XLI (Winter, 1956).

Bale, John. *The Image of Both Churches after the Revelation of Sainct John the Evangelist*. 1550.

243

Banks, Theodore H. *Milton's Imagery*. New York: Columbia University Press, 1950.

Barker, Arthur. *Milton and the Puritan Dilemma*. Toronto: University of Toronto Press, 1942.

Batsford, Harry and Fry, Charles. *The Greater English Church of the Middle Ages*. London: B. T. Batsford, 1943–44.

Bayley, Harold. *The Lost Language of Symbolism*. New York: Barnes & Noble, 1951.

Becon, Thomas. *The Catechism of Thomas Becon . . . with Other Pieces Written by him in the Reign of Edward the Sixth*, ed. for the Parker Society by the Rev. John Ayre. Cambridge: University Press, 1844.

————. *Prayers and Other Pieces of Thomas Becon*, ed. for the Parker Society by the Rev. John Ayre. Cambridge: University Press, 1844.

Benedict, Saint. "De humilitate," *Patrologiae Latinae*, LXVI.

Bernard, Saint. *The Steps of Humility*. Translated with an Introduction and Notes by George B. Burch. Cambridge [Mass.]: Harvard University Press, 1942.

The Bible Translated According to the Ebrew and Greeke, and Conferred with the Best Translations in Divers Languages (Geneva version). London, 1580.

The Holy Bible. The Authorised King James Version. London: Eyre and Spottiswoode, n.d.

The Interlinear Bible. The Authorised Version and the Revised Version. Cambridge: University Press, n.d.

The Interpreter's Bible. The Holy Scriptures in the King James and Revised Standard Versions with General Articles and Introduction, Exegesis, Exposition for each Book of the Bible. 12 vols. New York and Nashville: Abingdon-Cokesbury Press, 1952–57.

Binyon, Laurence. "A Note on Milton's Imagery and Rhythm," *Seventeenth Century Studies Presented to Sir Herbert Grierson*. Oxford: Clarendon Press, 1938.

Bowra, C. W. *Inspiration and Poetry*. London: Macmillan & Co., Ltd., 1955.

Bréhier, Louis. *L'Art Chrétien, son développement iconographique des origines a nos jours*. Paris: H. Laurens, 1918.

Broadbent, J. B. "Milton's Paradise," *Modern Philology*, LI (February, 1954).

————. "Milton's Hell," *English Literary History*, XXI (September, 1954).

Brown, John. *John Bunyan His Life, Times and Work*. London: Hulbert, 1928.

Bullinger, Heinrich. *A Hundred Sermons upon the Apocalips of Iesu Christe*. Translated by John Daws. 1561.

————. *The Decades of Henry Bullinger*, ed. for the Parker Society by the Rev. Thomas Harding. Cambridge: University Press, 1851.

Burns, John S. "Milton Criticism and the Biography, 1779–1909." Unpublished Master's thesis. Houston: The Rice Institute, 1953.

Bush, Douglas. *Mythology and the Renaissance Tradition in English Poetry*. Minneapolis: University of Minnesota Press, 1932.

————. *The Renaissance and English Humanism*. Toronto: University of Toronto Press, 1939.

————. *Paradise Lost in Our Time*. New York: Peter Smith, 1948.

————. *English Literature in the Earlier Seventeenth Century 1600–1660*. Oxford: Clarendon Press, 1952.

Calvin, John. *A Commentarie of John Calvin upon the first booke of Moses called Genesis*: Translated out of the Latine into English by Thomas Tymme. London, 1578.

Carver, P. L. "The Angels in *Paradise Lost*," *Review of English Studies*, XVI (October, 1940).

Casserley, J. V. Langmead. *The Retreat from Christianity in the Modern World*. London: Longmans, Green & Co., Ltd., 1952.

Cassian, Saint. "De Spiritu superbiae," *Patrologiae Latinae*, XLIX.

Cassiodorus, Saint. "Apocalypsis Sancti Joannis," *Patrologiae Latinae*, LXX.

Cawley, Robert R. *Milton and the Literature of Travel*. Princeton: Princeton University Press, 1952.

Chaning-Pearce, M. *The Terrible Crystal: Studies in Kierkegaard and Modern Christianity*. London: Kegan Paul, Trench, Trubner & Co., 1940.

Chester, Allan G. "Milton, Latimer, and the Lord Admiral," *Modern Language Quarterly*, XIV (March, 1953).

Chillingworth, William. *The Religion of Protestants. A Safeway to Salvation*. 4th ed. London, 1674.

Cobbett's Complete Collection of State Trials and Proceedings for High Treason and Other Crimes, Vol. III. London: T. C. Hansard, 1809.

Coleridge on the Seventeenth Century, ed. by Roberta Florence Brinkley. Durham: Duke University Press, 1955.

Conklin, George N. *Biblical Criticism and Heresy in Milton*. New York: King's Crown Press, 1949.

Cook, G. H. *Old S. Paul's Cathedral A Lost Glory of Mediaeval London*. London: Phoenix House, 1955.

Coulson, C. A. *Science and Christian Belief*. Chapel Hill, N.C.: University of North Carolina Press, 1955.

Coulton, G. G. *Ten Medieval Studies*. Cambridge: University Press, 1945.

————. *Art and the Reformation*. Cambridge: University Press, 1953.

Coverdale, Myles. *Remains of Myles Coverdale*, ed. for the Parker Society by the Rev. George Pearson. Cambridge: University Press, 1846.

Craigie, Sir William. *The Bible in Its Ancient and English Versions*, ed. by H. Wheeler Robinson. Oxford: Clarendon Press, 1940.

Cripps, Sir Stafford. *Towards Christian Democracy*. New York: Philosophical Library, 1946.

Crouch, Joseph. *Puritanism and Art*. London: Cassell and Co., 1910.

Curry, Walter C. *Milton's Ontology, Cosmogony, and Physics*. Lexington: University of Kentucky Press, 1957.

Daiches, David. *A Study of Literature for Readers and Critics*. Ithaca: Cornell University Press, 1948.

Darbishire, Helen. "Milton's Poetic Language," *Essays and Studies*, N.S., X. London: John Murray, 1957.

Davies, Godfrey. *The Early Stuarts 1603–1660*. Oxford: Clarendon Press, 1937.

Dawson, Christopher. *Religion and the Modern State.* New York: Sheed & Ward, Inc., 1938.

Dillistone, F. W. *Christianity and Symbolism.* Philadelphia: Westminster Press, 1955.

Donne, John. *The Sermons of John Donne,* ed. by George R. Potter and Evelyn M. Simpson. 7 vols. to date. Berkeley: University of California Press, 1953——.

Dorian, Donald C. "Milton's Two-Handed Engine," *PMLA,* XLV (March, 1930).

Du Bartas, Guillaume. *Du Bartas His Deuine Weekes and Workes.* Translated by Josuah Sylvester. London, 1611.

——. *Du Bartas His Diuine Weekes and Workes . . .* London, 1633.

Duncan, Joseph R. "Milton's Four-in-One Hell," *The Huntington Library Quarterly,* XX (February, 1957).

Dyson, A. E. "The Interpretation of *Comus,*" *Essays and Studies,* N.S., VIII. London: John Murray, 1955.

Edman, Irwin. *Philosopher's Holiday.* New York: Viking Press, 1938.

Eliot, T. S. "Milton," *Proceedings of the British Academy.* London: Oxford University Press, 1947.

Ellis-Fermor, Una. *The Frontiers of Drama.* New York: Oxford University Press, 1946.

Encyclopaedia of Religion and Ethics, ed. by James Hastings. XII. New York: Charles Scribner's Sons, 1922.

Eusebius (Pamphili). *The Ancient Ecclesiastical Histories of the First Six Hundred Years after Christ.* Translated by Meredith Hanmer. 4th ed. London, 1636.

Farnell, Lewis R. *The Attributes of God.* The Gifford Lectures. Oxford: Clarendon Press, 1925.

Farrer, Austin. *The Glass of Vision.* The Bampton Lectures. Westminster: Dacre Press, 1948.

——. "The Queen of Sciences," *The Twentieth Century,* CLVII (June, 1955).

Fell, Kenneth. "From Myth to Martyrdom," *English Studies,* XXXIV (August, 1953).

Fink, Zera S. *The Classical Republicans, an Essay in the Recovery of a Pattern of Thought in Seventeenth Century England.* Evanston: Northwestern University Press, 1945.

Fletcher, Harris F. *The Use of the Bible in Milton's Prose.* The University of Illinois Studies in Language and Literature, XIV (August, 1929). Urbana: University of Illinois, 1929.

Foss, Martin. *Symbol and Metaphor in Human Experience.* Princeton: Princeton University Press, 1949.

French, J. Milton. "Milton's Family Bible," *PMLA,* LIII (June, 1938).

——. "Milton's Two-Handed Engine," *Modern Language Notes,* LXVIII (April, 1953).

——. "The Digressions in Milton's *Lycidas,*" *Studies in Philology,* L (July, 1953).

—— (ed.). *The Life Records of John Milton.* Vols. I–IV to date. New Brunswick: Rutgers University Press, 1949–56.

246

Bibliography

Frye, Northrop (ed.). *Paradise Lost and Selected Poetry and Prose.* New York: Rinehart and Co., 1951.

Gardner, Helen C. "Walter Hilton and the Mystical Tradition in England," *Essays and Studies,* XXII. Oxford: Clarendon Press, 1937.

Garrison, W. E. *A Protestant Manifesto.* New York: Abingdon-Cokesbury, 1952.

Gilbert, Allan H. "The Theological Basis of Satan's Rebellion and the Function of Abdiel in *Paradise Lost.*" *Modern Philology,* XL (August, 1942).

Gill, John. *An Exposition of the New Testament.* 3 vols. London: Mathews & Leigh, 1809.

———. *An Exposition of the Old Testament.* 6 vols. London: Mathews & Leigh, 1810.

Goldschneider, Ludwig. *Michelangelo. Paintings, Sculptures, Architecture.* New York: Phaidon, 1953.

Gossman, Ann Mary. "Man Plac't in a Paradise: a Comparative Study of Milton, St. Ambrose, and Hugh St. Victor." Unpublished Master's thesis. Houston: The Rice Institute, 1954.

———. "The Synthesis of Hebraism and Hellenism in Milton's *Samson Agonistes.*" Unpublished Ph.D. dissertation. Houston: The Rice Institute, 1957.

Grenander, M. E. "*Samson's* Middle: Aristotle and Dr. Johnson," *University of Toronto Quarterly,* XXIV (July, 1955).

Grollenberg, L. H. *Atlas of the Bible.* London and New York: Thomas Nelson and Sons, 1956.

Hall, Joseph. *The Works of Joseph Hall.* Bishop of Exceter. . . . 3 vols. London, 1634–62.

———. *Divers Treatises, Written upon severall Occasions,* by Joseph Hall late Bishop of Norwich. The Third Tome. London, 1662.

Haller, William. *The Rise of Puritanism.* . . . New York: Columbia University Press, 1938.

———. *Liberty and Reformation in the Puritan Revolution.* New York: Columbia University Press, 1955.

Hanford, J. H. "The Temptation Motive in Milton," *Studies in Philology,* XV (January, 1918).

———. *A Milton Handbook.* 4th ed. New York: F. S. Crofts & Co., 1946.

———. *John Milton, Englishman.* New York: Crown Publishers, Inc., 1949.

——— (ed.). *The Poems of John Milton.* 2d ed. New York: Ronald Press, 1953.

Harbison, E. Harris. *The Age of Reformation.* Ithaca: Cornell University Press, 1953.

Hendel, Charles W. *Civilization and Religion.* New Haven: Yale University Press, 1948.

Hesiod, The Homeric Hymns and Homerica, with an English translation by Hugh G. Evelyn-White. London: W. Heinemann, 1914.

Hilton, Walter. *Scala perfectionis.* London, 1507.

———. *The Scale of Perfection.* Baltimore: Penguin Books, Inc., 1957.

The Holkham Bible Picture Book. Introduction and Commentary by W. O. Hassall. London: Dropmore Press, 1954.

Honorius of Autun. "Scala coeli major," *Patrologiae Latinae*, CLXXII.

Howard, Leon. "That Two-handed Engine Once More," *Huntington Library Quarterly*, XV (February, 1952).

Hughes, Merritt Y. "Myself Am Hell," *Modern Philology*, LIV (November, 1956).

———— (ed.). *John Milton Complete Poems and Major Prose*. New York: The Odyssey Press, Inc., 1957.

Huizinga, J. *The Waning of the Middle Ages*. Garden City, N.Y.: Double-day & Co., 1954.

Hunter, William B. "Prophetic Dreams and Visions in *Paradise Lost*," *Modern Language Quarterly*, IX (September, 1948).

Hürliman, Martin. *English Cathedrals*. Foreword by Geoffrey Grigson. Boston: Houghton Mifflin Company, 1950.

Huxley, Aldous. "Grace, Predestination and Salvation," *The Hibbert Journal*, L (July, 1952).

Inge, William Ralph. *Faith and Knowledge*, Edinburgh: T. & T. Clark, 1905.

————. *The Church in the World*. London: Longmans, Green & Co., Ltd., 1928.

————. *Christian Mysticism Considered in Eight Lectures delivered before the University of Oxford*. New York: Charles Scribner's Sons, 1933.

————. *Things New and Old*. London: Longmans, Green & Co., Ltd., 1933.

————. *Diary of a Dean*. New York: The Macmillan Company, 1950.

————. "An Old Man Looks at the World," *The Hibbert Journal*, L (July, 1952).

Isidore, Saint. "Liber Quintus de legibus et temporibus," *Patrologiae Latinae*, LXXXII.

James I. *The Workes of the Most High and Mightie Prince, Iames. . . .* London, 1616.

Jarrell, Randall. *Poetry and the Age*. New York: Vintage, 1955.

Jebb, Sir Richard. "*Samson Agonistes* and the Hellenic Drama," *Proceedings of the British Academy 1907–1908*. London: Oxford University Press, 1908.

Jonson, Ben. *Ben Jonson*, ed. by C. H. Herford and Percy Simpson. 10 vols. Oxford: Clarendon Press, 1925–50.

Jordan, W. K. *The Development of Religious Toleration in England from the Beginning of the English Reformation to the Death of Queen Elizabeth*. London: G. Allen & Unwin, 1932.

Joseph, Sister Miriam. "Orthodoxy in Paradise Lost," *Laval Théologique et Philosophique*, VIII (May, 1952).

Kelly, Maurice. *This Great Argument; a Study of Milton's De doctrina Christiana as a Gloss upon Paradise Lost*. Princeton: Princeton University Press, 1941.

Kendon, Frank. *Mural Paintings in English Churches during the Middle Ages*. London: John Lane, 1923.

Ker, William P. *The Art of Poetry: Seven Lectures 1920–1922*. Oxford: Clarendon Press, 1925.

Knowles, John A. *Essays in the History of the York School of Glass-Painting*. London: Macmillan & Co., Ltd., 1936.

Bibliography

Knox, John. *On the Meaning of Christ.* The William Belden Noble Lectures delivered at Harvard University. New York: Charles Scribner's Sons, 1947.

Krouse, F. Michael. *Milton's Samson and the Christian Tradition.* Princeton: Princeton University Press, 1949.

Latimer, Hugh. *Fruitfull Sermons: Preached by . . . Master Hugh Latimer.* London, 1584.

————. *Sermons,* ed. for the Parker Society by the Rev. George E. Corrie. Cambridge: University Press, 1844.

Lear, Floyd S. "St. Isidore and Mediaeval Science," *The Rice Institute Pamphlet,* XXIII (1936).

Le Comte, Edward S. "That Two-Handed Engine and Savonarola," *Studies in Philology,* XLVII (October, 1950).

Levi, Carlo. *Christ Stopped at Eboli.* New York: Farrar, Straus & Co., 1947.

Lewis, C. S. *A Preface to Paradise Lost.* London: Oxford University Press, 1946.

————. *English Literature in the Sixteenth Century Excluding Drama.* Oxford: Clarendon Press, 1954.

Lewis, Thomas Taylor (ed.). *Letters of the Lady Brilliana Harley.* London: The Camden Society, 1854.

Lovejoy, Arthur O. *The Great Chain of Being; a Study of the History of an Idea.* Cambridge [Mass.]: Harvard University Press, 1936.

Macaulay, Thomas B. "Milton," *The Edinburgh Review,* XLII (August, 1825).

Mackail, John W. *The Springs of Helicon. . . .* New York: Longmans, Green & Co., Inc., 1909.

Mâle, Émile. *L'Art Religieux de la Fin du Moyen Age en France.* Paris: Armand Colin, 1908.

————. *Religious Art in France, XIII Century.* 3d ed. Translated by Dora Nussey. London: J. M. Dent & Sons, 1913.

————. *Religious Art from the Twelfth to the Eighteenth Century.* New York: Pantheon, 1949.

Malorate, Augustine. *A Catholike and Ecclesiasticall Exposition of the holy Gospell after S. Mathewe, gathered out of all the singuler and approved Deuines which the Lorde hath giuen to His Churche.* Translated by Thomas Tymme. London, 1570.

Martin, L. C. "Thomas Warton and the Early Poems of Milton," *Proceedings of the British Academy.* London: Oxford University Press, 1934.

Martin, Saint. "Expositio libri Apocalypsis," *Patrologiae Latinae,* CCIX.

Mathew, David. *The Age of Charles I.* London: Eyre & Spottiswoode, 1951.

McColley, Grant. "Milton's Golden Compasses," *Notes and Queries,* CLXXVI (February, 1939).

————. *Paradise Lost An Account of Its Growth and Major Origins.* Chicago: Packard and Co., 1940.

McDill, J. M. *Milton and the Pattern of Calvinism.* Nashville: Private edition, 1942.

Menzies, W. "Milton: the Last Poems," *Essays and Studies,* XXIV. Oxford: Clarendon Press, 1939.

249

Migne, J. P. (ed.). *Patrologiae cursus completus sive bibliotheca universalis, integra, uniformis, commoda, oeconomica omnium S.S. patrum, doctorum scriptorumque ecclesiasticorum* . . . Series Latinae. . . . Paris: 1844——.

Miller, Milton. "*Paradise Lost*: the Double Standard," *The University of Toronto Quarterly*, XX (January, 1951).

Milton, John. *The Poetical Works of John Milton*, ed. by H. C. Beeching. London: Oxford University Press, 1900.

——. *The Works of John Milton*, Frank Allen Patterson general ed. 18 vols. and index 2 vols. New York: Columbia University Press, 1931–40.

——. *The Student's Milton*, ed. by Frank Allen Patterson. New York: F. S. Crofts & Co., 1933.

——. *Complete Prose Works of John Milton*, Don M. Wolfe general ed. Vol. I. New Haven: Yale University Press, 1953.

Moffatt, James. *An Introduction to the Literature of the New Testament*. 3d and rev. ed. Edinburgh: T. & T. Clark, 1949.

Moody, William V. (ed.). *The Complete Poetical Works of John Milton*. Boston: Houghton Mifflin Company, 1924.

Mottram, R. H. *The Glories of Norwich Cathedral*. London: Winchester Publications, 1948.

Münz, Ludwig. *Rembrandt*. New York: Harry N. Abrams, Inc., 1954.

Niebuhr, Helmut R. *Christ and Culture*. New York: Harper & Brothers, 1951.

Niebuhr, Reinhold. *Faith and History*. New York: Charles Scribner's Sons, 1949.

Osgood, Charles G. *Poetry as a Means of Grace*. Princeton: Princeton University Press, 1946.

Parish, John E. "Pre-Miltonic Representations of Adam as a Christian," *The Rice Institute Pamphlet*, XL (1953).

Parker, T. H. L. *The Oracles of God. An Introduction to the Preaching of John Calvin*. London: Lutterworth Press, 1947.

Parker, T. M. *Christianity and the State in the Light of History*. The Bampton Lectures. London: A. & C. Black, 1955.

Parker, W. R. "The Greek Spirit in Milton's *Samson Agonistes*," *Essays and Studies*, XX. Oxford: Oxford University Press, 1934.

——. *Milton's Debt to Greek Tragedy in Samson Agonistes*. Baltimore: Johns Hopkins Press, 1937.

Percival, H. M. (ed.). *Samson Agonistes by John Milton*. London: Macmillan & Co., Ltd., 1950.

Perkins, William. *The Workes of that Famous and Worthie Minister of Christ in the Universitie of Cambridge*. 3 vols. London, 1631.

——. *A Cloud of Faithfull Witnesses, Leading to the Heavenly Canaan*. London, 1608.

Perry, Ralph Barton. *Puritanism and Democracy*. New York: Vanguard, 1944.

Philippus Harvengius. "In Cantica Canticorum Moralitates," *Patrologiae Latinae*, CCIII.

Philips, Edward. *Certaine Godly and Learned Sermons*. . . . London, 1605.

Pico, Giovanni. "Oration on the Dignity of Man," *The Renaissance Philoso-*

Bibliography

phy of Man, ed. by Ernst Cassirer, Paul O. Kristeller, and John H. Randall, Jr. Chicago: University of Chicago Press, 1948.

Prince, F. T. *The Italian Elements in Milton's Verse*. Oxford: Clarendon Press, 1954.

Rajan, B. *Paradise Lost and the Seventeenth Century Reader*. London: Oxford University Press, 1947.

Rand, Edward K. *Founders of the Middle Ages*. Cambridge [Mass.]: Harvard University Press, 1928.

Rappoport, Angelo S. *Myth and Legend of Ancient Israel*. London: Gresham, 1928.

Raven, Charles E. *Natural Religion and Christian Theology*. The Gifford Lectures 1951. First Series: *Science and Religion*. Second Series: *Experience and Interpretation*. Cambridge: University Press, 1953.

Ray, Don E. "Milton and the Elizabethan Tradition of Christian Learning." Unpublished Ph.D. dissertation. Houston: The Rice Institute, 1957.

Read, Conyers. *Social and Political Forces in the English Reformation*. The Rockwell Lectures. Houston: Elsevier Press, 1953.

Richard Victor, Saint. "In Apocalypsim Joannis libri septem," *Patrologiae Latinae*, CXCVI.

Robins, Harry F. "Milton's 'Two-Handed Engine at the Door' and St. Matthew's Gospel," *Review of English Studies*, N.S., V (January, 1954).

Rogers, Richard. *Certaine Sermons Preached and Penned by R. Rogers. . . .* London, 1612.

Rogers, Thomas. *The Catholic Doctrine of the Church of England*. Cambridge: University Press, 1854.

Ross, Alexander. *Three Decades of Divine Meditations*. London, 1630.

Ross, Sir William David. *Foundations of Ethics*. The Gifford Lectures delivered at the University of Aberdeen. Oxford: Clarendon Press, 1939.

Rossetti, Christina. *The Face of the Deep: a Devotional Commentary on the Apocalypse*. 5th ed. London: Society for Promoting Christian Knowledge, 1907.

Rupert, Saint. "Apocalypsim Joannis Apostoli commentariorum liber tertius," *Patrologiae Latinae*, CLXIX.

Rushworth, John. *Historical Collections of Private Passages of State, Weighty Matters of Law, Remarkable Proceedings in Five Parliaments. . . .* 7 vols. London, 1721.

Russell, Bertrand R. *Mysticism and Logic*. London: Longmans, Green & Co., Ltd., 1913.

Salmi, Mario. *Italian Miniatures*. London: Collins, 1957.

Samuel, Irene. *Plato and Milton*. Ithaca: Cornell University Press, 1947.

———. "The Dialogue in Heaven: a Reconsideration of *Paradise Lost*, III. 1–417," *PMLA*, LXXII (September, 1957).

Sandys, Edwin. *The Sermons of Edwin Sandys . . . Archbishop of York*, ed. for the Parker Society by the Rev. John Ayre. Cambridge: University Press, 1842.

Santayana, George. *Interpretations of Poetry and Religion*. New York: Charles Scribner's Sons, 1900.

———. *Some Turns of Thought in Modern Philosophy. Five Essays*. Cambridge: University Press, 1933.

———. *The Philosophy of Santayana,* ed. by Irwin Edman. New York: Charles Scribner's Sons, 1953.

———. *The Life of Reason or the Phases of Human Progress.* New York: Charles Scribner's Sons, 1954.

Schanzer, Ernest. "Milton's Hell Revisited," *University of Toronto Quarterly,* XXIV (January, 1955).

Schultz, Howard. *Milton and Forbidden Knowledge.* New York: Modern Language Association of America, 1955.

Schweitzer, Albert. *Civilization and Ethics.* London: A. & C. Black, 1923.

———. *Out of My Life and Thought. An Autobiography.* New York: Henry Holt and Co., 1949.

———. "How Can We Attain the Kingdom of God?" *The Christian Century,* LXXII (September 7, 1955).

Sensabaugh, George F. "The Milieu of *Comus,*" *Studies in Philology,* XLI (April, 1944).

———. *That Grand Whig Milton.* Stanford: Stanford University Press, 1952.

Sheppard, J. T. *Music at Belmont.* London: Rupert Hart-Davis, 1951.

Shorr, Dorothy C. "The Role of the Virgin in Giotto's Last Judgment," *Art Bulletin,* XXXVIII (December, 1956).

Shuster, George N. *The English Ode from Milton to Keats.* New York: Columbia University Press, 1940.

Simpson, Alan. *Puritanism in Old and New England.* Chicago: University of Chicago Press, 1955.

Smart, John S. (ed.). *The Sonnets of Milton.* Glasgow: Macklehose, Jackson and Co., 1921.

Smith, Hallett, "No Middle Flight," *Huntington Library Quarterly,* XV (February, 1952).

Smith, Henry. *The Sermons of Master Henry Smith.* London, 1599.

Starnes, DeWitt T. and Talbert, Ernest W. *Classical Myth and Legend in Renaissance Dictionaries. . . .* Chapel Hill, N.C.: University of North Carolina Press, 1955.

Stauffer, Donald A. "Milton's Two-Handed Engine," *Modern Language Review,* XXXI (January, 1936).

Stein, Arnold. *Answerable Style. Essays on Paradise Lost.* Minneapolis: University of Minnesota Press, 1953.

———. *Heroic Knowledge.* Minneapolis: University of Minnesota Press, 1957.

Stoll, Elmer E. *Poets and Playwrights.* Minneapolis: University of Minnesota Press, 1930.

———. *From Shakespeare to Joyce.* Garden City, N.Y.: Doubleday & Co., 1944.

Strachan, James. *Early Bible Illustrations. A Short Study Based on Some Fifteenth and Early Sixteenth Century Printed Texts.* Cambridge: University Press, 1957.

Strype, John. *The History of the Life and Acts of the Most Reverend Father in God, Edmund Grindal, the First Bishop of London.* London, 1710.

Svendsen, Kester. *Milton and Science.* Cambridge [Mass.]: Harvard University Press, 1956.

Taylor, F. J. "Scripture and Tradition in the Anglican Reformation," *Scripture and Tradition.* London: Lutterworth Press, 1955.

Taylor, Henry O. *The Classical Heritage of the Middle Ages.* 3d ed. New York: The Macmillan Company, 1911.

———. *The Medieval Mind.* 4th ed. 2 vols. Cambridge [Mass.]: Harvard University Press, 1951.

Temple, William (Archbishop of Canterbury). *Christian Faith and Life.* London: S. C. M. Press, 1954.

———. *Christianity and the Social Order.* Harmondsworth: Penguin Books, 1956.

Thomas, George F. *Poetry, Religion, and the Spiritual Life.* The Rockwell Lectures. Houston: Elsevier Press, 1951.

Tillyard, E. M. W. *Milton.* New York: The Dial Press, Inc., 1930.

———. *The Miltonic Setting Past and Present.* Cambridge: University Press, 1938.

———. *Studies in Milton.* New York: The Macmillan Company, 1951.

———. *The Metaphysicals and Milton.* London: Chatto & Windus, 1956.

Trent, William P. (ed.). *John Milton's "L'Allegro," "Il Penseroso," Comus, and "Lycidas,"* New York: Longmans, Green & Co., Inc., 1895.

Trevelyan, George M. *England under the Stuarts.* London: Methuen & Co., Ltd., 1949.

Turner, Amy L. "The Visual Arts in Milton's Poetry." Unpublished Ph.D. dissertation. Houston: The Rice Institute, 1955.

Tuve, Rosamond. *Images and Themes in Five Poems by Milton.* Cambridge: Harvard University Press, 1957.

Tyndale, William. *The Whole Workes of W. Tyndale, John Frith, and doct. Barnes, three worthy martyrs, . . . of this churche of England. . . .* London, 1572–3.

———. *The Beginning of the New Testament Translated by William Tyndale,* 1525 . . . with an introduction by Alfred W. Pollard. Oxford: Clarendon Press, 1926.

———. *The New Testament Translated by William Tyndale; a Reprint of the Edition of 1534,* . . . ed. for the Royal Society of Literature by N. Hardy Wallis. Cambridge: University Press, 1938.

———. *Doctrinal Treatises and Introductions to Different Portions of the Holy Scriptures,* ed. for the Parker Society by the Rev. Henry Walter. Cambridge: University Press, 1848.

———. *Expositions and Notes on Sundry Portions of the Holy Scriptures together with the Practice of Prelates,* ed. for the Parker Society by the Rev. Henry Walter. Cambridge: University Press, 1849.

———. *An Answer to Sir Thomas More's Dialogue, . . .* ed. for the Parker Society by the Rev. Henry Walter. Cambridge: University Press, 1850.

Ussher, James. *A Body of Divinity, or the Summe and Substance of Christian Religion.* London, 1649.

Van Doren, Mark. *The Noble Voice.* New York: Henry Holt and Company, Inc., 1946.

Venturi, Lionelli. *Italian Painting. The Creators of the Renaissance. The Renaissance. Seventeenth and Eighteenth Centuries. Critical Studies by Lionelli Venturi. Historical Surveys by Rosabianca Skira-Venturi.* Translated by Stuart Gilbert. 3 vols. Geneva and Paris: Albert Skira, 1950–52.

Verity, A. W. (ed.). *Paradise Lost.* Cambridge: University Press, 1910, 1929.

Wallace, Ronald S. *Calvin's Doctrine of the Word and the Sacrament.* Edinburgh: Clarke, Irwin and Co., 1953.

Warton, Thomas. (ed.). *Poems upon Several Occasions, English, Italian, and Latin, with Translations, by John Milton . . . with Notes Critical and Explanatory, and other Illustrations,* by Thomas Warton. London, 1785.

Welsford, Enid. *The Court Masque; a Study in the Relationship between Poetry and the Revels.* Cambridge: University Press, 1927.

West, Robert H. *Milton and the Angels.* Athens, Ga.: University of Georgia Press, 1955.

Westcott, Brooke F. *A General View of the History of the English Bible.* 3d ed. Revised by William Aldis Wright. London: Macmillan & Co., Ltd., 1905.

Westlake, N. H. J. *History of Design in Mural Painting from the Earliest Times to the Twelfth Century.* London: E. P. Dutton & Co., 1905.

White, Andrew D. *A History of the Warfare of Science with Theology in Christendom.* New York: D. Appleton and Co., 1910.

White, Helen C. *The Metaphysical Poets. A Study in Religious Experience.* New York: The Macmillan Company, 1936.

Whitehead, Alfred N. *Symbolism Its Meaning and Effect.* New York: The Macmillan Company, 1927.

———. *Modes of Thought.* Cambridge: University Press, 1938.

Williams, Arnold. *The Common Expositor: An Account of the Commentaries on Genesis.* Chapel Hill, N.C.: University of North Carolina Press, 1949.

Williams, Charles. *James I.* London: Arthur Barker, 1951.

Winters, Yvor. "Problems for the Modern Critic of Literature," *The Hudson Review,* IX (Autumn, 1956).

Wolfe, Don M. *Milton in the Puritan Revolution.* New York: Thomas Nelson and Sons, 1941.

Woodhouse, A. S. P. *Puritanism and Liberty.* . . . London: J. M. Dent & Sons, 1938.

———. "The Argument of Milton's *Comus,*" *University of Toronto Quarterly,* XI (October, 1941).

———. "*Samson Agonistes* and Milton's Experience," *Transactions of the Royal Society of Canada,* XLIII (June, 1949).

———. "*Comus* Once More," *University of Toronto Quarterly,* XIX (April, 1950).

———. *Milton the Poet.* Toronto: J. M. Dent & Sons, 1955.

Wright, B. A. (ed.). *Shorter Poems of John Milton.* London: Macmillan & Co,, Ltd., 1950.

Zeno, Saint. "De somnio Jacob," *Patrologiae Latinae,* XI.

Zuntz, G. "Knowing—Learning—Living," *The Hibbert Journal,* LIV (July, 1956).

Index

255

DATE DUE

GAYLORD			PRINTED IN U.S A.